THE RENEGADO, OR, THE GENTLEMAN OF VENICE

KU-863-503

Philip Massinger

for the Lady Elizabeth's Men at the Cockpit

Edited by
MICHAEL NEILL

THE ARDEN SHAKESPEARE

LONDON • NEW YORK • OXFORD • NEW DELHI • SYDNEY

THE ARDEN SHAKESPEARE
Bloomsbury Publishing Plc
50 Bedford Square, London, WC1B 3DP, UK

BLOOMSBURY, THE ARDEN SHAKESPEARE and the
Arden Shakespeare logo are trademarks of Bloomsbury Publishing Plc

This edition of *The Renegado* edited by Michael Neill,
first published 2010 by Methuen Drama
Reprinted by The Arden Shakespeare 2018

A catalogue record for this book is available from the British Library.

ISBN: HB: 978-1-408-12518-2
       PB: 978-1-904-27161-1

Series: Arden Early Modern Drama

To find out more about our authors and books visit
www.bloomsbury.com and sign up for our newsletters.

The Editor

Michael Neill is Emeritus Professor of English at the University of Auckland. He is the author of *Issues of Death: Mortality and Identity in English Renaissance Tragedy* (1997) and *Putting History to the Question: Power, Politics, and Society in English Renaissance Drama* (2000). He has edited *Anthony and Cleopatra* and *Othello* for the Oxford Shakespeare and *The Changeling* for New Mermaids.

For Kubé, my faithful renegade

CONTENTS

LIST OF
ILLUSTRATIONS

GENERAL EDITORS' PREFACE

Arden Early Modern Drama (AEMD) is an expansion of the acclaimed Arden Shakespeare to include the plays of other dramatists of the early modern period. The series publishes dramatic texts from the early modern period in the established tradition of the Arden Shakespeare, using a similar style of presentation and offering the same depth of information and high standards of scholarship. We define 'early modern drama' broadly, to encompass plays written and performed at any time from the late fifteenth to the late seventeenth century. The attractive and accessible format and well-informed editorial content are designed with particular regard to the needs of students studying literature and drama in the final years of secondary school and in colleges and universities. Texts are presented in modern spelling and punctuation; stage directions are expanded to clarify theatrical requirements and possibilities; and speech prefixes (the markers of identity at the beginning of each new speech) are regularized. Each volume contains about twenty illustrations both from the period and from later performance history; a full discussion of the current state of criticism of the play; and information about the textual and performance contexts from which the play first emerged. The goal of the series is to make these wonderful but sometimes neglected plays as intelligible as those of Shakespeare to twenty-first-century readers.

AEMD editors bring a high level of critical engagement and textual sophistication to their work. They provide guidance in assessing critical approaches to their play, developing arguments from the best scholarly work to date and generating new perspectives. A particular focus of an AEMD edition is the play as it was first performed in the theatre. The title-page of each volume displays the name of the company for which the play was written and the theatre at which it was first staged: in the Introduction the play is discussed as part of a company repertory as well as of an authorial canon. Finally, each edition presents a full scholarly discussion of the base text and other relevant materials as physical and social documents, and the Introduction describes issues arising in the early history of the publication and reception of the text.

Commentary notes, printed immediately below the playtext, offer compact but detailed exposition of the language, historical context and theatrical significance of the play. They explain textual ambiguities and, when an action may be interpreted in different ways, they summarize the arguments. Where appropriate they point the reader to fuller discussions in the Introduction.

CONVENTIONS

AEMD editions always include illustrations of pages from the early texts on which they are based. Comparison between these illustrations and the edited text immediately enables the reader to see clearly what a critical edition is and does. In summary, the main changes to the base text – that is, the early text, most often a quarto, that serves as the copy from which the editor works – are these: certain and probable errors in the base text are corrected; typography and spelling are brought into line with current usage; and speech prefixes and stage directions are modified to assist the reader in imagining the play in performance.

Significant changes introduced by editors are recorded in the textual notes at the foot of the page. These are an important cache of information, presented in as compact a form as is possible without forfeiting intelligibility. The standard form can be seen in the following example:

31 doing of] *Coxeter;* of doing *Q;* doing *Rawl*

The line reference ('31') and the reading quoted from the present editor's text ('doing of') are printed before the closing square bracket. After the bracket, the source of the reading, often the name of the editor who first made the change to the base text ('*Coxeter*'), appears, and then other readings are given, followed by their source ('of doing *Q;* doing *Rawl*'). Where there is more than one alternative reading, they are listed in chronological order; hence in the example the base text Q (= Quarto) is given first. Abbreviations used to identify early texts and later editions are listed in the Abbreviations and References section towards the end of the volume. Editorial emendations to the text are discussed in the main commentary, where notes on emendations are highlighted with an asterisk.

Emendation necessarily takes account of early texts other than the base text, as well as of the editorial tradition. The amount of attention paid to other texts depends on the editor's assessment of their origin and importance. Emendation aims to correct errors while respecting the integrity of different versions as they might have emerged through revision and adaptation.

Modernization of spelling and punctuation in AEMD texts is thorough, avoiding the kind of partial modernization that produces language from no known period of English. Generally modernization is routine, involving thousands of alterations of letters. As original grammar is preserved in AEMD editions, most modernizations are as trivial as altering 'booke' to 'book', and are unworthy of record. But where the modernization is unexpected or ambiguous the change is noted in the textual notes, using the following format:

> 102 trolls] *(*trowles*)*

Speech prefixes are sometimes idiosyncratic and variable in the base texts, and almost always abbreviated. AEMD editions expand contractions, avoiding confusion of names that might be similarly abbreviated, such as Alonzo/Alsemero/Alibius from *The Change-ling*. Preference is given to the verbal form that prevails in the base text, even if it identifies the role by type, such as 'Lady' or 'Clown', rather than by personal name. When an effect of standardization is to repress significant variations in the way that a role is conceptualized (in *Philaster*, for example, one text refers to a cross-dressed page as *Boy*, while another uses the character's assumed name), the issue is discussed in the Introduction.

Stage directions in early modern texts are often inconsistent, incomplete or unclear. They are preserved in the edition as far as is possible, but are expanded where necessary to ensure that the dramatic action is coherent and self-consistent. Square brackets are used to indicate editorial additions to stage directions. Directions that lend themselves to multiple staging possibilities, as well as the performance tradition of particular moments, may be discussed in the commentary.

Verse lineation sometimes goes astray in early modern playtexts, as does the distinction between verse and prose, especially where a wide manuscript layout has been transferred to the narrower measure of a printed page. AEMD editions correct such mistakes. Where a verse line is shared between more than one speaker, this series follows the usual modern practice of indenting the second and subsequent part-lines to make it clear that they belong to the same verse line.

The textual notes allow the reader to keep track of all these interventions. The notes use variations on the basic format described above to reflect the changes. In notes, '31 SD' indicates a stage direction in or immediately after line 31. Where there is more than one stage direction, they are identified as, for example, '31 SD1', '31 SD2'. The second line of a stage direction will be identified as, for instance, '31.2'. A forward slash / indicates a line-break in verse.

We hope that these conventions make as clear as possible the editor's engagement with and interventions in the text: our aim is to keep the reader fully informed of the editor's role without intruding unnecessarily on the flow of reading. Equally, we hope – since one of our aims is to encourage the performance of more plays from the early modern period beyond the Shakespeare canon – to provide texts which materially assist performers, as well as readers, of these plays.

PREFACE

In the course of preparing a scholarly edition, one accumulates more and greater debts than one can readily discharge in a short preface. In the case of *The Renegado*, I am particularly conscious of how much I owe to the support of my General Editors – to Gordon McMullan and Suzanne Gossett for their critical acumen and intellectual generosity, and above all to John Jowett for his meticulous advice and unsurpassed mastery of all things textual. The editorial team at Arden have been unfailingly helpful, despite the burden laid on them by a difficult period of transition involving two changes of ownership. I am especially indebted to the patience and good humour of Margaret Bartley, to the sharp eye of Jane Armstrong – perhaps the most accomplished copy editor I have been lucky enough work with – and to the perseverance of Charlotte Loveridge and Anna Brewer in helping to gather the illustrations. Thanks, too, to Jason Gray and Martin Coombs for the map on p. 3. Perhaps my largest debt is to Gwyn Fox for her translation of Cervantes's stylistically tricky play *Los Baños de Argel*, part of which is included as an appendix to this edition.

Needless to say, I am grateful for the assistance of the excellent staff at the several libraries where I worked on the edition: the Cambridge University Library, the British Library, the libraries of Trinity and King's College, Cambridge, the Auckland University Library and the Folger Shakespeare Library (where Georgianna Ziegler and Betsy Walsh have, as always, been wonderfully obliging).

I began work on *The Renegado* whilst on sabbatical leave from the University of Auckland in 2005; and I received invaluable support from Trinity College, Cambridge (where I was a Fellow

Commoner for most of that year), and subsequently from the Folger Shakespeare Library where I held a short-term fellowship until mid-2006. In 2008 Vanderbilt University generously enabled me to travel to Cambridge for the summer, where Trinity once again provided me with accommodation and technical assistance. For their intellectual support and unstinting hospitality, I owe more than I can say to my Cambridge hosts, Anne Barton and Adrian Poole. I am indebted to Katherine Duncan–Jones for information about the family of George Harding, Baron Berkeley, to whom Massinger dedicated *The Renegado.*

It is always useful to try out arguments on one's peers, and I am grateful to the organizers of two conferences who made it possible for me to present material from the Introduction to unusually discriminating audiences: Subha Mukherji and Raphael Lyne invited me to their Cambridge conference on tragicomedy in 2005, while Heather James and Albert Braunmuller asked me to join a two-day seminar on drama and politics at the Huntington in 2009.

A great deal of what goes into an edition such as this derives, needless to say, from conversation and occasional correspondence with friends and colleagues. In this connection, I should particularly like to mention Colin Gibson, Nabil Matar, Michael Questier, Benedict Robinson and Daniel Vitkus. I have also benefited enormously from the ideas and expertise of Süheyla Artemel, Richmond Barbour, Kate Belsey, Anston Bosman, Graham Bradshaw, Jonathan Burton, Thomas Cogswell, Jane Degenhardt, Jean Feerick, Jonathan Gil Harris, Jean Howard, John Kerrigan, Peter Lake, Leah Marcus, Linda McJannet, Patricia Parker, Gail Kern Paster, Linda Peck and David Schalkwyk. To them, and to the many others from whose friendship and support I have benefited, I offer my warmest thanks.

INTRODUCTION

THE PLAY

The Renegado is one of the most entertaining plays of its period: the variety of its situations and characters, the liveliness of its plot and its shamelessly theatrical brio help to explain how Massinger emerged as the most commercially successful dramatist of his day, rising to become the successor of William Shakespeare and John Fletcher as principal dramatist for the King's Men. Building on a number of texts by Miguel de Cervantes, in which the Spanish writer drew on his own experiences as a captive in Algiers, Massinger's play was pitched at a theatre audience that took particular pleasure in the vicarious enjoyment of colourful foreign locations.[1] Looking forward to such better-known oriental extravaganzas as Mozart's *The Abduction from the Seraglio*, *The Renegado* introduced the eroticized captivity narrative to the English stage, combining it with the long-popular romance motif of a Christian wooer's conquest of an exotic princess. Onto these Massinger grafted the story of a Venetian renegade who, like a number of notorious English sea-captains, has 'turned Turk' and thrown in his lot with the corsairs of the Barbary Coast. For the original audience, the presence of the renegade, together with the inclusion of an English eunuch amongst the princess's slaves, must have given the play a more urgently contemporary twist, since the corsairs were pirates and slave raiders whose forays reached the coasts of Britain and Ireland, reminding their populations that no part of Christendom could remain entirely isolated from the

---

1 See the remarks of the Swiss visitor Thomas Platter, in Clare Williams (ed.), *Thomas Platter's Travels in England, 1599* (1937), 170.

struggles of the Mediterranean world. Thus, even as it indulges in romantic fantasy, *The Renegado* exploits real anxieties occasioned by the endemic conflict between trade-hungry Europe and the expansionist Ottoman Empire (Fig. 1) – a conflict that involved competition for control of Eastern commerce as well as battles for territorial supremacy, but that was typically interpreted as an extension of the long war between Christendom and Islam that stretched back to the beginning of the Crusades. To the extent that English involvement in a revived crusading impulse was a significant focus of King James's ecumenical aspirations, *The Renegado* also appealed to immediate national concerns. At the same time, the play's carefully articulated theological arguments show a playwright alert to the contentious sectarian politics of the mid-1620s. As the energetic satire of such plays as *A New Way to Pay Old Debts* and *The City Madam* demonstrates, Massinger knew how to tap in to the liveliest social, political and religious issues of his time, whilst avoiding the open controversy that landed contemporaries like Ben Jonson, John Marston and Thomas Middleton in such trouble. Massinger seems to have written *The Renegado* early in 1624, at the height of the extended political crisis provoked by King James's attempt to negotiate a Catholic marriage for his heir; yet although he placed a Jesuit priest at the moral centre of its action, the play's first performances seem to have passed off without any public furore. Perhaps this had something to do with the distraction created by its ostentatious anti-Mahometanism on the one hand, and the shamelessly theatrical brio of its romantic plotting on the other.[1]

Although the play's title seemingly identifies the renegade Grimaldi as its protagonist, the main plot centres on Vitelli, a gentleman of Venice, who has travelled to Tunis in search of his missing sister, Paulina. In order to avoid the suspicion of the Ottoman authorities he has disguised himself as a merchant,

---

1 Throughout this edition I use the old forms 'Mahomet' and 'Mahometan' to distinguish seventeenth-century English constructs of the Islamic world from the historical realities of Islamic peoples and their faith.

suspicion
Suspicion

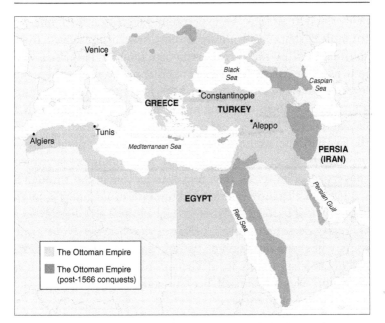

1 Map showing the expansion of the Ottoman Empire, 1300–1700

with his manservant, Gazet, posing as his apprentice. Shortly after his arrival, Vitelli learns from his friend and counsellor, the Jesuit Francisco, that Paulina was abducted by Grimaldi and that she has been sold to the Turkish Viceroy, Asambeg. The Viceroy now dotes upon his beautiful Christian slave and is determined to conquer her virtue. With the aid of a powerful relic given her by Francisco, Paulina is able to resist Asambeg's lustful designs. Her brother, however, proves less fortunate: as he peddles his tawdry trade-goods in the market-place of Tunis, Vitelli attracts the attention of Princess Donusa, niece of the Turkish Sultan, who lures him to her palace and seduces him. The dangerous bravado with which Vitelli abandons himself to his desire for this alluring unbeliever ('Though the Devil / Stood by and roared, I follow!', 2.4.134–5) initially recalls Faustus's surrender to the demonic Helen of Troy in Marlowe's popular tragedy. But Massinger

3

deliberately frustrates the expectation he creates, for Donusa's triumph is short-lived: the besotted Christian is rescued from spiritual peril by the earnest remonstrations of Francisco, and returns to the palace determined to break off his liaison; here the lovers are surprised by Donusa's Moorish suitor, Mustapha, and a furious Asambeg, who announces that the penalty for such a liaison is death. In the scenes that follow, Vitelli's steadfastness in the face of his persecutors so impresses Donusa that she abandons her efforts to undermine his faith and announces her own conversion. The action then moves to its conclusion through a sequence of elegantly symmetrical reversals of fortune: Paulina's chaste refusal to 'turn Turk' is set against the Turkish princess's voluntary decision to turn Christian; Vitelli carries Donusa off to Italy in a neat inversion of the original abduction of Paulina; and his assistant in this act of virtuous piracy is none other than Grimaldi, who has himself been brought to repentance by the ministrations of Francisco.

This elaborate braiding of plots is further complicated by subsidiary actions involving the frustrated ambitions of Mustapha and the fortunes of a gallery of servant figures – notably the hero's ambitious, conniving, but absurdly naive manservant, Gazet. The pleasures of exotic romance are sharpened by a number of devices designed to sheet the action home to its English audience. Vitelli's merchant guise and the commercial setting in which he enters the play invite a reading of his rich prize as an allegory of mercantile desire, while Grimaldi's ferocious piracy animates the dark side of such ambition, reminding seventeenth-century playgoers of the threat to English enterprise posed by corsairs who included renegade Englishmen (such as the notorious John Ward, also known as Yusuf Reis). The satiric commentary placed in the mouths of Gazet and the English eunuch Carazie repeatedly links the action to contemporary critiques of English vice and folly, while the presence of a Jesuit priest as spiritual adviser to Vitelli and Grimaldi raises theological issues closely bound up with the fierce religious controversies attending the final years of James I's reign – especially those provoked by his efforts to secure a Catholic marriage for his son and successor, Charles. The inclusion of such potentially explosive material at a time of political crisis might have invited the kind of trouble that befell the King's Men later in the same year, when they staged Thomas Middleton's satiric allegory of the abortive Spanish match, *A Game at Chess*; but Massinger's deft interweaving of disparate materials, combined with a mastery of tone that enables *The Renegado* to insist on its ultimately playful status as a sentimental fantasy, seems to have protected it from both Protestant opprobrium and official sanction.

The pace and verve of the play's action, the unexpected turns and counterturns of its plot and the effortless shifts of tone through which the voices of its various characters are realized, all mark *The Renegado* as the work of a consummate professional – one whose long apprenticeship as a collaborator with the leading playwrights of his day (Fletcher, Middleton and Thomas Dekker among them) had given him a sure feel for managing the pleasures of an audience. Massinger's well-honed skills, like those of Middleton and other contemporaries, have for too long been obscured by the extraordinary pre-eminence of Shakespeare; but successful revivals of several of his plays, including *The Roman Actor*, *Believe as You List* and *A New Way to Pay Old Debts*, have demonstrated the sharpness of his theatrical instinct. Perfectly adjusted to the tastes of the elite 'private' playhouse for which it was written, *The Renegado* is equally well calculated to delight modern playgoers; and its involvement with the long and troubled history of relations between the Christian West and Islamic East make it a text of peculiar interest to the present time.

CRITICAL APPROACHES

For a long time, critical and theatrical attention to Massinger's extensive *oeuvre* has tended to concentrate on a small number of relatively well-known plays: the lively social satire of his comedies *A New Way to Pay Old Debts* and *The City Madam*, and the metatheatrical reflexiveness of his tragedies *The Roman Actor* and *Believe as You List*, in particular, have attracted the interest of critics and, to some extent, of theatre directors; but the tragicomedies have been less well served. *The Renegado*, despite its obvious theatrical flair, has suffered peculiar neglect, barely rating a mention in the two books that set out to reawaken interest in Massinger towards the end of the twentieth century.[1] Over the last decade, however, a number of convergent factors have combined to remedy this situation. Most conspicuously, perhaps, anxieties about the so-called 'clash of civilizations' have stimulated an interest in literature that mirrors the vexed history of relationships between Christian Europe and the Muslim world. This in turn has provided a new direction for the longstanding critical concern with works that reflect or refract England's emerging preoccupation with mercantile enterprise and dreams of empire – a preoccupation that was often complicated by envious awareness of the belated and fragile character of English expansionism.[2] At the same time, various critics, perplexed by the choric role allotted to the Jesuit priest, Francisco, have attempted to situate the play's conflict of faiths in the complicated religious politics of the early 1620s and the anxieties stirred up by the prospect of a Catholic marriage for the Prince of Wales.

Generic play: The Renegado *as tragicomedy*

The title-page of the 1630 Quarto identifies *The Renegado* as

1 Douglas Howard (ed.), *Philip Massinger: A Critical Reassessment* (Cambridge, 1985), and Ira Clark, *The Moral Art of Philip Massinger* (Lewisburg, 1993).

2 Two important studies that place writing about Moors and Turks in the wider contexts of European imperial desire are Barbara Fuchs's wide-ranging *Mimesis and Empire: The New World, Islam, and European Identities* (Cambridge, 2001) and Jonathan Burton's more closely focused study (Burton, *Traffic*). See also Daniel J. Vitkus, 'Trafficking with the Turk: English travelers in the Ottoman Empire during the early seventeenth century', in Kamps and Singh, 35–52. In the opening chapter of *Turning Turk*, Vitkus sensibly stresses the gap between England's emerging idea of empire and the lack of 'a real, material empire on the ground' (6).

'*A Tragicomædie*', advertising its affiliation with the Italianate genre that had been developed in England by Massinger's mentor and frequent collaborator, Fletcher. The play is Fletcherian in its exploitation of exotic romance motifs, as well as in its deployment of the structural conceits celebrated by contemporaries in their relish of 'the Plots swift change, and counterturn'[1] – that witty orchestration of peripeties by which an apparently tragic sequence of events is raised to a pitch of danger before being brought to a miraculously happy conclusion. Praising the craftsmanship of *The Renegado*'s elaborately symmetrical design, Maurice Chelli observes that in its piling up of 'disguises, surprises, naive ruses, swift and touching conversions, sudden and burning amours . . . this play has everything necessary to make it a perfect epitome of conventional tragicomedy.'[2] It is, moreover, unusually self-conscious in the way it handles the conventions of the form.

Tragicomedy is by definition a mixed mode, but one of the distinctive things about the design of Massinger's play is the way its unexpected switches of tone and direction are produced by yoking together elements from a wide variety of genres and subgenres – as if in defiance of Sir Philip Sidney's famous strictures on this 'mongrel' kind.[3] Apart from its links to voyage drama and to other Turk plays,[4] *The Renegado* recalls Marlovian heroic tragedy in the blustering rant of the renegade Grimaldi (see, for example, 1.3.42–6), and revisits citizen romance through Vitelli's bourgeois disguise as 'A poor mechanic pedlar' (3.3.80) who wins the love (and dowry) of an oriental princess. Even more striking are the disorienting recollections of city comedy: Massinger's Tunis is a very different city from the Algiers remembered by Cervantes; its symbolic centre has shifted from the prison to the market–place – a point that Massinger underlines

---

1   The phrase is from William Davenant's epilogue to *The First Day's Entertainment at Rutland House* (London, 1656).
2   Chelli, 132 (editor's translation).
3   Sir Philip Sidney, *An Apology for Poetry*, in Edmund Jones (ed.), *English Critical Essays (Sixteenth, Seventeenth and Eighteenth Centuries)* (1947), 46.
4   The designation is borrowed from Daniel Vitkus, whose introduction to *Three Turk Plays from Early Modern England* includes a useful discussion of the genre.

by casting his Christian characters as citizens of Venice, a republic famous for the wealth it garnered from trade with the Orient, and by introducing his hero as a Venetian merchant, come with his apprentice to set up shop in the Tunis bazaar.

Beneath his disguise, of course, Vitelli is '*The Gentleman of Venice*' invoked by the play's original subtitle, but he opens the play with a blunt demand better fitted to the commercial world satirized in Jacobean city comedy than to the aristocratic and romantic ambience conventionally associated with Fletcherian tragicomedy: 'You have hired a shop, then?' (1.1.1). The dialogue of 1.1 and 1.3 compounds this generic confusion: capitalizing on the 'free trading' allowed to foreigners in the 'mart-time' (1.1.45–6), and whipping up custom for their 'toys and trifles' (1.3.105) with the pedlar's cry of 'What do you lack?' (1.3.1, 5, 35, 92, 99), Vitelli and Gazet lay out their stock of 'choice China dishes . . . pure Venetian crystal . . . and curious pictures of the rarest beauties of Europa' (1.3.1–5). The glass and china may be flawless (1.1.1–4), but the same cannot be said for their supposed court portraits – images which they seek to pass off as masterpieces of that 'great Italian workman' Michelangelo (1.3.131–2), even as they privately identify them as mere 'figures / Of bawds and common courtesans in Venice' (1.1.4–13), cheap paintings of the kind used for advertisement in the Venetian sex trade.[1] This milieu of fleshly appetite, commercial appetancy and petty fraud is immediately reminiscent of Jonson and Middleton; and Gazet, in particular, who takes his name from a small Venetian coin, is a character whose combination of opportunism, naivety and greed would not be out of place in *Bartholomew Fair* or *A Chaste Maid in Cheapside*.

By contrast, the subtitle's identification of Massinger's protagonist as '*The Gentleman of Venice*' invites comparison with two very different plays: *The Merchant of Venice* and

---

1   See, for example, Angelica Bianca's use of a portrait to advertise her charms in Aphra Behn's *The Rover*.

Othello – otherwise known as *The Moor of Venice*.[1] The story of Grimaldi – a Venetian Christian turned Turk who repents and returns to his former allegiance – resembles a reverse image of Shakespeare's Moor-turned-Christian whose tragic destiny is (in his own imagination at least) to 'turn Turk' again. By the same token, the successful enterprise of a young Venetian who wins himself an exotic bride endowed with fabulous wealth recalls the rich matches achieved by Bassanio and Lorenzo in *The Merchant of Venice* – not least in the way that Vitelli successfully elopes with a convertite bride whose dowry, like Jessica's, consists of rich jewels and a casket crammed with treasure. Yet even as *The Renegado*'s subtitle highlights its relation with *The Merchant of Venice*, it distances the action from the milieu of commerce by emphasizing that the play's real concern is with the fortunes of a 'gentleman', whose true rank fits him to the more elevated world of Fletcherian tragicomedy;[2] and, while both plays pivot on a scene of narrowly averted execution in which an infidel turns Christian, the model for Donusa's spectacular conversion lay closer to hand, in the work of Massinger's old collaborator Fletcher.

Fletcher's *Island Princess* had been staged by the King's Men little more than a year before *The Renegado* was performed by their rivals, the Lady Elizabeth's Men, at the Cockpit, and it seems likely that Massinger's play was conceived partly in response to the success of this oriental fantasy. Fletcher's tragicomedy also centres on the fortunes of a gentleman adventurer who achieves his ends by assuming the guise of a merchant – a device that conveniently validates English commercial ambitions, even as the play ostensibly disavows them with the pretence that merchant enterprise is no more than a convenient cover for old-fashioned chivalric heroism (Neill, 'Materiall flames'). Both plays exploit

---

1   This appellation appears not only as the play's subtitle in both Q1 and F, but as the full title for the 1604 court performance recorded in the account book of Edmund Tilney, Master of the Revels.
2   On status divisions in the play, see Barbara Fuchs: 'the world of *The Renegado* . . . tolerates conversions far better than it does change in social status' (Fuchs, 64).

the glamour of exotic settings; and like *The Renegado*, *The Island Princess* climaxes in the conversion of an infidel princess who is so moved by her Christian lover's fortitude that she surrenders herself to his inspirational faith.[1] Considered as a theatrical meta-commentary on Fletcher's play, however, *The Renegado* exhibits some important differences – not least in its attitude towards cultural contact. The precipitate escape of Massinger's Venetians from Tunis contrasts with the amity and 'universal gladness' celebrated by the triumphant Portuguese and their East Indian allies at the end of *The Island Princess*, where the King of Tidore is sufficiently impressed by Armusia's steadfast courage, and by his own sister's conversion, to contemplate turning Christian himself. But Massinger's Mahometan potentates, while they may admire Vitelli's unwavering refusal to betray his faith, feel no such admiration for Donusa's apostasy; nor do they ever falter in their determination to punish the offenders. As a result, where the final scene of *The Island Princess* brings Tidoreans and Portuguese together in a circle of cross-cultural reconciliation, *The Renegado* deliberately frustrates conventional tragicomic expectation by concluding on a note of enraged bafflement and mutual recrimination, as Mustapha and Asambeg discover the captives' escape and face the prospect of exile or torture at the hands of their 'incensed master', the Sultan (5.8.31–9).[2] In this, it departs even from the ending of its principal dramatic source, Cervantes's *Los Baños de Argel* (*The Prisons of Algiers*), which

1 The parallel was first noted in Marvin T. Herrick, *Tragicomedy* (Chicago, 1955), 291.
2 Benedict Robinson, likening the Venetians' flight to the abandonment of Prospero's island at the end of *The Tempest*, argues that Massinger 'abandons the possibility of any legitimate contact with "Turks", because such intercourse can only be 'contaminating' ('Commodities', 141). However, given that the hero departs with a sizeable fortune in Ottoman jewels – the portion of a princess who has herself been figured as the choicest commodity of all – the conclusion we are to draw about his adventuring is not, perhaps, quite so clear-cut: in fact, it might well seem that Massinger's fugitives are allowed to have it both ways, returning from their enterprise laden with wealth even as they celebrate their departure from Tunis by launching a defiant 'broadside' at their infidel pursuers. Such equivocation is in accord with the divided attitude towards Ottoman Turkey described by Burton, who shows how 'a discourse of captivity and degeneracy' competed with more positive reactions designed to encourage trade – sometimes within the same text (*Traffic*, 24).

focuses on the happiness of its reunited lovers as they flee the scene of their captivity.

Turks, renegades and merchants: the Islamic context

By Massinger's time, European anxiety about the Islamic East already had a long history, stretching back through the Crusades to the Moorish conquest of the Iberian peninsula in the eighth century. The recurrent presence of a lavishly attired 'King of Moors' in medieval street pageants, a figure at once fearful and glamorously exotic, served as a sign of the ambivalent fascination that the Muslim world exercised upon the popular imagination – a fascination that later fed into Christopher Marlowe's characterization of oriental despotism in *Tamburlaine*. In the fifteenth and sixteenth centuries, the rapid expansion of Ottoman Turkey gave a fresh immediacy to such attitudes: overrunning the remains of the Byzantine Empire, Ottoman armies pushed west, reaching as far as the walls of Vienna in 1529 (see Fig. 1).[1] The traumatic fall of Constantinople in 1453 had turned the

---

1   Richard Knolles prefaces his *Generall Historie of the Turkes* (1603) by lamenting 'The long and still declining state of the Christian Commonweale, with the utter ruine and subversion of the Empire of the East' (sig. A4ʳ), and by expressing his consternation at an empire 'growne to that height of pride, as that it threatneth destruction unto the rest of the kingdomes of the earth . . . [and] holdeth all the rest of the worlde in scorne, thundering out nothing but still bloud and warre' (sig. A4ᵛ); he goes on to blame the members of the 'Christian Commonweale' for ignoring their common interests as members of a single body, and for being 'so divided among themselves with endlesse quarrels, partly for questions of religion . . . partly for matters touching their own proper state and sovereigntie . . . that they could never as yet . . . joyne their common forces against the common enemie' (sig. A4ᵛ). The author does, however, conclude his massive work with 'A briefe discourse of the greatnesse of the Turkish Empire' designed to show to 'the zealous Christian' how the signs of its decadence and ultimate fall are already apparent, since the empire is 'not much unlike the overgrowne tree, at the greatnesse whereof every man wondereth . . . Which although it be indeed verie strong . . . yet is by many probably thought to be now upon the declining hand, their late emperors in their owne persons so far degenerating from their warlike progenitors, their souldiers generally giving themselves to unwonted pleasures, their ancient discipline of war neglected, their superstition not with as much discipline as of old regarded . . . [Turkey exhibits] all the signs of a declining state . . . the greatnesse of the empire being such, as that it laboureth with nothing more then with the weightinesse, it must needs . . . of it selfe fall, and againe come to nought, no man knowing when or how so great a worke shall be brought to passe, but hee in whose deepe counsells all those great revolutions of Empires and Kingdomes are from eternitie shut up' (sigs 6C1ʳ–7C8ʳ).

attention of Humanist scholars to this new Islamic menace. The picture of the Turkish Empire that emerged from their studies was laced with contradictions: as the memory of recent disasters merged with legend, romance and religious dogma, Turks might be denounced 'as amoral barbarian[s], inhuman scourge[s], and even [as the] anti-Christ' (Burton, *Traffic*, 23). Seen as responsible for destroying the great monuments of classical civilization, feared as ruthless slave raiders and corsairs (Fig. 2), they were nevertheless often stigmatized as indulgent sensualists, adherents of 'a sham religion founded on violence and unrestrained lust' (Bisaha, 15). Their spectacular military and political success, however, invited more positive reactions: praised for their 'learning . . . arts, civility, and government', they were sometimes held up as 'paragon[s] of order, piety, and strength', exponents of 'a virtuous, austere culture' (Fig. 3) who were not only 'worthy and capable adversaries', but might even be courted as potential allies (Burton, *Traffic*, 28, 23; Bisaha, 6–9). Thus Ottoman Turkey became in many respects the defining other of Tudor and Stuart culture, functioning, in Burton's words, 'as a discursive site upon which contesting versions of Englishness, Christianity, masculinity, femininity and nobility [were] elaborated and proffered' (*Traffic*, 28). In some respects this response prefigured the later constructions of oriental alterity famously described by Edward Said;[1] but, as both Burton and Richmond Barbour have stressed, the deep ambivalence of English attitudes makes any attempt to view early modern encounters with the Islamic world through a Saidian lens perilous – a misleading 'back-formation' that disguises the fear and anxious sense of inferiority that characterized early modern responses to Turkish power.[2]

The work of Nabil Matar, in particular, has done much to

---

1 See Edward Said, *Orientalism* (New York, 1979).
2 See Vitkus, *Turning Turk*, 10–11, 19, Richmond Barbour, *Before Orientalism: London's Theatre of the East, 1576–1626* (Cambridge, 2003), 3–5, and Burton, *Traffic*, 12. Barbour, whilst acknowledging that pre-enlightenment 'orientalisms' were in some important respects ancestral to later formations, nevertheless insists that they 'expressed material, political, and discursive relations profoundly different from those Said finds typical of modernity' (3). See also McJannet, 2–6.

2 'Turkish Pirate', from Cesare Vecellio, *Habiti antichi, e moderni di tutto il Mondo*, 1598

reveal and explain the extraordinary place occupied by Ottoman Turkey and the Barbary states in the Tudor and Stuart imaginary.[1] On the one hand, Turkey controlled crucial trade routes to the silks and spices of the East and was a source of coveted luxuries in its own right; on the other, it was the seat of a powerful

1 See Nabil Matar, *Islam in Britain, 1558–1685* (New York, 1998), *Turks, Moors, and Englishmen in the Age of Discovery* (New York, 1999) and *Britain and Barbary, 1589–1689* (Gainesville, 2005).

3   Lecherous Christian couple with a Turk preparing to kill them, from André Friedrich, *Emblemes Nouveaux*, Frankfurt, 1617

expansionist empire vying for control of Mediterranean trade routes, and exercising suzerainty over the Levant, Greece, the Balkans and most of the North African littoral (see Fig. 1). The protracted struggle between a dangerously divided Europe and Ottoman power had climaxed in the Christian victory at the battle of Lepanto (1571) that forms part of the background to Shakespeare's *Othello*. Barely had this much trumpeted success been achieved, however, than surrender of the Venetian-controlled island of Cyprus announced a further erosion of Christian territory. Although the main burden of this fighting was borne by Catholic powers to which the Protestant English were normally inimical, it was nevertheless viewed as part of a contest in which all of Christian Europe was pitched against an aggressive Islam. James I, the self-proclaimed *rex pacificus*, who in his youth had written a poem celebrating the triumph of Lepanto, was temperamentally attracted to the idea of a Christendom united against the Muslim enemy; while for the English at large, though the main battles might be far away, the Islamic threat was given frightening immediacy not only by the attacks of Barbary corsairs on English shipping but by their sporadic coastal slave raids.

England's relationship with the Arab-Berber states of North Africa was further complicated by a number of factors, both political and commercial. On the one hand, Elizabethan diplomacy had sometimes seen the Moors (like their nominal suzerains in Constantinople) as potential allies against Catholic Spain; on the other, the Barbary ports harboured lawless pirates and renegades – among them English pirates like the Tunis-based John Ward, the infamous anti-hero of Robert Daborne's play *A Christian Turned Turk* (1609–12) – who were the subject of numerous pamphlets, ballads and plays. In 1620 King James had actually joined with the Spanish in an unsuccessful attack on Algiers which attempted to release the thousands of Christian prisoners enslaved by these very pirates (Malieckal, 25–6). But at the same time, the cities of the North African littoral were attractive commercial entrepôts, whose importance had been recognized in 1585 when Queen Elizabeth granted a monopoly to the Barbary Company, giving it control of a trade which (until North Africa was overtaken by New World plantations in the mid-seventeenth century) included England's main supply of sugar. There were good material and ideological reasons, then, why – quite apart from the glamour of exotic romance – London audiences would have been interested in

Massinger's carefully limned picture of Tunis and its Turkish overlords.

In the half-century before the appearance of *The Renegado*, the ambiguous allure of the Muslim world had been demonstrated in at least sixty plays and dramatic entertainments featuring Islamic locations, characters and themes.[1] As Jack D'Amico and others have recognized, however, Massinger's tragicomedy is unusual in the seriousness with which it attempts to re-create its exotic locale. Although earlier studies had recognized the play's significant dependence on documentary sources, with Samuel Chew praising its 'accurate and realistic orientalism',[2] D'Amico's brief account of *The Renegado*, in his pioneering study of the figure of the Moor in English Renaissance drama, was the first to give full weight to Massinger's picture of ethnic and religious conflict: 'more than any other play,' he argued, 'it dramatizes a direct confrontation between characters representative of Christian and Islamic values, as those values are seen from the point of view of the West' (D'Amico, 120). D'Amico's approach has since been extended by a number of critics, notably Daniel Vitkus, who explores the play's relation to pirate literature and to narratives of captivity and conversion, including a range of 'Turk plays'.[3] For Vitkus,

1 Burton, *Traffic*, 11. See also Lawrence Danson, 'England, Islam, and Mediterranean drama: *Othello* and others', *JEMCS*, 2 (2002), 1–25. For interesting surveys of early modern English attitudes to the Turks written from a Turkish perspective, see two essays by Süheyla Artemel: '"The Great Turk's particular red herring": the popular image of the Turk during the Renaissance in England', *Journal of Mediterranean Studies*, 5 (1995), 188–208, and 'The view of the Turks from the perspective of the Humanists in Renaissance England', in Mustafa Soykut (ed.), *Historical Image of the Turk in Europe: 15th Century to the Present* (Istanbul, 2003), 149–73.
2 S. C. Chew, *The Crescent and the Rose: Islam and England during the Renaissance* (New York, 1965), 536. A less flattering view is taken by Nabil Matar, who insists that, because of the dependence on foreign models, 'from the *Battle of Alcazar* . . . to *Othello* . . . English playwrights, despite their imaginative brilliance, invented stage Muslims without any historical or religious verisimilitude' (in Vitkus, *Piracy*, 4).
3 See Vitkus, *Turk Plays*, 1–53. Nabil Matar places English renegade plays in the context of a wider literature of apostasy in 'The renegade in English seventeenth-century imagination', *SEL*, 33 (1993), 489–506. A lively and economical survey of the plays discussed by Vitkus and Matar can be found in Lois Potter, 'Pirates and "turning Turk" in Renaissance drama', in Jean-Pierre Maquerlot and Michele Willems (eds), *Travel and Drama in Shakespeare's Time* (Cambridge, 1996), 124–40. See also Mary C. Fuller, 'English Turks and resistant travelers: conversion to Islam

The Renegado is best understood as one of a group of dramas –
including Kyd's *Soliman and Perseda* (1592), Heywood's *1 Fair
Maid of the West* (*c.* 1597–1610) and Daborne's *A Christian Turned
Turk* (1609–12) – preoccupied with apostasy and conversion,
in which Islam is presented as 'a religion of temptation' with a
culture that is at once 'powerful, wealthy, and erotically alluring'
(Vitkus, *Turning Turk*, 108). In each play Christians are subjected
to the enticements of this hazardous world; but even when (as
with Daborne's Ward) their fall proves irreversible, the example
is offset by the triumphant conversion of Mahometans or the
reconversion of penitent apostates. Women play a pivotal role
in these encounters: where Eastern females appear as dangerous
sirens, their chaste Christian sisters 'speak truth to patriarchal
power, targeting an "Islamic" form of the raging male libido' (126).
Sometimes (as with Heywood's Bess or Massinger's Paulina) they
may even appear to exercise a quasi-magical influence of the sort
traditionally attributed to virginity.

So striking are *The Renegado*'s parallels with *A Christian Turned
Turk*, Vitkus argues, that it might even have been composed as a
deliberate riposte to Daborne's tragedy,[1] 'rewriting' the original
as 'A Turk Turned Christian', and 'revers[ing its] outcome . . . by
affirming the power of Christianity to "'redeem" both Muslims and
renegades'.[2] In this reading, the fatal liaison between the English
pirate Ward and the Moorish temptress Voada 'is reconfigured in the
happy outcome of the Vitelli–Donusa relationship', while Grimaldi
represents an amalgam of the ruthless Ward and the repentant
Dutch corsair Dansiker (Vitkus, *Turk Plays*, 41–3).

Vitkus pays some attention to the play's mercantile setting,
noting how 'the desire for profit leads to other lusts', exposing the

and homosocial courtship', in Kamps and Singh (66–73), and Jean E. Howard,
'Gender on the periphery', in Tom Clayton, Susan Brock and Vicente Forés (eds),
Shakespeare and the Mediterranean (Newark, 2004), 344–62.

1 Massinger had once worked alongside Daborne as a hack writer for the unscrupulous
theatre manager Philip Henslowe; in 1613 the pair, with Nathaniel Field, appealed to
Henslowe in the hope that he might bail them out of debtors' prison.

2 Vitkus, *Turk Plays*, 43; for another reading that also sees Massinger as 'rewriting'
Daborne, see Parker.

Paggi del Signore.

4   Eunuchs: 'Slaves of the Sultan and Pashas', from Cesare Vecellio, *Habiti antichi, e moderni di tutto il Mondo*, 1598

4 *(contd.)*

market-place as 'a site of temptation and potential contagion'.[1] It is in the market that Donusa and Vitelli first meet, establishing the connection between her extravagant wealth and her dangerous sexual allure that is borne out in their subsequent encounter, where she heaps 'imperial coin' and '[Indian] gems' upon her 'royal merchant' (2.4.82–94). But if lust is potentially the instrument of Christian downfall, it is also imagined as 'the definitive Turkish vice', which, through Asambeg's infatuation with Paulina, not only 'proves a weak point for the Christians to exploit',[2] but (one might add) enables them to enjoy the profit of Ottoman trade without any ultimate cost to their own virtue.

Burton extends Vitkus's approach to the Islamic setting of *The Renegado* by stressing the symbolic importance of castration in the play's moral economy. A recurrent source of anxiety not merely in Turk plays but in innumerable texts dealing with the Muslim world, eunuchism here becomes the focus of fantasies that help to shape Massinger's entire design.[3] The conspicuous role of Carazie in Donusa's household not only bodies forth the threat to which Gazet is comically exposed, but stands as a brutally physical equivalent for the unmanning that threatens Vitelli through his surrender to his Turkish enchantress. The fact that Carazie is also the play's sole Englishman serves to sheet the menace home to Massinger's audience. The anxieties attendant upon English weakness in the face of Ottoman power are thus expressed as a fear of feminization and ultimate emasculation; for 'rather than being embodied in powerful Muslim men, the principal threat to Christian men in the stage's imaginary world of trafficking comes in the form of an alluring, feminized Islam' (Fig. 5).[4] The triumphant effect of the plot's crucial counterturns, in Burton's

1 Vitkus, *Turning Turk*, 158; cf. *Turk Plays*, 41.
2 Vitkus, *Turk Plays*, 43; cf. *Turning Turk*, 159.
3 Burton, *Traffic*, chs 2 and 3, and 'English anxiety and the Muslim power of conversion: five perspectives on "turning Turk" in early modern texts', *JEMCS*, 2 (2002), 35–67; see also Malieckal.
4 Burton, *Traffic*, 127. Women were apparently sometimes offered to Christian captives in an attempt to make them 'turn Moor' – see e.g. the narrative of Richard Hasleton, in Vitkus, *Piracy*, 71–95, esp. 90.

5 The dangerous oriental temptress: 'Roxolana, Solyman his best beloved wife', from Richard Knolles, *The Generall Historie of the Turkes*, 1603

analysis, is to redirect these anxieties onto the Turks themselves: in their first scene together, Asambeg is made to confess that his abject passion for the unyielding Paulina has undone his masculinity – precisely as Christian men feared that Turks might rob them of their own manhood – putting him in the position of 'a eunuch or bought handmaid' (2.5.148):

> There is something in you
> That can work miracles (or I am cozened),
> Dispose and alter sexes: to my wrong,

In spite of nature, I will be your nurse,
Your woman, your physician and your fool,
Till with your free consent – which I have vowed
Never to force – you grace me with a name
That shall supply all these . . .
                              Your husband!
                                 (149–56)

The upshot, as Burton suggests, is that while 'the virtuous Christian man overcomes temptation by converting lechery into propriety and the Muslim temptress into a Christian wife . . . lechery is displaced from the former temptress onto the Muslim man whose foolhardy obsession with an unattainable Christian woman enables the escape of all his Christian captives' (Burton, *Traffic*, 153).

Jonathan Gil Harris expands and complicates Burton's arguments by suggesting ways in which the play's castration fantasies are specifically linked to its mercantile preoccupations.[1] Citing Carazie's dubious reassurance to Gazet that the 'price' of becoming a court eunuch is nothing more than 'parting with / A precious stone or two' (3.4.51–2), and noting the way in which Gazet's name equates his unmanning with coin-clipping, Harris observes how 'castration is . . . associated throughout the play with economic loss' (157). This threat is directly linked to English economic concerns by the figure of Carazie, whose castration, like Clem's in *1 Fair Maid of the West*, 'not only metaphorically deprives England of its precious stones but also arbitrarily removes wealth in the form of human capital from circulation'; since, moreover, all the play's Christian males are menaced by Turkish tyranny, all are potential castrati (158). So it seems that 'the only way in which a male Christian visitor . . . can fully avert the risk of castration is to receive the largesse of a powerful Turkish princess who, by filling his testicular purse with precious stones, also restores his manly vigor' (158). So

1   Harris, 154, 157–61; see also Fuchs, 63.

6   Amurath III, engraving from Richard Knolles, *The Generall Historie of the Turkes*, 1603

long as the price of those stones is effeminating subjection to female will, however, they remain an ambiguous restorative – rendered acceptable only through the play's concluding fantasy in which the escapees, loaded down with Turkish treasure, represent 'a transnational community of Christian venturers liberated not only from Islamic masters but also from the emasculating sway of the state in general' (159). Harris's *Renegado* proves to be as much about the discontents of English merchant adventurers, chafing under the restrictive controls of the Jacobean state, as it is about exotic romance or fears

7   Aga, 'captain general of the Janizaries', from Nicolas de Nicolay
[Daulphinois], *The Navigations, Peregrinations and Voyages, made into Turkie*,
trans. T. Washington the younger, 1585

The Ianissarie or Ianissarler, being a souldier on foot, and of the ordinary gard of the great Turk.

8   A janizary, from Nicolas de Nicolay [Daulphinois], *The Navigations, Peregrinations and Voyages, made into Turkie*, trans. Thomas Washington the younger, 1585

9   A beylerbey, from Cesare Vecellio, *Habiti antichi, e moderni di tutto il Mondo*, 1598

10   A kapiaga, from Cesare Vecellio, *Habiti antichi, e moderni di tutto il Mondo*,
     1598

fears
of the Islamic other; and when his Grimaldi rails against the
'unmanly' potentate who idles at home while the much abused
corsairs 'run abroad all hazards [to] bring . . . home new pillage
/ For the fatting his seraglio' (2.5.13–16), it is the complaints
of early free marketeers about the treatment of entrepreneurial
merchants that the pirate articulates. 'In a dark way,' as Barbara
Fuchs observes, '[piracy] mimics the incredible accumulation

that was the goal of all mercantile (ad)ventures' (47). Grimaldi, of course, makes precisely this connection when he contrasts the freebooting extravagance of the corsair fraternity with the avaricious accumulation of merchants:

> No, no, my mates, let tradesmen think of thrift
> And usurers hoard up; let our expense
> Be, as our comings-in are, without bounds.
> We are the Neptunes of the ocean,
> And such as traffic shall pay sacrifice
> Of their best lading. I'll have this canvas
> Your boy wears lined with tissue, and the cates
> You taste served up in gold. Though we carouse
> The tears of orphans in our Greekish wines,
> The sighs of undone widows paying for
> The music bought to cheer us, ravished virgins
> To slavery sold for coin to feed our riots,
> We will have no compunction.
>
> (1.3.64–76)

For all Grimaldi's professed disdain for merchant parsimony, the dramatic function of his rhetoric is to emphasize the uneasy parallels that *The Renegado* repeatedly suggests between the corsairs' 'trade' (2.5.6) in treasure and human commodity and the material and erotic vending of the market-place.

For the bulk of Massinger's audience, however, the danger posed by the Tunis bazaar must have seemed as much religious as it was sexual or economic. Gazet's mock piety may present it as an arena for the 'meritorious work' of abusing the Turkish infidel (1.1.21–3), but the market is a place of perilous fungibility, where the bartering of commodity may all too easily extend to the spiritual exchange of 'turning Turk' (1.1.38–41).

Religious conversion and sectarian controversy

In 2.6, following his seduction by Donusa, Vitelli reappears dressed in the 'rich suit' that proclaims him 'turn[ed] courtier' and followed by a 'train [of] Turks' (2.6.2, 9–10). This ostentatious makeover announces a sexual renegadism that matches the blasphemous apostasy of Grimaldi. Each in his way has turned Turk; and, as the action unfolds, both Gazet and Paulina will be tempted to follow their example – he in reality and she in appearance only. A counter-action begins, however, with the disgrace of Grimaldi for having 'blasphemed the Ottoman power' – an action expressly linked to the scene of his original irreligious outrage (2.5.78–80); and this continues through the scenes of Vitelli's penitence (3.2), Grimaldi's recantation (3.2, 4.1) and Donusa's conversion (4.3, 5.3). The spiritual transformations of Grimaldi and the physical metamorphoses of Vitelli (from Venetian gentleman to shopkeeper, to lavishly dressed Turkish courtier, to prisoner in penitential garb) serve to foreground the importance of conversion in a play whose action reaches its climax in the Christianization of an Ottoman princess.

It seems highly significant that there are no real precedents for Massinger's treatment of apostasy and conversion, either in Cervantes or even in *The Island Princess*. In *Los Baños* they are merely part of the background against which the action unfolds: the renegade's inward conflict may reflect the outward strife between Costanza's abductor, Yzuf, and the repentant renegade Hazen; but Hazen's killing of Yzuf is quickly discovered and the penitent executed before he can contribute anything further to the story. If Cervantes shows no interest in the psychological consequences of apostasy, he seems equally uninterested in the processes of conversion. Unlike Vitelli, Don Lope has no need to turn Zahara Christian, since she has long ago been converted by a slave woman: as a result, the Spanish play offers no equivalent to the sensational counterturn produced by Donusa's renunciation of Mahomet in Act 4 of *The Renegado*. The dramatic prominence accorded to this episode becomes especially striking when it is compared with its model in *The Island Princess*.

In Fletcher's play, Quisara's change of faith is accomplished in four rather perfunctory lines ('Your faith, and your religion must be like ye . . . I do embrace your faith sir, and your fortune', 5.2.118–21); by contrast, Massinger extends Donusa's across two scenes, climaxing it with a carefully improvised baptism that turns the hero from a passive example of Christian endurance into a kind of surrogate priest. This disparity reveals the extent to which the clash between the play's European and Turkish worlds is imagined in religious rather than racial terms. Unlike Fletcher's East Indians, who are distinguished from his Portuguese adventurers primarily by their 'tawny' skins and by the lamentable want of 'temperance' of which their colour appears to be the outward sign (see Neill, 'Materiall flames'), Massinger's Turks are set apart from his Europeans by faith and customs rather than by colour: Donusa may scorn her Moorish suitor Mustapha for his 'wainscot face' and 'tadpole-like complexion' (3.1.48, 50), but (as the play's title indicates) the crucial distinctions between Venice and Tunis are cultural, political and, above all, spiritual.

For Massinger, what is at issue does indeed appear to be a clash of civilizations: making use of what were to become some of the most enduring tropes of Orientalism, the dramatist stresses the difference between the social 'liberty' enjoyed by Christians and the untrammelled 'licence' claimed by their Mahometan rivals.[1] Where Christian liberty is seen as contingent upon voluntary self-control, Mahometan licence paradoxically registers enslavement to the senses and the passions; where licence permits tyranny over others, liberty depends upon a regime of voluntary service. Thus, on the political level, Massinger contrasts the 'bondage' imposed by the arbitrary, passion-driven whims of Turkish autocracy with the 'freedom' enjoyed by rational Europeans.

---

1 On the endlessly recycled myths of Mahometan licence and lust, see Vitkus, *Turning Turk*, 115–19, and 'Conversion', 155–9.

The humiliations of Ottoman slavery are set against the good 'service' that governs relations among the citizens of Venice; the 'unbounded' power of the Sultan (2.4.89) and his tyrannous subordinates is opposed to the voluntary submission and self-restraint exemplified by the Venetian hero; and the 'free' conduct allowed to Christian women – even if it sometimes leads to the libertine excess satirically attributed to domineering English wives (1.2.27–48) – is contrasted with the repressive 'restraint of freedom' to which

11 Mustapha Pasha, engraving from Richard Knolles, *The Generall Historie of the Turkes*, 1603

12   'A Favourite of the Sultan', from Cesare Vecellio, *Habiti antichi, e moderni di tutto il Mondo*, 1598

A Woman Moorisque of Alger in Barbarie, as she goeth in the streetes.

13   Female Moorish slave from Algiers, from Nicolas de Nicolay [Daulphinois], *The Navigations, Peregrinations and Voyages, made into Turkie*, trans. T. Washington the younger, 1585

their Turkish sisters are subjected by a religion that, while ostensibly 'allow[ing] all pleasure' to its adherents, actually confines the 'free enjoyment' of desire to men (1.2.16–50; 4.2.126–9).

It is the ideological thoroughness of the opposition that Massinger establishes between these competing societies that accounts for the problematic nature of commerce between the

A Woman Turke going through the Citie.

14 Veiled Turkish woman, from Nicolas de Nicolay [Daulphinois], *The Navigations, Peregrinations and Voyages, made into Turkie*, trans. T. Washington the younger, 1585

15   Turkish woman of 'the better sort', from George Sandys, *A Relation of a
     Journey begun Anno Domini 1610*, 1621

two, even though each is imagined as the focus of the other's
material and erotic desires. For those who would venture
across the boundaries of faith and manners, the only options,
it would appear, are to 'turn Turk' or become Christian. It
is these religious 'turnings' that supply the crucial peripeties
upon which Massinger's tragicomic design depends; and they

help to account for the crucial role allotted to Francisco, who manages the sequence of redemptive conversions.

The Jesuit is a character with no equivalent in the sources.[1] Of course the addition of such a choric moralizer is something that might be expected from a dramatist of Massinger's somewhat didactic bent, but his choice of a Jesuit in the role seems at first sight astonishing – especially in the wake of the ferocious anti-Catholic feeling stirred up by King James's efforts to secure a Spanish match for his son Charles in 1623.[2] From the foundation of the order, members of the Society of Jesus had been the objects of peculiarly intense suspicion in England by virtue of the fact that, alone amongst Catholic clergy, they swore allegiance directly to the Pope, thereby voiding their loyalty to crown and nation. Anathematized by all God-fearing Protestants, and disliked even by loyalist fellow-Catholics, with their treachery amply demonstrated by their apparent implication in the Gunpowder Plot, Jesuits were routinely denounced as masters of treacherous equivocation and disguise (Shell, 113–18). In fact the Society of Jesus had been singled out for special execration in one of Massinger's sources, William Biddulph's *Travels* (108–12, 120–1); and only a few months after the appearance of *The Renegado*, the papist conspiracies of Middleton's *A Game at Chess* were ushered in by none other than Ignatius Loyola,

---

1 Observing Massinger's extensive use of such Catholic practices as belief in relics, lay baptism and confession, oddly combined with solecisms like the appearance of a Jesuit in a bishop's costume, Maurice Chelli (328–31) concluded that the dramatist showed such a 'deplorable ignorance' of Catholicism that the invention of Francisco could only be explained as an attempt to provide more local colour. By contrast, Burton has suggested that Francisco's role may have been partially inspired by the story of an English Jesuit who was responsible for the reconversion of the English renegade Sir Francis Verney, who was active as a corsair in Algiers from 1608 to 1615 before falling prey to the desperate illness that prompted his remorse (*Traffic*, 149–50). For documentation of the liberty allowed by Barbary authorities to Catholic priests ministering to prisoners, see Matar, in Vitkus, *Piracy*, 19.

2 The choice is surprising even if (or perhaps especially if) Massinger was the closet Catholic suspected by Gifford, rather than the whiggish Protestant imagined by Coleridge. See Gifford, 1.xliv, 2.122; and Dunn, 49–51, 184–91.

founder of the order, whose malign spirit presides over the Induction with his faithful servant Error. Yet Massinger presents his Francisco as an entirely admirable character: far from the papist Machiavel of theatrical convention, he is not only the steadfast friend and spiritual counsellor saluted by Vitelli as the 'stay of my steps in this life / And guide to all my blessed hopes hereafter' (1.1.64–5), but the holy confessor whose redemption of Grimaldi ultimately makes possible the escape of all the play's Christians from their Turkish captors.[1]

To idealize a Jesuit in this way would have been problematic at any time; yet – in contrast to the furore provoked by *A Game at Chess* – *The Renegado* seems neither to have attracted censorship nor to have roused any conspicuous public debate. Benedict Robinson has sought to address this anomaly by proposing a rather strained 'allegorical displacement' whereby the audience would '[read] Islam as a stand-in for Catholicism, and . . . forget the actual Catholicism of the main characters'.[2] This seems improbable, however – not least because the dramatist actually seems to go out of his way to highlight the characters' religious allegiance by introducing a number of controversial points of Catholic doctrine, including justification by works (1.1.23; 4.1.96, 129), the role of confession and penance (3.2.1–11), the significance of the Mass and of ritual vestments (4.1.31–2, 81–2), the magical

---

1 Claire Jowitt, while acknowledging the apparent anomaly of presenting a 'heroic' Jesuit 'at a time [of] such strong anti-Catholic . . . feeling', nevertheless attempts to argue (unconvincingly, in my view) that details of the plot expose him as 'an untrustworthy machiavel' (Jowitt, *Voyage*, 182).

2 See Robinson, 'Commodities', 129. Robinson elaborates the proposal originally made by Doris Adler that 'Massinger dramatized a Christian-pagan conflict as an analogy for a Catholic-Protestant conflict' (see Adler, 57); Adler discovers 'a bleak analogical undertone' in Donusa's conversion and Paulina's invincible virginity: 'The educated ruler has taken a converted wife, but the virgin of the land remains unhusbanded. The play holds out the hope that Prince Charles will make a good wife of Henrietta Maria, but little hope that he will truly "husband" England' (59). A similar approach is taken by Claire Jowitt, who reads the play as 'a geographically displaced account of recent anxieties about Charles's vulnerability to conversion to Catholicism whilst negotiating a marriage with the Infanta' (*Voyage*, 178). For further discussion of the play's relation to James's negotiations for the Spanish and French matches, see Jowitt, 'Another woman'.

power of relics (1.1.146–53; 2.5.161–3) and the continuing possibility of miracles (2.5.150). Most conspicuously of all, Massinger makes the crucial 'counterturn' of his tragicomic plot depend upon the efficacy of lay baptism (5.1.29–41; 5.3.110–16) – a ritual strictly necessary only for those committed to the Catholic belief in the miraculous efficacy of the sacraments.[1]

All of this – especially given the boldness of Massinger's decision to enact so controversial a sacrament before the very eyes of his audience – would surely have given an electric charge to the play's theology at the time of its first performance; for in the first months of 1624 the King was on a collision course with Parliament over Catholic toleration and the Jesuit presence. A possible explanation for Massinger's apparent daring is suggested by historians such as Nicholas Tyacke and Thomas Cogswell, who have demonstrated the exceptional fluidity and complexity of English religious politics at the time of the play's composition and first performances. Already, by the second decade of the seventeenth century, the broadly 'Arminian' reaction against official Calvinism, which would reach its apogee under the archbishopric of William Laud, had begun

---

1   For Catholics or Arminians, baptism was a sacrament that bestowed grace *ex opere operato* (it conferred grace of itself) and not *ex opere operantis* (its efficacy was not dependent on the conferrer). Thus in 'cases of necessity' (where an unbaptized person might be about to die and no priest was available), baptism by a lay person was considered an essential recourse. So it is that Francisco licenses Vitelli to 'do that office' for Donusa as she faces execution, assuring him not only that 'Midwives upon necessity perform it', but also that 'knights that in the Holy Land fought for / The freedom of Jerusalem . . . have made their helmets / The font out of which . . . their holy hands . . . drew . . . heavenly liquor' (5.1.29–39). By contrast, for Calvinist predestinarians, who denied the *ex opere operato* nature of sacraments, baptism was a ritual that confirmed the already established covenant of grace between God and the elect. It was perhaps the belief in the transformatory power of the sacrament that made the Roman Church, as Dunn notes, so much 'more rigorous in proselytizing' than its Protestant rivals (187). By attaching the principal 'counterturn' of its plot to a layman's baptism of a Turkish convertite, *The Renegado* makes its opposition to Calvinist orthodoxy as overt as possible. For a summary of contemporary debate on lay baptism, see Cressy, 117–23. As Robinson notes, the 1604 Hampton Court Conference had sought to confine the performance of baptism to 'the Minister of the Parish, or any other lawfull Minister' (*Turks*, 237, n.51).

to gather head, attracting powerful supporters both inside and outside the Church. The direction in which the official wind was beginning to blow was marked by the publication of Richard Montagu's anti-Calvinist *A New Gagg for an Old Goose* early in 1624, shortly before *The Renegado*'s theatrical debut.[1] Montagu (who was to become one of Laud's bishops) was particularly anxious to dissociate the Anglican Church from the rigid predestinarianism associated with the Thirty-Nine Articles; and his book was accordingly denounced in a petition to Parliament as 'full fraught' with the 'dangerous opinions of Arminius'; however, Montagu's claim that his book was printed 'by King James's speciall warrant' suggests that his views enjoyed powerful support, and that the King himself had begun to shift towards a more Arminian position (Tyacke, 103–4, 147–51). Montagu, who (like James) seems to have envisaged Christian unity as a necessary bulwark against Islam, had denounced the Turks in his earlier publication, *Apello Caesarem* (1623), as 'the grand professed enemies of Christians, Christianity, [and] CHRIST'; and in his insistence that Rome was, despite everything, 'a true church and the Pope not demonstrably an Antichrist', Montagu reflected the increasingly tolerant official attitude towards Catholicism at the beginning of the 1620s, when James's efforts to conclude a Spanish match had led to a considerable relaxation of the penal laws against Catholics (Tyacke, 149; and see Patterson, 317). As polemicists on both sides began to appeal for the greater ecumenical understanding to which the pacific James himself was attracted (Shell, 144; Patterson, 343–4), 1623 became the year when (in the words of one contemporary) 'the Romish foxes came out of their holes'. With prosecutions for recusancy now abandoned, Catholic priests – especially Jesuits – had begun to appear openly in both London and the provinces, and

---

1   Since Massinger's earlier play *The Bondman* was not licensed for performance until 3 December 1623, it seems reasonable to assume that the writing of *The Renegado* must belong substantially to the first three months of 1624.

were proselytizing with considerable success in the court and beyond.[1]

These developments could have emboldened Massinger and the Cockpit company – or those in whose interests they may have been working – to risk a play whose doctrinal attitudes are not merely compatible with Arminianism, but in open sympathy with Catholic religion, whilst inviting open admiration for an heroic Jesuit. Yet such a move was still a potentially dangerous one, and those associated with the play can hardly have been unaware of the gathering Protestant reaction, stoked by rumours of an impending French marriage for the Prince, that found voice in the fiercely anti-Catholic Petition of Religion drawn up by Parliament on 3 April.[2] The initial staging of the play must have coincided with the angry debate over the King's reply which dominated Parliament from 17 to 24 April, culminating in James's reluctant acceptance of the petition, and the ensuing proclamation of 6 May banning the Jesuits – those 'Janizaries of his Holynesse' as John Castle, using a loaded Turkish analogy, called them.[3] From this perspective, *The Renegado* looks as though it may have been intended as one shot in a campaign, supported by James, for tolerance and Christian unity. For this reason, it may also have formed part of the skirmishing between the King and the Prince of Wales, who (along with Buckingham) had at this juncture temporarily thrown his support behind the

1 See Cogswell, 37–8 (the quotation is from stanza 40 of John Vicar's *Englands Hallelu-jah*, 1631). In a private communication, Michael Questier has reminded me that 'although Charles's and Buckingham's return from Spain was, politically, the end of the Spanish match project, the king was still thinking in terms of an Anglo-Spanish treaty, and did so more or less to the end of his life. All during 1624 there were rumours that Gondomar was about to return to England, and that Buckingham would be displaced. James was deeply distrustful of the U-turn performed by Charles and Buckingham, and thought that the war policy was a serious mistake.'

2 See Roger Lockyer, *Buckingham: The Life and Political Career of George Villiers, First Duke of Buckingham, 1592–1628* (New York, 1981), 199.

3 Cogswell, 246–53; Castle's words are from a letter dated 14 May 1624 (cited in Cogswell, 253).

Calvinists.[1] This embroilment in religious politics – rather than the professional quarrel with Davenant and Carew to which it is normally ascribed[2] – may have been what attracted the hostile attention referred to in Shirley's commendatory verses, where he writes of 'A tribe who in their wisdoms dare accuse / This offspring of thy Muse' (22–3). But any difficulties experienced either by the dramatist or the players presumably dissolved quite quickly in the wake of Charles's accession (2 February 1625), his marriage to the French Catholic Henrietta Maria (13 June 1625) and his increasing commitment to the Arminian cause. As a result, *The Renegado*'s published text would have seemed less controversial to its readers. Then too, as Jane Degenhardt has argued, it is possible that the mysterious power which the play attributes to relics and the sacramental rite of baptism was rendered less contentious by a felt need for 'tangible and material' symbols powerful enough to counter the conspicuously embodied and sexualized form given to the Muslim threat in European fantasy.[3] If the temptation of apostasy is conventionally imagined through the seductive magic of a Mahometan beauty, then some even more potent physical charm will be needed to counter it.

Certainly it is *The Renegado*'s open allegiance to the magical power of relics and sacraments that underlies its repeated reference to the various kinds of false or misapprehended magic which produce the deceptive 'turns' of a plot that is ushered to its happy conclusion by the transformatory 'counterturn' of conversion and baptism. The Turks' religion is stigmatized as the work of

1 However, it would be dangerous to assume that members of the Prince's circle were necessarily hostile to the Jesuits *per se*: Questier, noting that 'the Society, while seen by many as the prime representative of popery, described itself at this stage as primarily non-political and also broadly supportive of the regime', points out that there were prominent Catholics in Buckingham's own circle who favoured Jesuit priests as chaplains – including the Countess herself, whose conversion was engineered by John Percy SJ (private communication).

2 See e.g. Oxf, 5.140, and Adler, 73–80.

3 Like the present editor, Degenhardt is inclined to see the play's proto-Arminianism as symptomatic of a gathering 'breakdown of the Calvinist consensus in ways prior to and separate from the ecclesiastical ramifications of Laud and the Durham House group' (Degenhardt, 79).

an 'Impostor' (5.3.133), a 'juggling Prophet' whose impotent 'sorceries' are contrasted with the 'pious miracle[s]' associated with Francisco (4.3.115, 125; 5.7.18).[1] Not for nothing is the chamber where Donusa seduces Vitelli compared to the Prophet's tomb in Mecca by the infatuated Mustapha (1.2.60–2);[2] for the supposedly fraudulent pretences of his religion are associated with the base transformations wrought by unlicensed desire – just as, for those who turn Christian, profane love is shown to become an instrument of miraculous grace. Thus Asambeg feels himself 'Transformed' by the 'charm' of Paulina and the 'angelical sounds' of 'her enchanting tongue' which seem to 'invade and take possession of my soul', convincing him that there is 'something in [her] / That can work miracles' (2.5.104, 110, 114, 132–4, 149–50).

In much the same way, Donusa, overcome on her first encounter with Vitelli by the 'sudden change' that makes her 'turn roarer' and vandalize the Venetians' shop (2.1.5; 1.3.145–7), attributes this unaccountable passion to a 'magic [that] hath transformed me from myself' (2.1.23). In each case, erotic fascination shadows the possibility of the more profound alteration that grace might effect: Asambeg's desire for his 'sweet saint' Paulina (2.5.164), the play intimates, arises partly as an unrecognized (and therefore ineffectual) response to the greater magic represented by the holy talisman given her by Francisco, 'a relic ... which has power ... To keep the owner free from violence' (1.1.147–9); Donusa's desire, on the other hand, ultimately gives way to the 'holy motion' that begins the process of her conversion at the end of Act 4.[3]

1   For the propagandist association of Mahomet with magic and sorcery, see Parker.
2   In the European imagination, the Prophet's tomb – where his casket was reputedly suspended in mid-air by what Christians regarded as some dubious spell – was strongly associated with sinister magic.
3   For a reading that explores the sexual relationships in the play as a response to intense gender anxieties aroused by encounters with the Turkish world, see Burton, *Traffic*, chs 2, 3: 'Asambeg experiences at Paulina's hands the effeminization that Christian men feared suffering in their encounters with Muslims' (114); 'the virtuous Christian man overcomes temptation by converting lechery into propriety and the Muslim temptress into a Christian wife. At the same time lechery is displaced from the former temptress onto the Muslim man whose foolhardy obsession with an unattainable Christian woman enables the escape of all his Christian captives' (153).

Faced with the prospect of execution for her dalliance with an infidel, Donusa seeks to evade her fate by relying on what Asambeg calls 'the magic of her tongue' in order to 'turn this Christian Turk and marry him' (4.2.184, 161). Instead, she finds herself so overwhelmed by Vitelli's 'unanswerable' arguments against her faith (4.3.138) that the hero, sensing victory, draws on the power of his own transformatory magic and marks her with the sign of the cross – 'The sacred badge [God] arms his servants with' (142) – ensuring that it is she rather than he who, to Asambeg's horror, now stands ready to 'turn apostata' (159). Surrendering herself to the shackled Venetian as his moral 'prisoner' (149), the princess yields to the 'heavenly prompter' within her (140), defies the Viceroy's threats and renounces her religion in a gesture of extreme profanity: 'thus I spit at Mahomet' (158). Then, in the final act, as the lovers prepare to take leave of life in a martyr's 'wedding', Vitelli completes his mistress's conversion with an improvised baptism: assured of its sacramental efficacy by his Jesuit mentor, he throws water on her face, producing the miraculous effect that metamorphoses the Mahometan princess into 'another woman':

> till this minute
> I never lived, nor durst think how to die.
> How long have I been blind! Yet on the sudden,
> By this blest means, I feel the films of error
> Ta'en from my soul's eyes. O divine physician . . .
> Let me kiss the hand
> That did this miracle
>
> (5.3.121–5, 128–9)

The violent contempt with which Donusa repudiates her faith is evidently designed as the reverse counterpart of the insolent sacrilege that announced Grimaldi's apostasy – that act of 'wanton, irreligious madness' in St Mark's, when he snatched the Host from the priest's sanctified hands and 'Dashed it upon the pavement' (4.1.29–33); and when baptism confirms

Donusa's release from 'the cruellest of prisons – / Blind ignorance and misbelief' (5.3.131–2), it is as if Grimaldi's violation of one sacrament has been symbolically cancelled out by Vitelli's performance of another. But, as we have seen, Grimaldi too is subject to a process of conversion: cashiered for his insolence to the Viceroy, he descends from atheistic Tamburlainean rant into Faustian despair, calling on fire, earth, air and sea for the blessing of annihilation – only to be rescued by Francisco. Moving through the proper stages of contrition, confession and penance, the renegade's transformation comes to its own dramatic climax in a scene that deliberately challenges the Calvinist dismissal of ritual as empty and impious histrionics. By interrupting Grimaldi's desperate meditations dressed in the same 'sacred vestments' he had worn during the Mass at which the apostate performed his original blasphemous outrage, the Jesuit stuns him into a recognition of the redemptive power of grace. The renegade confesses his sins – including his assault upon the very 'shape' (Francisco in his ecclesiastical cope) who now stands before him (4.1.72–80) – and then falls to his knees before the Jesuit, who grants him forgiveness, with the penitential proviso that he 'Purchase it / By zealous undertakings' (80–8). Wondering at the mysterious transformation that ensues, Grimaldi goes on to meditate upon the efficacy of good works as an instrument of salvation:[1]

> What celestial balm
> I feel now poured into my wounded conscience!
> What penance is there I'll not undergo –
> Though ne'er so sharp and rugged – with more pleasure
> Than flesh and blood e'er tasted? Show me true Sorrow,
> Armed with an iron whip, and I will meet
> The stripes she brings along with her as if

---

1 In a neat gloss on the play's mercantile setting, Robinson suggests that 'Francisco's theology, according to which grace can be "purchased" by works, also preserves at its heart a kind of commerce, suggesting that commerce and conversion are versions of each other' ('Turks', 230).

They were the gentle touches of a hand
That comes to cure me. Can good deeds redeem me?
I will rise up a wonder to the world,
When I have given strong proofs how I am altered

(4.1.88–98)

Francisco's appearance in the splendid cope that renders him *'like a bishop'* (4.1.72 SD) is a transparently theatrical device that nevertheless becomes indistinguishable from the sacramental magic that overwhelms Grimaldi here. Earlier in the play, however, the plot appears to associate 'personation' and role-playing with less admirable forms of transformation – above all, through the protagonist's merchant disguise, with the deceits and doubtful exchanges of the market-place. In the dialogue that opens the play, Gazet declares his allegiance to a commercial regime in which religion seems to be as subject to 'free trading' as any other commodity: 'Live I in England, Spain, France, Rome, Geneva,' he declares, 'I am of that country's faith' (1.1.36–7). It is only his fear of being 'caponed' that dissuades him from immediately 'turn[ing] Turk' in Tunis (1.1.58, 38); and before long that is the very path both he and his master will take. First Vitelli establishes himself as 'a royal merchant' – in both senses of that quibbling oxymoron – when he trades his virtue for the favours of a Turkish princess (2.4.94). After Donusa has capriciously destroyed the glassware in his shop, Vitelli is summoned to meet her in the palace, where she tempts his sight with an array of treasure laid out on her table (2.4.0): looking for all the world like a more sumptuous version of the 'commodities' displayed on his own shop-counter, these bags of 'imperial coin' and Indian gems are ostensibly offered as recompense for 'The trespass I did to thee' (2.4.82–5), but are soon identified as 'seeds' of a more bountiful 'harvest' – the 'tender' (as she puts it) of her own person (97–9, 101).[1]

1   A similar point is made about Donusa's 'self-commodification' by Robinson ('Turks', 221).

If Donusa has felt herself inwardly changed by her sudden infatuation with this Christian – 'What magic hath transformed me from myself' (2.1.23) – Vitelli is subject to his own outward transformation by the 'rich suit' and train of attendant Turks that mark his new-found status as a 'citizen turn[ed] courtier' (2.6.9–10, 2). Where the Statutes of Apparel had once sought to regulate social mobility by defining the costumes and materials allowable to various ranks and professions, Massinger describes a world of sartorially fluid identity in which (as Donusa contemptuously suggests to Mustapha) any French tailor can 'new create' a man (3.1.57–8), Vitelli himself appears so 'strangely metamorphosed' that Gazet can barely recognize him as 'mine own natural master', thinking him perhaps 'some French ambassador' (2.6.20, 19, 9). It is as if 'the gentleman of Venice' were himself becoming the renegado of the title: clad in what he later calls 'the proud livery / Of wicked pleasure' (3.5.50–1), he is visibly in thrall to a mistress whose religion itself 'Allows all pleasure' (1.2.50); and from the perspective of Francisco, at least, his protégé appears 'lost' to salvation (2.6.1), as though to turn courtier in this extravagant oriental fashion were indeed to turn Turk.

The effect of Vitelli's makeover on his impressionable servant is immediate: having been released from his apprenticeship and made master of their shop (2.6.25–7), Gazet sets about turning himself into 'A city gallant' (3.2.50) by dressing himself in his master's clothes and insisting that there is now no difference between them:

> They fit me to a hair, too: let but any
> Indifferent gamester measure us inch by inch
> Or weigh us by the standard, I may pass;
> I have been proved and proved again true metal.
>
> (3.4.11–14)

To imagine the scales of social judgement thus turning in his favour is not enough, though: for Gazet next resolves to 'change

[his] copy' (3.4.32) and to follow his master into the Turkish court. The parallel between the two is reinforced by the way that preferment in both cases is not only imagined in the language of trade, but made contingent on a form of sexual exchange. Gazet, who earlier confessed his fear of losing 'A collop of that part my Doll enjoined me / To bring home as she left it' (1.1.39–40), now evinces himself willing to 'sell my shop . . . And all my wares' to secure the supposedly lofty office of eunuch. In his ignorance he appears not to recognize – even when the English eunuch Carazie assures him that the real 'price' is 'but parting with / A precious stone or two' (3.4.50–2) – that he is about to barter the one 'commodity' he has hitherto reserved from the market (see 4.1.151–6n.). Undertaking, if necessary, to 'part with all my stones', he innocently declares himself 'made', even as Carazie prepares his surgical unmaking (3.4.53–6).[1]

The initial transformations of both Vitelli and Gazet, beginning as they do in the promiscuous transactions of the bazaar, perfectly reflect those anxieties about the dangerous fungibility of the self in a market-dominated world of 'limitless profit' and 'radically unbalanced exchange' that Benedict Robinson describes.[2] But equally important is the way in which the standard satirical motif of tradesman turning courtier is so rapidly linked to the idea of turning Turk – and hence to the apostasy and reconversion of Grimaldi. Gazet's behaviour not only mimics his master's folly, but serves to parody the twists and turns of Grimaldi's renegadism: dismissing even the deep inward promptings of conscience as though they too were a form of degrading costume, mere 'scrupulous rags . . . Invented only to keep churchmen warm' (1.3.48–50), Grimaldi is a man so free

1   In a reading of the play that fascinatingly explores the relationship between gender anxieties and trade, Harris highlights Massinger's use of castration as a figure for economic loss (see pp. 22–3).

2   See Robinson, 'Turks', 221; Robinson further notes that the 'metaphorical and literal sexiness' of Vitelli's ware suggests 'that there is something promiscuous about buying and selling' and that 'the play continually sexualizes trade, drawing out the simultaneously mercantile and erotic associations of words like "commerce" and "commodity"' (219); see also Robinson, 'Commodities', 118–22.

of any loyalty that, when he is slighted by his Turkish masters, he can contemplate 'turn[ing] honest and forswear[ing his] trade' (2.5.6), as readily as he once turned Turk and forswore his natal faith.

But just as true repentance and counter-apostasy are only made possible for Grimaldi by Francisco's ministrations, so the Jesuit's spiritual counselling produces a redemptive turnabout in the hero's own progress. In Act 3, just as his apprentice is about to follow his example and turn courtier, Vitelli stages a second sartorial metamorphosis. Responding to Francisco's spiritual counselling, he returns to Donusa's chamber to 'deliver back the price / And salary of [her] lust' (3.5.48–9): first returning her casket of jewels, he then tears off his cloak and doublet, as if they were 'Alcides' fatal shirt', and announces himself free 'Of sin's gay trappings' (53, 50). To Donusa, this volte-face represents a kind of treason or apostasy: 'you turn rebel to / The laws of Nature . . . and deny allegiance / Where you stand bound to pay it' (17–20); and she hits back by vowing to Asambeg that she will 'turn this Christian Turk' (4.2.161).[1] The hero's new-found resolve proves unshakeable, however, and in the final stage of his transformation he is hauled from the palace dungeon in the chains and soiled garments of a prisoner – a costume that Francisco hails as the splendid robe of a martyr:

> I never saw you
> Till now look lovely . . .
> All Roman Caesars that led kings in chains
> Fast bound to their triumphant chariots, if
> Compared with that true glory and full lustre
> You now appear in, all their boasted honours,

1 In '"Best play with Mardian": eunuch and blackamoor as imperial culturegram', *Shakespeare Studies*, 34 (2006), 123–57, Anston Bosman interprets Vitelli's rejection of Donusa's seductions (and the jewels she heaps on him) as a kind of 'voluntary eunuchism, albeit of the spiritual variety', in which the hero learns, in his own words, 'To put off the condition of a man' (3.2.9) – rather as Gazet does when he offers to surrender his own 'jewels'.

Purchased with blood and wrong, would lose their names
And be no more remembered!

(4.3.9–10, 15–20)

Underlying these visible transformations, of course, is another
even more important one, since Vitelli has been from the beginning a man in disguise. The audience is given a clue to the
merchant-protagonist's real identity as early as the second half
of 1.1: enraged by the news that his sister, 'the virtuous Paulina',
has been sold by Grimaldi to the Viceroy's seraglio (1.1.109–17),
Vitelli swears to discard his 'borrowed shape' (154) and prove
his 'noble' condition by exacting revenge on his enemy (119–20).
Francisco, however, dissuades him (140–58), ensuring that Vitelli
remains cloaked in his merchant role until the climactic moment
of discovery in Act 5, when (to Donusa's evident relief) Paulina
at last reveals her brother to be no merchant at all, but 'a gentleman / Of the best rank in Venice' (5.5.12–13).[1] A disguised hero
is, of course, a conventional device of romance – so much so that
Vitelli's Turkish rival, Mustapha, feels bound to discredit the
possibility that Donusa's lover is a 'prince disguised' by repeatedly insisting that he is 'no man of mark nor honour . . . But . . .
A poor mechanic pedlar', 'a delinquent of . . . mean condition'
(3.3.77–80; 5.3.4). But, while in romance 'disguised greatness'
(5.3.6) frequently masks in humility, it rarely adopts such a real-
istically bourgeois guise – a 'sordid shape' as Asambeg thinks it
(5): even in *The Island Princess*, Armusia's merchant imposture
is a only a fleeting camouflage to enable his heroic rescue of the
King of Tidore, and one that compromises neither the hero's
identity nor the play's chivalric fantasy. By contrast, Vitelli's extended pretence not only installs the market at the centre of *The
Renegado*, but makes his successive transformations – from shopkeeper to courtier, from sexual minion to penitent moralist and
helpless prisoner, from prospective apostate to intending martyr

1 It is possible that Massinger's emphasis on Vitelli's status was influenced by
Cervantes's story 'The Liberall Lover', in which the lady Halima is impressed by a
rumour that her new slave, 'Mario', is actually 'a Gentleman' (147).

and from merchant to 'Gentleman of Venice' – significant turning-points in the action.

The importance of Paulina's disclosure of her brother's true identity lies in its implicit appeal to an essential self that remains unchanged beneath the casual alterations effected by disguise and theatrical imposture or driven by the powerful currents of desire and fear. Responding to Francisco's applause, Vitelli at first envisages his prospective martyrdom as a histrionic performance of heroism – like that of Paris, the player-protagonist of Massinger's *The Roman Actor* – at the sight of which 'a thousand full-crammed theatres / Should clap their eager hands to witness that / The scene I act did please' (4.3.22–4), but then insists that it is proof of something much less ephemeral: ''Tis not in man / To change or alter me' (53–4). Even his torturer and intending executioner, Asambeg, is made to marvel that this Christian will not 'Be altered in his soul for any torments / We can afflict his body with' (5.3.25–6).

Donusa's progress through the play follows a similar trajectory. Vitelli's theatrical metaphors call to mind his earlier dismissal of the princess's amorous overtures as a 'personated passion' (2.4.67), as well as her vain insistence on the veracity of the performance as 'A part in which I truly act myself' (74); and this echo is a reminder that the turns of fortune involve the heroine in a parallel set of transformations, which (like Vitelli's) culminate in another of the play's spectacular changes of costume. In 4.2, Asambeg orders Donusa to be stripped of her court finery and to be led forth 'In black as to her funeral' (4.2.65). Donusa's mourning dress is symbolically linked both to the deadly vehicle of 'the Grand Signor's pleasure' – the sinister *'black box'* which contains her sentence (59, 57 SD) – and to the Black Tower (Fig. 16) from which the condemned Vitelli makes his escape in the penultimate scene; but the princess's 'sad livery of death' (75) proves – like her lover's discarded 'livery / Of . . . pleasure' (3.5.50–1) – to stand for a more inward metamorphosis: as

A. *The Blacke Tower.* C. *Thracian Bosphorus.* E. *Part of Bythinia.*
B. *The oppofite Caftle.* D. *Part of Thrace.*

16 'The Castles commanding the Bosphorus', showing the Black Tower, from
George Sandys, *A Relation of a Journey begun Anno Domini 1610*, 1621

Vitelli persuades the Princess to 'turn apostata' (4.3.159), her
black gown becomes the penitential robe that announces her
death to the world of sin, before being identified in 5.3 as her
wedding garment. Together with her 'choicest jewel' (5.1.25),
the baptismal cross with which Vitelli marks her forehead and
which takes the place of the rich jewels of the seduction scene,
it signifies her union not merely with her chosen husband,
but with the Christian Church whose agent he has now
become.

It is just at this point, as bride and groom prepare to welcome
martyrdom, that Massinger adds one last extravagant counterturn
to his plot. Scarcely has Donusa's sacramental transformation

been effected, than the virtuous Paulina denounces it as a piece of empty theatre:

> Who can hold her spleen,
> When such ridiculous follies are presented –
> The scene, too, made religion?
>
> (5.3.140–2)

To Massinger's Jacobean audience this might have sounded like a sudden concession to Protestant indictments of Church ritual; but it proves to be the prelude to an even more astounding turnabout – one that seemingly reveals Paulina's iconoclastic scorn to be an expression not of Puritan but of Mahometan leanings. Having up to now resisted Asambeg's tyrannic efforts to make her 'turn apostata to the faith / That she was bred in' (1.1.138–9), Paulina suddenly announces herself ready to 'turn Turk' (5.3.152), demanding that the renegade princess change places with her and become her slave, while she adorns herself in Donusa's 'choice and richest jewels' (5.3.166). Only one short scene elapses, however, before the Christian virgin is made to reveal that this seeming transformation was, after all, only one last theatrical imposture, designed to secure a reprieve for her brother's bride:

> no way was left me
> To free you from a present execution
> But by my personating that which never
> My nature was acquainted with.
>
> (5.5.4–7)

Like her revelation of Vitelli's true identity a few lines later, Paulina's invocation of her own 'nature' appeals to an idea of essential, unchanging selfhood that seems amply warranted by her resolute defiance of all Asambeg's efforts to make her yield to his importunities and 'turn Turk'.[1] But then we remember that it

---

1 The phrase 'turning Turk' is indicative of the strangely fluid conceptions of 'race' or ethnic identity in this period, according to which an apostate could be imagined as having become that paradoxical creature, 'an English Turk' – see, for example, the narrative of John Rawlins in Vitkus, *Piracy*, 96–120, esp. 104.

was only the mysterious power of Francisco's relic that enabled such chaste constancy, just as it was the sacramental influence of which the Jesuit is the primary conduit that secured the conversion of Donusa, the recovery of Vitelli's and Grimaldi's 'true' selves, and their escape from the world of ceaseless transformation and exchange epitomized by the seductions of the Turkish market-place.

The way in which Massinger's plot comes to turn on episodes of conversion or religious 'turning' demonstrates a crucial symmetry between the play's doctrinal stance and its dramatic form. It is not, I think, entirely coincidental that the conventional 'change, and counterturn' of tragicomic design should have become the vehicle for a drama of apostasy and conversion just as English Arminianism was beginning to test its strength against Calvinist orthodoxy; nor is it surprising that tragicomedy should have gone on to become such a favoured genre during the Arminian ascendancy (see Neill, 'Turn'). For if the impossibility of effective repentance in such works as *Doctor Faustus* and *The Duchess of Malfi* points to a natural affinity between Calvinism and tragedy, then the sudden reversals and metamorphoses of *The Renegado* suggest that tragicomedy may have its own doctrinal affiliations. Once we are alert to them, some interesting formal patterns begin to emerge. I have tried to show how in *The Renegado* the structural bond that ties turning-as-conversion to turning-as-peripety is linked to a pervasive preoccupation with various forms of metamorphosis, disguise and theatrical pretence: the resulting pattern contrasts the superficial alterations produced by the 'juggling sorceries' and enchantment of infidel Turks with the deeper transformations wrought by sacramental Christian magic. This aspect of Massinger's design looks even more carefully calculated in the light of the dramatist's conspicuous alterations to his source material – not just the unlikely invention of a Jesuit priest as the moral anchor of his fable, but the prominence which his title gives to the role of the renegado himself, and the relocation of the play's symbolic centre from the prison of Algiers, where Cervantes's Spanish captives languish, to the Tunis bazaar, where Massinger's Venetians drive their ambiguous trade.

SOURCES

Close examination of the text shows that Massinger read widely whilst assembling material for his tragicomedy: for background information on the Ottoman world, the dramatist consulted Richard Knolles's *The Generall Historie of the Turkes* (1603) and George Sandys's *A Relation of a Journey begun Anno Domini 1610* (1615) (Fig. 17) – both republished in 1621 – as well as William Biddulph's *The Travels of certaine Englishmen into Africa, Asia, Troy, Bithynia, Thracia, and to the Blacke Sea* (1609).[1] A number of significant details clearly derive from these sources – especially from Knolles, whose contributions appear to include the names of Asambeg (Asam-Beg), Carazie (Caraza) and Manto (Fig. 18). Other travel narratives that Massinger probably knew include a translation of Nicolas de Nicolay's *The Navigations, Peregrinations and Voyages, made into Turkie* (1585), William Lithgow's *Discourse of a Peregrination in Europe, Asia, and Affricke* (1614) and Fynes Moryson's *An Itinerary* (1617).[2] Details of likely borrowings from these texts are recorded in the commentary.

For his plot, Massinger was substantially dependent on a group of closely related fictions by Cervantes – two prose stories and two plays – all of them drawing on the Spanish writer's own experience as a prisoner in Algiers. From Cervantes Massinger borrowed the two main elements of his design: the story of a Christian maiden's abduction by a renegade, followed by the efforts of her grief-stricken brother to rescue her from the Turks; and the story of an infatuated Turkish woman's pursuit of a

1 The most detailed account of Massinger's source material is in Rice, 65–75.
2 For an account of the translations of Greek, Arabic and Turkish texts available to early modern writers on the Islamic world, see Linda McJannet, '"History written by the enemy": Eastern sources about the Ottomans on the continent and in England', *ELR*, 36 (2006), 396–429.

17   Title-page with the figure of Sultan Ahmed I ('or the tyrant') with orb, yoke
     and broken scales of justice, from George Sandys, *A Relation of a Journey
     begun Anno Domini 1610*, 1621

18   Manto, from Richard Knolles, *The Generall Historie of the Turkes*, 1603

handsome Christian lover. The best known of these fictions is 'The Captive's Tale', from *Don Quixote* (Pt 1, chs 39–40), which Massinger may have discovered in the translation first published in 1612. He had probably also read 'The Liberall Lover', from *Novelas ejemplares* (1613), which became available in a French version in 1615, although it was not translated into English until 1640. Cervantes's plays, however, Massinger could only have read in Spanish. It is impossible to be sure that he knew *El Trato de Argel* (*The Traffic of Algiers*), since even in Spain it was not published until 1784, although it has been suggested that he might somehow have obtained a manuscript copy. There can be no doubt, however, that he was familiar with *Los Baños de Argel*, which appeared in a collection of eight *comedias* in 1615. Indeed, this seems to have been the version of Cervantes's captivity narrative that most gripped the English playwright's imagination. In *Los Baños*, Moorish corsairs, operating on behalf of Hassan Pasha, King of Algiers, and led by the renegade Yzuf, abduct a group of Spaniards in a slave raid on Yzuf's home town on the Spanish coast. Their prisoners include a betrothed couple, Costanza and Don Fernando, who are sold separately to the Captain of Algiers, Caurali, and to his wife, Halima. Caurali is attracted to Costanza, and Halima to Fernando, and the two Christians become the objects of lascivious attention from their owners, which they determinedly resist. The chaste and resolute Costanza is clearly the model for Massinger's constant Paulina, while Fernando's situation partially resembles that of Vitelli. Vitelli's true counterpart, though, is Don Lope, a prisoner wooed by the wealthy and aristocratic Zahara, who (like Donusa) is the chosen bride of a Mahometan potentate – in this case Muley Maluco, King of Fez. Zahara first excites Don Lope's interest by sending him secret messages accompanied with gifts of gold, and then contrives to meet him in the street: overwhelmed by Zahara's beauty when she unveils herself, Don Lope is at once determined to possess her; and Zahara in turn longs only for the handsome stranger to take her to Spain, where they can be married. At the end of the play the couple escape with the other principal captives on a Spanish ship, Don Lope's bride formally declaring her conversion with the announcement that she is 'Zahara no more – my name is Maria'.

Beyond the broad outlines of his plot, Massinger owes relatively little to Cervantes: he borrows occasional striking details, such as the *coup de théâtre* in 1.3, where Donusa unveils her dazzling beauty to make Vitelli fall in love with her (see Appendix 1); but otherwise his debt is confined to one or two touches of characterization: the eponymous figure of the renegado, for example, seems to represent a loose amalgam of the cruel Yzuf with a penitent renegade named Hazen; and Vitelli's clownish servant, Gazet, may have been partly inspired by Cervantes's buffoon-figure, the sacristan. But Gazet's naive desire to advance himself by becoming a court eunuch suggests a closer link to the tribulations of Clem in Heywood's *1 Fair Maid of the West*.

There are no other substantial sources for *The Renegado*, but its link to *1 Fair Maid* is a reminder of the fact that Massinger's tragicomedy belongs to a subgenre of voyage plays whose action focuses on European encounters with the Ottoman world – a group that Vitkus has dubbed 'Turk plays'. Its generic ties, however, are by no means confined to that group; indeed, as my discussion of *The Renegado* as tragicomedy has indicated, it makes sense to think of Massinger's play as being, like many plays of the 1620s and 1630s, in loose 'conversation' with a variety of dramatic predecessors. Such self-consciousness was something to which the knowing, often playful style of Jacobean tragicomic romance was particularly receptive.

DATE OF COMPOSITION

On 17 April 1624 Sir Henry Herbert, the *de facto* Master of the Revels, issued a licence to the Lady Elizabeth's Men at the Cockpit playhouse for the performance of '*The Renegado, or the Gentleman of Venice*: Written by Messenger.' Since Herbert had licensed another of Massinger's tragicomedies, *The Bondman*, for the same company a little more than four months earlier, it is reasonable to suppose that *The Renegado* was written at some time between early December 1623 and late March 1624. The apparent allusion at 2.6.9 to the sartorial extravagance of a French nobleman who visited King James's court in December–January 1620–1, supports a date in the early 1620s; and, as we shall see, the play's sympathetic treatment of the Jesuit priest Francisco, together with its apparent endorsement of a number of points of Catholic doctrine, provides additional support for a date between late 1623 and April 1624, during the brief period in which James's government relaxed constraints on the practice of the Roman religion (see pp. 38–40).

PERFORMANCE HISTORY

Massinger designed his play for performance by a company of at least eighteen actors: there are substantial speaking roles for eleven adults and three boys, while the parts of the Gaoler and the First and Second Turks, together with the ensemble of Janizaries, Guards and Sailors, call for a minimum of four supernumeraries. Except amongst these extras, the play's structure allows for no doubling; but it is relatively frugal in its staging demands, requiring little beyond the usual trapdoor, which provides the entrance to Vitelli's dungeon in 4.3, a curtained discovery space (or perhaps a stage booth) to serve as his shop, and a gallery (or 'tarras') for scenes in which characters appear 'above', including the climactic 5.7, where the hero makes his escape from the Black Tower by means of a rope-ladder. A table and chairs are needed for the display of Donusa's wealth in 2.4 and for Paulina's banquet in 5.5; but there is no scene that could not be easily performed on the comparatively bare Jacobean stage.

Like most of Massinger's work in this phase of his career, *The Renegado* was written for the Cockpit playhouse (sometimes called the Phoenix after its rebuilding in the wake of a serious fire in 1617). This was one of those relatively exclusive indoor theatres that catered for elite tastes in later Jacobean and Caroline London. Owned and managed by the impresario Christopher Beeston, and home to a succession of acting companies, the theatre provided the main competition to the Blackfriars, the so-called 'private playhouse' owned by Shakespeare's old troupe, the King's Men. In 1622 Prince Charles's Men, for whom Massinger seems to have written his first independent play, had surrendered it to the Lady Elizabeth's Men, who were re-establishing themselves in London after several years of provincial touring. Their repertory included major plays by George Chapman, Jonson, Fletcher and Middleton, the last of whom collaborated with William Rowley to give them their most distinguished tragedy, *The Changeling*, in 1622. Massinger wrote at least two other plays for the Lady Elizabeth's Men – *The Bondman* (1623) and *The Parliament of Love* (1624) – before the advent of Charles I saw them replaced by a company under the patronage of his queen, Henrietta Maria – Queen Henrietta's Men, or the Queen's Majesty's Servants. The ownership of the Lady Elizabeth's Men's repertory apparently passed into the hands of the new company along with the theatre; and when Queen Henrietta's Men were in turn replaced by the King and Queen's Young Company (sometimes known as Beeston's Boys) in 1637, *The Renegado* duly became their property.

The title-page of the 1630 Quarto promised prospective buyers the text 'As it hath beene often acted by the Queenes Maiesties servants, at the private Play-house in *Drurye-Lane*', thereby drawing attention to its fashionable auspices (see Fig. 21); but although this edition contains a list of actors opposite its *Dramatis Personae* (see Fig. 22), the absence of Richard Perkins and other leading members of Queen Henrietta's Men suggests that the cast-list belongs to one of the company's earlier productions (*c.* 1625), before those actors had joined (Bentley, 1.220–2). Of the actors named in the Quarto, Blaney, Sumner, Bowyer, Allen, Robins and Bourne were all (or were all to become) prominent members of the company. Robins was a well-known comic actor whose parts included Antonio, the eponymous 'changeling' in Middleton and Rowley's tragedy. Theophilus Bourne (or 'Bird') – who must have been at least seventeen when he played Paulina, his first recorded part – went on to a long career as an adult actor, stretching into the Restoration. The careers of the other actors remain obscure: Reynolds, according to Bentley (2.543), may have been a musician; Shakerley is known to have been acting before 1624, but no other records of his performances have survived; Edward Rogers appeared as '*Milliscent, Cardonae's* daughter' in Queen Henrietta's Men's production of James Shirley's *The Wedding* (1626), but is otherwise unknown.

The Renegado remained an important part of the Cockpit repertory until at least 1639, when Christopher Beeston's son William valued it highly enough to include it in a list of plays that 'all other Companyes of Actors' were forbidden 'to intermedle wth or Act'.[1] The evident popularity of 'the sweet Renegaddo', as Samuel Sheppard nostalgically dubbed it in 1646,[2] survived the closure of the playhouses during the Civil War and Interregnum: continuing interest in the play is indicated by the inclusion of a version of its plot in William Chamberlayne's 'heroick poem' *Pharonnida* (1659) (Rice, 74–5); and it was among the pre-war plays chosen for revival by Thomas Killigrew's King's Men in the early years of the Restoration. It opened on 6 August 1662 at the Vere Street theatre in Lincoln's Inn Fields (the former Gibbon's Tennis Court). William Browne recorded paying half a crown to see it there at some time before the company moved to their new theatre in Bridges Street (6 May 1663) – though the number of performances it achieved is unknown, and there are no records of any further revivals.[3]

The Bodleian Library possesses a manuscript of an undated revision of the play (MS Rawl. poet. 20), which was evidently prepared for a Restoration performance, since it contains a number of new stage directions, some of them specifically tailored to the possibilities of the new scenic stage – as for example at 3.5.67 SD, where Asambeg's and Mustapha's entry '*above*' to spy on Vitelli and Donusa is replaced by a sequence in which the lovers are 'discovered' in a scene of deep perspective and then surprised by the two potentates, who comment on 'their

1 See *Malone Society Collections*, 2.3 (1931), 389–90.
2 Samuel Sheppard, *The Times Displayed*, cited in Bentley, 4.814.
3 A possible hint of *The Renegado*'s standing in the Restoration is contained in a copy of the 1630 Quarto held in the British Library (C.83.b.6) which is bound with six other Massinger plays (*Emperor*, *Great Duke*, *Duke of Milan*, *Dowry*, *City Madam*, *Combat*). The flyleaf of the volume is inscribed with a list of titles annotated as being in the hand of Charles II, the patron of Killigrew's company; however, staff at the library's Manuscript Room are sceptical of the attribution.

wanton dallyance' from the forestage. This text was put together using a copy of Q, whose errors (such as 'alledge' ('alleadge' Q) for 'alleged' at 3.1.81) it sometimes unthinkingly repeats. The manuscript was evidently not a fair copy, since it transcribes passages from Q, as well as proposed revisions and additions, that were subsequently marked for deletion; and a substantial blank on its final page suggests that the revision remained incomplete. Its exact connection – if any – with the Vere Street revival is impossible to determine,[1] but the text has a good deal to reveal about the ways in which changing taste must have affected post-Interregnum performances of the play.

Some of its extensive changes to Massinger's text are relatively trivial: Gazet's name is changed to Iseppo; Act 3 begins (for no very obvious reason) with Q's 2.6; documentary details are fashionably updated, so that Vitelli's trade-goods now include 'fine Japan works'; and some parts are rewritten to make them conform more readily to the Restoration taste for 'easy', colloquial language, whilst Massinger's longer speeches are typically broken up with short passages of dialogue. In keeping with the Restoration taste for theatrical display, the 'lusty strain' of music called for by Donusa in 1.2 and the song she requests from Carazie in 2.4 are replaced by elaborate musical interludes performed by a troupe of 'dancing Eunuchs and . . . Grecian women'. But more substantive changes are also involved. The play's potential for arousing sectarian controversy is minimized by the removal of all references to Paulina's protective relic and to Francisco's role as confessor; while the magic of Catholic sacraments is played down, so that the water in which Vitelli baptizes Donusa, for example, is identified as a mere symbol, the 'perfect *sign* of innocence'. Presumably as a concession to sharpening racial sensitivities, Donusa is spared the humiliation

---

1 See W. J. Lawrence, '*The Renegado*', *TLS*, 24 October 1929, 846, and J. G. McManaway, 'Philip Massinger and the Restoration drama', in Richard Hosley, Arthur C. Kirsch and John W. Velz (eds), *Studies in Shakespeare, Bibliography, and Theater* (New York, 1969), 3–30, esp. 14–15.

of courtship by a black Moor: no longer disdaining Mustapha for his 'wainscot face' and 'tadpole-like complexion' (3.1.48, 50), she now dislikes him merely for his weatherbeaten 'soldierlike complexion'.

Extensive cuts are made throughout, but big scenes are often extended to increase their dramatic impact: the rewriting of 3.5, for example, in which Vitelli repents his surrender to Donusa and returns her jewels, not only adds a hundred lines to the original, but includes a new ending in which Donusa vows to rescue Paulina from Asambeg and to 'partake with her the sweets of liberty'. The reviser prunes much of Massinger's bawdy comedy, including all references to Vitelli's courtesan portraits as well as Gazet's scheme to achieve the office of eunuch (3.4); episodes of more elevated eroticism, by contrast, are often enlarged to intensify their effect: thus the temptation scene (2.4) is expanded by thirty lines to allow Vitelli to rhapsodize on the impending satisfaction of his desires, whilst the hundred lines added to the baptism scene (5.3) ratchet up the sexual tension created by Paulina's apparent surrender to Asambeg – a thrill intensified by the addition of some thirty-five lines at the end of 5.6, where her adoring appeal to 'my noble Vice-roy, my Asambeg' shows off her skill in histrionic 'personation'.

The revised trial scene (4.2) is not merely sixty lines longer, but now climaxes in an elaborate judgement tableau, centring on an entirely new character, the Mufti – an Islamic judge, whose Koran takes the place of Massinger's black box. The Mufti is included mainly to enhance the opportunity for solemn spectacle, but another new character, the 'Spye-Eunuch', is introduced to add more excitement to the action, when he and Mustapha are made to observe Vitelli's covert departure from Donusa's boudoir. A number of other changes also affect the plot: careful to flatter the aristocratic bias of the Restoration audience, the reviser is at pains to let them know from the beginning that Vitelli's 'mean habit' is a mere disguise; in 3.1, Manto's reluctant collusion with Mustapha is given added plausibility by reference to a previous affair between the two; and the action of 4.3 is altered so that Paulina and Vitelli come dangerously close to revealing their kinship. Most strikingly of all, Massinger's rather abrupt ending is transformed by rewritten, much expanded versions of 5.7 and 5.8: Paulina and Donusa are brought to Vitelli's cell by Asambeg and Mustapha, only for the Turks to fall into a trap laid by Grimaldi and his followers; the Christians make their glad escape, while their captors are left locked up in their own prison.

However carefully this revision attempted to cater for the palates of the Restoration playgoers, it was insufficient to save Massinger's tragicomedy, for soon after its 1662 revival, *The Renegado* seems, like most pre-Civil War plays, to have been swept aside by the tide of theatrical fashion. Since then it has been left to languish in undeserved theatrical obscurity, though a staged reading in 2003, as part of Shakespeare's Globe's 'Read Not Dead' series, marked a hesitant revival of interest.

THE PLAYWRIGHT

Although he enjoyed his greatest celebrity as principal dramatist for the King's Men during the reign of Charles I, Philip Massinger belonged to an earlier generation than the other leading playwrights of that period, James Shirley (b. 1596) and William Davenant (b. 1606). A near contemporary of the great Jacobeans Thomas Middleton (b. 1580), John Webster (b. 1580) and John Ford (b. 1586), he was born in Salisbury, where he was baptized at the church of St Thomas on 24 November 1583. His father, Arthur, was educated at St Alban Hall, Oxford, and became a fellow of Merton College (1573–9), from where he seems to have joined Sir Humphrey Gilbert's unsuccessful voyage to America in 1578. Surrendering his fellowship after his marriage to Anne Crompton, the daughter of a Staffordshire mercer, Arthur Massinger entered the service of Henry Herbert, Earl of Pembroke, rising to become his general agent and a Member of Parliament. Massinger's memories of the trials and humiliations (as well as the rewards) of service in a great Elizabethan household must have contributed to the picture of domestic life in what is arguably his greatest play, *A New Way to Pay Old Debts* (*c*. 1625). Later in life he was presumably able to capitalize on this family connection to secure the patronage of Herbert's son, Philip, Earl of Montgomery, one of the dedicatees of Shakespeare's First Folio, to whom he dedicated *The Bondman* in 1624. The Herberts were a strongly Protestant clan, but Massinger's own religious affiliations remain a matter of debate: the prominence given to a virtuous Jesuit in *The Renegado*, combined with the interest in Catholic hagiography exemplified in *The Virgin Martyr*, has led to speculation that he may have been a closet Catholic. Certainly one of his maternal uncles was a convicted recusant, and another a suspected papist, whilst his own circle of friends included such prominent Catholics as the playwright James Shirley (who wrote encomiastic verses for *The Renegado*) and the courtier-dramatist Sir Aston Cokayne. George Harding, Lord Berkeley, to whom Massinger dedicated *The Renegado*, had Catholic connections: following the death of his grandfather in 1613, Berkeley was made ward to his mother's uncle, the Catholic Earl of Northampton, and he may himself have had sympathies with the old religion. But Berkeley had affiliations with Puritan families as well: he was related by marriage to the Earl of Huntingdon, the leader of a strongly Puritan anti-Buckingham faction, to whose sister Massinger had dedicated *The Duke of Milan* in 1623. Massinger's other dedicatees included the Catholic Earl of Caernarvon, to whom he offered *A New Way to Pay Old Debts* in 1633; but the dedication invokes the dramatist's ties to Caernarvon's guardian and father-in-law, the Puritan Earl of Pembroke, whom Massinger's father had served as steward. Contradictory as they are, these indications serve only to demonstrate that, like so many people in early modern England, Massinger is likely to have had divided loyalties where religion was concerned; and (as with Shakespeare) there is as much in his writing that seems distinctively Protestant as there is evidence of Catholic sympathies.

Philip Massinger was admitted to his father's former college, St Alban Hall, in 1601–2, but left Oxford without taking a degree. Nothing is known about his early years in London, but he must have begun writing for the theatre before 1613, when he, along with the playwrights Robert Daborne and Nathaniel Field, appealed from debtors' prison to the theatrical entrepreneur Philip Henslowe, seeking payment for a play the three had written together. Surviving records suggest that until about 1620 Massinger worked mainly as a journeyman-playwright, collaborating with a number of other practitioners, including Field and Fletcher. The most important of these partnerships was with Fletcher, Shakespeare's successor as principal dramatist for the King's Men, whose preferred collaborator he became; but Massinger also worked extensively for the succession of companies at Beeston's Cockpit, and even collaborated with Dekker to write *The Virgin Martyr* (*c.* 1620) for the notoriously rowdy Red Bull theatre. In the early 1620s, Massinger began to establish himself as an independent dramatist, dividing his efforts between the King's Men and the Lady Elizabeth's Men at the Cockpit. It was for the Cockpit that he wrote his earliest known independent play, *The Maid of Honour*, first staged *c.* 1621, and so perhaps performed by Prince Charles's Men, rather than the Lady Elizabeth's, who replaced them in 1622. Several more sole-authored plays followed – including the three for the Lady Elizabeth's Men – as well as collaborations with Fletcher, before Massinger succeeded to the latter's position with the King's Men in 1625. From then until his own death in 1640, Massinger seems to have worked entirely on his own, although he apparently undertook several revisions of Fletcher plays. He was a prolific writer: in addition to the numerous collaborations, seventeen of his independent plays have survived, while at least nine more have been lost. Massinger's unusually varied apprenticeship made him adept in several genres: amongst his finest works are two energetic comedies in the satiric tradition of Marston, Jonson and Middleton – *A New Way to Pay Old Debts*

(1625) and *The City Madam* (1632) – as well as two superbly theatrical tragedies, *The Roman Actor* (1626) and *Believe as You List* (1631); his forte, however – as one might expect from a protégé of Fletcher – was in romantic tragicomedy, the genre to which *The Renegado* belongs.

PUBLICATION AND TEXTUAL HISTORY

Six years elapsed between the earliest performances of *The Renegado* and the moment when, under the aegis of the bookseller John Waterson, it first appeared in print. Before it could be published, *The Renegado* was required, like any other play, to be submitted to the Revels Office for censorship. On 22 March 1630, having been inspected by Sir Henry Herbert and deemed free of offensive matter, it was duly entered in the Stationers' Register:

> Mr Ioh: Waterson. Entred for his Copie vnder the
> handes of Sr Henrye Harbert and Mr Purfoote warden
> A play called the Runegado by Phil: Messenger.

Later in the same year the play was printed for Waterson by 'A.[ugustine] M.[atthews]', using the quarto format common to most published playtexts in the period. The play appeared with a dedicatory epistle that bears testimony to Massinger's sense of investment in the publication of his own work – something that is borne out by the material facts of its preparation; for, somewhat unusually, the dramatist himself seems to have been involved in the process of correcting what was, by and large, a quite carefully produced edition. In addition to routine corrections, a number of substantive, presumably authorial, alterations were made to the text in the course of printing. On top of these changes, Massinger, evidently anticipating a second edition, made another thirty-two manuscript changes – among them three substantive textual alterations – which are preserved in one of the surviving copies of the Quarto, the Folger Harbord copy (Figs 19, 20).

The Renegado.

Your bafe vnworthy fall,from your high vertue.
  Donu. I doe appeale to *Amurah.*
  Afam. We will offer
No violence to your perfon,till we know
His facred pleafure,till when vnder gard
You fhall continue heere.
  Donufa. Shall ?
  Afam. I haue faid it.   *The Gard leades off Donufa.*
  Donu. We fhall remember this.
  Afam. It ill becomes
Such as are guilty to deliuer threats
Againft the innocent. I could teare this flefh now,
But tis in vaine,nor muft I talke but do :
Prouide a well made galley for Conftantinople,
Such fad newes neuer came to our great Mafter ;
As hee directs,we muft proceed,and know
No will but his,to whom what's ours we owe.

                                    Exeunt.

mann'd (margin annotation)

The end of the third Act.

Actus Quartus, Scæna Prima.

             Enter Mafter, Botefwaine.

  Mafter. He does begin to eate ?
  Botef. A little, Mafter,
But our beft hope for his recouery,is that
His rauing leaues him, and thofe dreadfull words,
Damnation,and defpayre,with which he euer
Ended all his difcourfes are forgotten.
  Maft. This ftranger is a moft religious man fure,
And I am doubtfull whether his charity,
In the relieuing of our wants,or care
To cure the wounded confcience of *Grimaldi,*

                                 Deferues

19, 20   Massinger's manuscript alterations in two pages from the Folger
Harbord copy of Q, 1630, sigs G2ʳ, H1ᵛ

The Renegado.

Or height of blood could thaw, fhould now fo far
Be hurried vvith the violence of her luft,
As in it burying her high birth and fame,
Bafely defcend to fill a Chriftians armes
And to him yeeld her Virgin honour vp,
Nay fue to him to take't.

   Afam. A Chriftian?

   Muft. Temper
Your admiration: and vvhat Chriftian thinke you?
No Prince difguis'd; no man of marke, nor honour,
No daring vndertaker in our feruice,
But one vvhofe lips her foote fhould fcorne to touch,
A poore Mechanicke-Pedler.

   Afam. Hee?

   Muft. Nay more,
Whom doe you thinke fhe made her fcout, nay baude,
To finde him out but me? What place makes choyce of
To wallow in her foule and lothfome pleafures,
But in the pallace? Who the inftruments
Of clofe conueyance, but the captaine of
Your gard the *Aga*, and that man of truft
The warden of the inmoft port? I'll proue this,
And though I fayle to fhew her in the act,
Glew'd like a neighing ~~ftallion to her ftallion~~, *make to be a proue ftallion*
Your incredulity fhall be conuinc'd
With proofes I blufh to thinke on.

   Afam. Neuer yet,
This flefh felt fuch a feuer, by the life
And fortune of great *Amurah*, fhould our prophet
(Whofe name I bow to) in a vifion fpeake this,
T'would make me doubtfull of my faith; leade on,
And when my eies, and eares, are like yours, guilty,
My rage fhall then appeare, for I will doe
Something; but what, I am not yet determin'd.

                Exeunt.

G.3   *Actus.*

Although a small number of printer's errors escaped even this second round of correction, the Harbord copy shows that Massinger's attention to the text was frequently meticulous, extending even to minor details of spelling – as at 3.5.5, where he took the trouble to insert a second *m* in 'immaculate' by means of a macron. The planned re-publication never took place, however, and *The Renegado* remained out of print until 1759, when it appeared in Thomas Coxeter's collected edition of Massinger's plays.

Waterson's edition was apparently set by a single compositor, using twenty-four formes arranged in two skeletons. The typesetting was generally of a good standard, with fewer casual errors than is usual in a publication of this kind, and there is evidence that the text was quite carefully corrected: as many as fifty-eight amendments are distributed across eleven formes and some sheets have been altered several times, existing in up to five states.[1] In my collations I have recorded the readings of both uncorrected (Qa) and corrected (Qb) states; where a correction has itself been corrected in a later state, this is shown as Qc. Some aspects of the punctuation suggest that it was set up from an autograph manuscript – probably a fair copy rather than a playhouse manuscript, since the stage directions are generally more descriptive than the playhouse required, but in the case of group entries often lack the numerical specificity that the playhouse book-keeper would require. The directions for some entries have the vagueness characteristic of authorial drafts ('*Enter Aga . . . Boteswaine, etc.*', 2.5.0.1–2), while others supply costuming details in a more precise form than the playhouse normally expected ('*Enter Francisco in a Cope like a Bishop*', 4.1.72 SD).

The present edition has been prepared from the Folger Harbord copy, which has been collated with two other Folger copies and four copies held in the British Library, as well as individual copies from the Cambridge University Library and the library of King's College, Cambridge. I have also consulted the manuscript revision of the play prepared for a Restoration theatre and held in the Bodleian Library at Oxford (MS Rawl. poet. 20). The reviser responsible for this text clearly worked from a copy of the 1630 Quarto, and made some sensible

1 For full details of the variant forms, see Oxf, 5.

emendations to it; while these have no independent authority, they deserve consideration as part of an intelligent response to the play by a near-contemporary of the dramatist. The collation does not record literal variants except where they derive from Massinger's own MS corrections in the Folger Harbord copy, since these reveal the sometimes minute (albeit intermittent) attention which the dramatist gave to the task of proofing his work. Non-substantive alterations to the Q stage directions are not collated, but are marked by square brackets in the text.

Like any modern editor of the play, I am extensively indebted to the work of earlier scholars – to the collected editions of Coxeter, Mason, Gifford, Coleridge and Cunningham, to Daniel Vitkus's modernized text in *Three Turk Plays*, and especially to Philip Edwards and Colin Gibson's definitive Oxford edition of the *Plays and Poems of Philip Massinger.* Shirley's commendatory verses have been collated with the version subsequently printed in his *Poems &c* (1646).

THE
RENEGADO,
A TRAGÆCOMEDIE.

As it hath beene often acted by the
Queenes Maiesties seruants, at
the priuate Play-house in
Drurye-Lane.

By PHILIP MASSINGER.

LONDON,
Printed by *A. M.* for *Iohn Waterson,*
and are to be sold at the *Crowne* in
Pauls Church-Yard. 1630.

21   Title-page from the Folger Harbord copy of Q, 1630

Dramatis Perſonæ.	The Actors names.
ASAMBEG, *Viceroy of* Tunis.	Iohn Blanye.
MVSTAPHA, *Baſha of* Aleppo.	Iohn Sumner.
VITELLI, *A Gentelman of* Venice *diſguis'd.*	Michael Bowier.
FRANCISCO, *A Jeſuite.*	William Reignalds.
ANTHONIO GRIMALDI *the* Renegado.	William Allen.
CARAZIE *an Eunuch.*	William Robins.
GAZET *ſervant to* Vitelli.	Edward Shakerley.
AGA.	
CAPIAGA.	
MASTER.	
BOTESVVAINE.	
SAYLORS.	
IAILOR.	
3. TVRKES.	
DONVSA, *neece to* AMVRATH.	Edward Rogers.
PAVLINA, *Siſter to* Vitelli.	Theo. Bourne.
MANTO, *ſervant to* Donuſa.	

22 List of *Dramatis Personae* from the Folger Harbord copy of Q, 1630. The
list follows the usual seventeenth-century convention whereby characters
were listed according to social rank rather than dramatic importance. The
catalogue of female roles invariably followed that of males, after a space
indicating that they belonged to a separate (and secondary) hierarchy. The
fact that female parts were played by boys no doubt tended to reinforce this
conventional subordination.

To the Right Honourable George Harding, Baron Berkeley of Berkeley Castle and Knight of The Honourable Order of the Bath

My good Lord,

To be honoured for old nobility or hereditary titles is   5
not alone proper to yourself, but to some few of your
rank who may challenge the like privilege with you; but
in our age to vouchsafe, as you have often done, a ready

Dedicatory epistle The practice of attaching dedicatory epistles (as well as encomiastic verses and other prolegomenary material) to printed plays, rare in the 16th century, became increasingly common in the Jacobean and Caroline periods. A dedication of this sort could serve a number of purposes: it was designed to attract the attention or to acknowledge the generosity of some wealthy and influential personage who might either assist the playwright materially or simply help to protect him from the attention of hostile claques in the theatre. In a deferential society, it enhanced the prestige of the published play by implying the approval of a distinguished patron. It might also provide a vehicle for the playwright to vent his own opinions on literary or social matters.

1–2 *George Harding, Baron Berkeley* (1601–58) A cousin of Massinger's first known patron, Lady Katherine Stanhope (1609–67), Harding succeeded to his ancient title in 1613, becoming 18th Baron Berkeley, and was made a Knight of the Bath in 1616. He studied at Oxford (1619–23) and subsequently at Gray's Inn. A royalist in the Civil War, Berkeley nevertheless contrived, by his caution in its later stages, to preserve his family estates. 'An amiable nonentity,' according to the family historian, 'bent for the most part on peacefully administering the estates left to him by his grandfather', he seems, however, to have been something of a literary patron: he found a living for Robert Burton, who dedicated *The Anatomy of Melancholy* to him in 1621; and he received further dedications from both the strongly Protestant John Webster (*The Duchess of Malfi*, 1623) and the Catholic James Shirley (*The Young Admiral*, 1637). There are striking parallels between Webster's and Massinger's dedications in their emphasis on the superior distinction conferred by Harding's generous patronage as opposed to his 'hereditary titles' – a theme echoed in Burton's epistle. Among the letters in the Berkeley family archive is one from his sister, Theophila Coke, asking young George to send her playbooks from London – a detail that suggests that his theatrical enthusiasms were well known to his family.

Berkeley's eldest son, George, having married the daughter of its Treasurer, went on to become a prominent member of the East India Company, but there is no evidence that the father had any direct connections with trade to the Orient. For further information on the Harding family, see Falk and Smyth.

2 *Berkeley Castle* the family seat of Lord Berkeley in Gloucestershire

To the . . . Massinger] *misbound after encomiastic verses in BL 162.d.17*

hand to raise the dejected spirits of the contemned sons
of the Muses – such as would not suffer the glorious fire   10
of poesy to be wholly extinguished – is so remarkable
and peculiar to your lordship that with a full vote and
suffrage it is acknowledged that the patronage and
protection of the dramatic poem is yours – and almost
without a rival. I despair not, therefore, but that my   15
ambition to present my service in this kind may in your
clemency meet with a gentle interpretation. Confirm
it, my good lord, in your gracious acceptance of this
trifle, in which – if I were not confident there are some
pieces worthy the perusal – it should have been taught   20
an humbler flight, and the writer, your countryman,
never yet made happy in your notice and favour, had
not made this an advocate to plead for his admission
among such as are wholly and sincerely devoted to your
service. I may live to tender my humble thankfulness in   25
some higher strain, and till then comfort myself with
hope that you descend from your height to receive
    Your honour's commanded servant,

                    Philip Massinger

---

9   **contemned** despised, slighted

13 **suffrage** vote in favour of some person or thing; consensus of opinion
(*OED n.* 4; 8a)

16 **service** In early modern England the
relation between patron and client was
understood as a variant of the master–
servant relationship; but Massinger's
rhetorical stress on service and its
obligations wittily foregrounds their
prominence in the play itself (cf. pp.
30–1).

17 **gentle** kindly; but also indicating the
sort of response to be expected from
one of Berkeley's gentle birth

19 **trifle** Massinger, with playful self-
deprecation, implies an equivalence

between the play he offers Harding
and the commercial 'trifles' that
Vitelli offers Donusa (1.3.105, 130,
153).

21 **your countryman** 'Country' here
means 'county': Massinger, born
in Wiltshire, the county adjacent to
Gloucestershire, is taking a slight liberty with the facts.

26 **higher strain** Presumably Massinger,
who seems to be echoing Virgil's
announcement of a 'loftier song'
(*'paulo maiora canamus'*) at the opening of the Fourth Eclogue, has in mind
a tragedy, ranked as the most elevated
dramatic kind, above the middle mode
of tragicomedy (cf. pp. 6–7).

To my honoured friend Master Philip Massinger upon his Renegado

Dabblers in poetry that only can
Court this weak lady or that gentleman
   With some loose wit in rhyme,   5
   Others that fright the time
Into belief with mighty words that tear
   A passage through the ear,
      Or nicer men
That through a perspective will see a play   10
   And use it the wrong way –
      Not worth thy pen –

Encomiastic verses The inclusion of commendatory material of this sort has some analogies with the modern commercial practice of including endorsements and excerpts from well-known reviewers on book jackets; but (like the printing of dedicatory epistles, prefaces and other paratextual material) it was also a way of insisting on the growing *literary* prestige of plays, formerly regarded as largely ephemeral performance texts.

   This poem was republished in a slightly revised form in 1646 in Shirley's collected *Poems &c.* Oxf claims that it was also printed with Shirley's *Triumph of Beautie* (1646), but it does not appear in any copy inspected by this editor, although *The Triumph* itself is bound with the Folger copy of *Poems &c*, which may be the source of the confusion.

   The rhetorical stress on honorifics (*honoured, Master, worthy*), on worth and merit and on friendship, in both the titles and verses of Shirley's and Lakyn's poems, is designed to balance the language of deference expected of a dedication. The defensive tone of both pieces suggests that the play may have had a mixed reception in the theatre.

7 **mighty words** Poets and critics in the Caroline period, reacting against what they saw as the wayward rhetorical extravagance of Elizabethan and Jacobean playwrights, typically valued purity and simplicity of style. Here Shirley presumably has in mind the 'mighty line' famously attributed to Marlowe by Jonson in his encomiastic verses attached to Shakespeare's First Folio – a trick of style sometimes mimicked by inferior contemporaries.

9 **nicer men** i.e. minutely attentive playgoers (ironic)

10 **perspective** stress on first syllable (the usual pronunciation at this time); an optical instrument designed to magnify or playfully distort objects and images. Here the term is used as a metaphor for the kind of textual 'application' that led to the discovery of veiled contemporary references, and so to supposedly false personal and political interpretations of a work.

1–2 *To my . . .* Renegado] *Q; To M*. Phil. Massenger *on his Renegado* | *Shirley*

Though all their pride exalt 'em, cannot be
Competent judges of thy lines or thee.

I must confess I have no public name   15
To rescue judgement, no poetic flame
    To dress thy Muse with praise
    And Phoebus his own bays;
Yet I commend this poem and dare tell
    The world I liked it well;   20
      And if there be
A tribe who in their wisdoms dare accuse
    This offspring of thy Muse,
      Let them agree,
Conspire one comedy, and they will say   25
'Tis easier to commend than make a play.

James Shirley

18 **Phoebus . . . bays** i.e. the wreath of bay or laurel leaves worn by (Phoebus) Apollo, god of poetry, to signify the immortality of art

22 **tribe** Cf. the sobriquet which Jonson bestowed on his followers, 'The Tribe of Ben'. Oxf suggests that Shirley – like Lakyn, with his talk of *scornful malice* and *envy* (18, 26) – 'was responding to a general attack on the plays and players of his company made by Thomas Carew and his followers, which had drawn in Massinger'. The Cavalier poet Thomas Carew was a prominent member of Jonson's 'Tribe'; however, the attacks referred to here sound more personal, and it is possible that Massinger had

suffered criticism because of the play's perceived pro-Catholic tendency (see pp. 40–1).

25 **Conspire** unite in producing (*OED v.* 5)

27 **James Shirley** (1596–1666) prominent Caroline dramatist. A protégé of Laud, and ordained as an Anglican priest in 1619, Shirley converted to Catholicism in 1623 and worked as a schoolmaster before beginning his career as a dramatist for Queen Henrietta's Men in 1625. Massinger contributed his own set of encomiastic verses for Shirley's *The Grateful Servant*, also published in 1630, and entered on the Stationers' Register a month before *The Renegado*.

13 'em] them *Shirley*   15 public] glorious *Shirley*   22 wisdoms] wisdom *Shirley*   23 This] The *Shirley*   27 James Shirley] *not in Shirley*

To his worthy friend Master Philip Massinger, on his play called The Renegado

The bosom of a friend cannot breathe forth
A flattering phrase to speak the noble worth
Of him that hath lodged in his honest breast   5
So large a title: I, among the rest
That honour thee, do only seem to praise,
Wanting the flowers of art to deck that bays
Merit has crowned thy temples with. Know, friend,
Though there are some who merely do commend   10
To live i'th' world's opinion such as can
Censure with judgement, no such piece of man
Makes up my spirit; where desert does live,
There will I plant my wonder, and there give
My best endeavours to build up his story   15
That truly merits. I did ever glory
To behold virtue rich, though cruel Fate
In scornful malice does beat low their state
That best deserve, when others that but know
Only to scribble, and no more, oft grow   20
Great in their favours that would seem to be
Patrons of wit and modest poesy.
Yet, with your abler friends, let me say this:
Many may strive to equal you but miss
Of your fair scope. This work of yours men may   25
Throw in the face of envy, and then say
To those that are in great men's thoughts more blest:
'Imitate this, and call that work your best.'
Yet wise men in this and too often err

3–9 **The bosom . . . with** Lakyn implicitly contrasts the *noble worth* deriving
from Massinger's art and from his
title of friend with the *old nobility*
and *hereditary titles* acknowledged in
the dramatist's dedication to Lord
Berkeley.

8 **that bays** (see 18n. above). The
singular form results from the fact
that *bays* is an abbreviation of 'wreath
or garland of bays'.

16, 32 **merits** With a complimentary
flourish, Lakyn plays on one of the
play's own key terms (see 1.1.23n.).

When they their love before the work prefer.   30
If I should say more, some may blame me for't –
Seeing your merits speak you, not report.

Daniel Lakyn

33 **Daniel Lakyn** (1606–54) physician, and author of two medical treatises. Lakyn's MS on the treatment of venereal disease (British Museum, Sloan 2818) mentions his travels to Morocco, Constantinople and the Black Sea area.

23   Wenceslas Hollar, portrait of a Turk, etching, Antwerp, 1645

THE RENEGADO,
OR,
THE GENTLEMAN
OF VENICE

VITELLI	*a gentleman of Venice (disguised as a merchant)*	
GAZET	*servant to Vitelli*	
FRANCISCO	*a Jesuit*	
PAULINA	*sister to Vitelli, enslaved to Asambeg*	
DONUSA	*niece to Amurath, the Ottoman Sultan*	5
MANTO	*waiting-woman to Donusa*	
CARAZIE	*a eunuch, enslaved to Donusa*	
ASAMBEG	*Viceroy of Tunis*	
MUSTAPHA	*Pasha of Aleppo, suitor to Donusa*	
AGA	*Captain of the Janizaries*	10
KAPIAGA	*Chief Porter of the palace*	
GAOLER		
Two TURKS		
GUARDS		
Antonio GRIMALDI	*the renegado*	15
MASTER BOATSWAIN }	*leading Grimaldi's crew*	

Janizaries, Sailors

Two TURKS] 3 Turkes *Q*   GUARDS] *this edn*   Janizaries] *this edn*

1 VITELLI a name perhaps derived (as Oxf suggests) from that of Alexander Vitellius, 'a most famous captaine' sent from Italy with an army of 'three thousand chosen footmen' by Pope Paul III to assist in the campaign against Suleiman the Magnificent in Austria and Hungary. Vitellius so distinguished himself at the siege of Budapest (1541) that during a truce 'a notable captaine of the Turks, desired to see *Vitellius*, who being shewed unto him . . . ran to embrace him for his honour' (Knolles, sigs 3Q5ʳ, 3Q6ᵛ).

2 GAZET The servant's disguise as a merchant's apprentice suggests that his name is meant to recall that of a small Venetian coin (worth less than an English penny), but for some it will also have recalled the scandalous news-sheets, or *gazzette*, published in Venice from the mid-16th century, whose name is likely to have derived from their price. It is probably significant that the *OED*'s earliest example of the English form of the word, in a reference to 'rediculous Italian Gazetts', is dated 1623, and that there had been an explosion in the publication of such news-sheets in London from *c.* 1618.

3 FRANCISCO the name of the father of two captives in Cervantes's *El Trato de Argel* and of a martyred boy-prisoner in his *Los Baños de Argel*; but perhaps meant to be evocative of the gentle St Francis of Assisi, founder of the Franciscan order. The presence of a priest in Tunis is not as arbitrary a device as it seems, since (as Vivanco observes in *Los Baños*), 'these faithless dogs allow us to observe our religion . . . [and] to say our mass, although in secret'. Even in the slave prisons of North Africa, priests were permitted to say Mass and minister to the spiritual needs of captives.

Jesuit Founded in 1533 by St Ignatius Loyola, the Society of Jesus was a principal instrument in the Counter-Reformation struggle waged by the Vatican against Protestant reformers. Hated in Protestant Europe, the Jesuits were frequently regarded as suspect even in Catholic countries because of their cultivation of the rich and powerful, their endorsement of Machiavellian policy to gain their ends and their unscrupulous use of casuistry in politico-religious debate (hence 'Jesuitical'). Massinger's positive characterization of the Jesuit is especially unexpected, given the particular odium in which the Society of Jesus was held in England following the implication of its English superior, Father Garnet, in the Gunpowder Plot (1605). One of Massinger's documentary sources, Biddulph's *Travels*, devotes several pages to execration of the Order generally and of the Jesuits the author encountered in the Levant in particular (sigs R1ᵛ–R3ᵛ, S4ʳ⁻ᵛ). Only months after the first staging of *The Renegado*, popular loathing of the order was fanned by Middleton's anti-Catholic *succès de scandale*, *A Game at Chess*, which is introduced by the figure of Loyola and his sinister companion, Error.

4 PAULINA In a play so much concerned with miracles and conversion, the saintly Paulina's name is perhaps meant to recall that of the first great missionary saint, Paul, the apostle whose travels criss-crossed the Mediterranean. However, Rice (74) cites a passage in Knolles describing the fate of a Christian captive, the daughter of Paulus Ericus, governor of the captured city of Chalcis, who 'for her rare perfection' was handed over to Sultan Mahomet 'as the mirrour of beautie': failing to win her 'by flattering words and faire persuasion', he threatened her 'with death, torture, and force, worse than death it selfe; if shee would not otherwise yeeld unto his appetite. Whereunto the constant virgin . . . answered so resolutely, and so contrarie to the tyrants expectation, that he being therewith enraged, commaunded her to be presently slaine.'

5 DONUSA perhaps derived (as Rice suggests) from 'Ionuses', the name of a jealous pasha in Knolles (sigs 3B3ʳ–3B4ʳ) who murders his wife

'Manto' (Fig. 18); see 6n.

Amurath Amurath (or Murad) IV had ascended the Ottoman throne in 1623, but since he was still a child, Massinger probably had in mind Amurath III (1574–95), sultan at the time of Cervantes's captivity (Fig. 6). The Ottoman sultanate, founded by Osman I at the beginning of the 14th century, overran the Byzantine Empire (what remained of the Eastern Empire of Rome), capturing Constantinople in 1453. By Massinger's day it was the most powerful empire in the world, controlling most of the Middle East, North Africa, the eastern Mediterranean, Greece and the Balkans, as well as making deep inroads into Europe that had carried Ottoman armies to the walls of Vienna in 1529 and would do so again in 1683. Shortly before Massinger began writing *The Renegado*, moreover, Turkish troops had joined in a Hungarian siege of that same city. Admired and envied by Europeans for its wealth, and cultivated by merchants as a source of luxury goods, including silk and other textiles, carpets, spices and coffee, the Ottoman Empire was also feared as a threat to Christendom and denigrated for its autocratic politics, its luxury and supposed decadence. English attitudes towards the Turks were ambiguous: James I had written a well-known poem celebrating the Battle of Lepanto (1578) as a triumph of Christian Europe over its infidel enemy, and English writers liked to contrast Turkish 'tyranny' (both political and domestic) with English liberty; yet English diplomacy (notably under Elizabeth) had also flirted with the idea of the Turks as allies in the struggle against Catholic Spain and the power of the Pope – as indeed the Hungarians had been in 1621.

6 MANTO borrowed from the name of a beautiful Greek captive of whom the pasha Ionuses became so enamoured that he married her (Fig. 18). However, the old man's jealousy was such that Manto 'determined secretly

to depart from him, and so to returne again into her own country'; betrayed by one of her own eunuchs, she was murdered by her enraged husband (Knolles, sig. 3B4ʳ).

7 CARAZIE Following Rice (73), Oxf suggests that the name derives from that of Caraza, an old Turkish captain in the war against Scanderbeg under Mahomet (Mehmed) the Great (Knolles, sig. 2K8ᵛ); while Knolles's text associates Caraza with Asam-beg (see 8n.), the name is more likely to be borrowed from another of Mahomet the Great's commanders, Carazies Bassa, killed at the siege of Belgrade (1456) (sig. Hh5ʳ). Christian captives who 'turned Turk' were normally given Muslim names. Jonathan Burton comments: 'that Carazie is both the sole Englishman in the play and a castrated eunuch is a mark of the play's interest in women's power and the weakness of English men abroad' (*Traffic*, 106).

8 ASAMBEG The name probably derives from Hassan Baxi (or Pasha), the King of Algiers in Cervantes's play *Los Baños de Argel*, who also appears as Hassan Aga in 'The Captive's Tale', where he is identified as a Venetian renegade. An actual renegade of this name, Hasán Baxá (sometimes known as Hasán Veneciano), was the beylerbey (ruler) of Algiers 1577–80 and 1583–5 (see Fig. 9). Another beylerbey named Hasán Agha had inflicted a catastrophic defeat on the besieging fleet of Charles V in 1541. However, Massinger's form of the name (Asambeg) seems to have been determined by that of one of Sultan Mahomet the Great's commanders, Asam-beg (Knolles, sig. 2K6ʳ). Knolles describes the beylerbey of Tunis as 'a Viceroy, [who] commaundeth all that great and large kingdome' (sig. 6C6ʳ).

In Massinger's day the cities of the Barbary Coast, including Algiers and Tunis, were notorious as bases for the corsairs (privateers), who preyed on Mediterranean shipping and

84

conducted slave raids on European coasts, including the British Isles, and ultimately reached as far as Iceland. Owing nominal suzerainty to the Ottoman sultan in Constantinople (modern Istanbul), these North African fiefdoms operated in many respects as independent states.

9 MUSTAPHA then, as now, among the more common Turkish names (see Biddulph, sig. P4ʳ). An Ottoman official known as Mustapha, presenting himself as a chiaus (or messenger) of the Sultan, arrived in England in July 1607, seeking the King's help to control the activities of English corsairs in the Levant (Burton, *Traffic*, 248–9). James's reluctance to receive the ambassador caused tensions with the Levant Company. Massinger will also have encountered the name in various literary contexts: he is likely to have known Fulke Greville's closet drama *Mustapha* (*c.* 1594–6); and Sandys, after describing how the pashas married to Turkish princesses are given to them by the sultan to be treated like their slaves, mentions '*Mustapha* and *Hadir*, (two of the *Vizers* of the Port) [who] haue married this *Sultan* [Ahmed]'s sister, and neece' (sig. H2ʳ). Knolles describes the career of Mustapha Bassa, a general whom Amurath (or Murad) II sent against the Albanian hero Scanderbeg (1404–68) (sigs 2D1ʳff.). He also writes of an even more prominent general of the same name who served under Suleiman the Magnificent (1520–66), and later under Amurath III (sigs 3C3ʳff.) (see Fig. 11).
Pasha a title (variously represented as Bashaw or Bassa in early modern texts) borne by senior military commanders and provincial governors in the Ottoman Empire
Aleppo Among the most cosmopolitan cities of the Ottoman Empire, Aleppo was a major hub for European trade in the Levant.

10 AGA commander, 'a place of high trust, and third in repute through the Empire' (Sandys, sig. E6ʳ) (see Fig. 7)

11 KAPIAGA apparently deriving from *kapi* = gate, so perhaps originally the principal officer in charge of entrance to the palace. Knolles speaks of 'the *Capiaga* or chiefe porter, a man ever of great authoritie in the Turks court' (sig. 4Q5ᵛ) (see Fig. 10). Biddulph defines the '*Cappagie*' as a 'Pursevant' (pursuivant), i.e. a royal messenger with the power to execute warrants (including, in this case, warrants of execution – see 4.2.61–2n.). According to Sandys, the sultan's train included 500 'Capagies' (sig. H2ʳ), whose tasks included guarding the royal harem where they 'waite by fifties at euery gate' (sig. H1ʳ).

13 Two TURKS Although Q's *Dramatis Personae* specifies '3 Turkes', only two speaking parts are allocated in 1.3.

15 GRIMALDI Perhaps derived (as Oxf suggests) from the Grimolda, one of the great houses of Genoa, but 'Grimaldi' itself is an established Italian surname to which Massinger was possibly attracted by its punning suggestiveness in an English context; tellingly, the name was later chosen by John Ford for one of the villains of his tragedy *'Tis Pity She's a Whore* (*c.* 1632). Burton finds an analogue for Grimaldi's story in the career of the renegade Sir Francis Verney, an English corsair in Algiers (1608–15), who, having fallen 'desperately sick', was rescued by an English Jesuit (*Traffic*, 149–50).
renegado See LN, p. 235.

16 MASTER in merchant vessels the ship's captain, but in naval vessels the officer in charge of a ship's navigation, as opposed to its commander in naval operations (*OED n.*[1] 2a, b)

17 BOATSWAIN officer in charge of a ship's sails and rigging, responsible for summoning the crew to their duties (*OED n.* 1); at this time still sometimes pronounced as spelled, but more usually 'bos'n'

18 **Janizaries** elite body of Turkish infantry from whom the sultan's palace guard was drawn (see Fig. 8) – made up of some renegades, but drawn chiefly

from the ranks of former Christians who had been sent as children to the sultan by way of tribute. According to Sandys (whose description may give some clues as to the costuming envisaged by Massinger), 'the *Ianizaries* (a name that signifies new soldiery) are those that beare such great sway in Constantinople: insomuch that the *Sultans* themselues haue bene sometimes subiect to their insolencies . . . These are flower of the Turkish infantry, by whom such wonderful victories have bene atchieued . . . They serue with harquebushes, armed besides with cymiter, and hatchets. They weare on their heads a bonnet of white felt, with a flap hanging downe behind to their shoulders; adorned about the browes with a wreathe of metall, gilt, and set with stones of small value; hauing a kind of sheathe or socket of the same erected before, wherein such are suffered to sticke plumes of feathers as haue behaued themselues extraordinarie brauely. They tucke vp the skirtes of their coates when they fight . . . They haue yearely giuen them two gownes apeece, the one of violet cloth, the other of stammel' (sigs E6^v–F1^r). See also Knolles (sigs 6B6^v–6B7^r, 6C3^r–6C4^r).

THE RENEGADO,
OR, THE GENTLEMAN
OF VENICE

The scene Tunis

1.1   *Enter* VITELLI *and* GAZET.

VITELLI
You have hired a shop, then?
GAZET   Yes, sir, and our wares –
Though brittle as a maidenhead at sixteen –

TITLE See LN, p. 235.

0 **Tunis** Massinger's reason for shifting the action of his play from Cervantes's Algiers to another infamous depot of the Barbary corsairs may be related to the fact that his play is in part a riposte to *A Christian Turned Turk* (1612), Robert Daborne's dramatization of the life of the infamous English renegade John Ward, which had made Tunis a familiar location to English audiences. Despite the activities of the corsairs, the Barbary Company (founded in 1551 and granted a monopoly by Queen Elizabeth in 1585) conducted an extensive trade with the Barbary Coast, from which most of England's sugar derived. The play's documentary detail, however, derives almost entirely from contemporary accounts of Ottoman cities in the Levant, notably Constantinople and Aleppo.

1.1 Location: a street in Tunis

1 **hired a shop** It is not clear how much knowledge Massinger had of the actual conditions of European commerce in Tunis and elsewhere: hiring a shop and paying for one's ground (1.3.77) sounds as if simply adapted from English practice, and Massinger probably has in mind a booth like those used in Jonson's *Bartholomew Fair* (1614), though English market squares were often surrounded by permanent shops. 'N.H.', in *The Complete Tradesman* (1684), indicates that shopkeepers normally rented rather than owned their premises (9, 35).

2 **brittle ... sixteen** a proverbial-sounding phrase; Oxf cites the anonymous poem 'A Maidenhead', in *Merry Drollery* (1661), where virginity is 'At fifteen rare, at eighteen strange'. Cf. also *Maid of Honour*, 2.2.10–12, and *Emperor*, 2.1.255.
  brittle liable to break, fragile. Cf. Middleton, *Fair Quarrel*, comparing a daughter's 'brittle niceness' to 'a mere cupboard of glasses, / The least shake breaks or cracks 'em' (1.1.8–9).

TITLE OR, THE GENTLEMAN OF VENICE] *Herbert's licence; not in Q* 1.1] *(Actus primus. Scena Prima.)*

87

Are safe unladen: not a crystal cracked
Or China dish needs soldering; our choice pictures
As they came from the workman, without blemish.   5
And I have studied speeches for each piece,
And, in a thrifty tone to sell 'em off,
Will swear by Mahomet and Termagant

3 **crystal** crystal glass – at this time a relatively novel luxury in England (*OED*'s earliest citation is 1594). Despite strenuous efforts to develop a native industry, high-quality glass was typically associated with the Venetian glass industry in Murano from where it was mostly imported (Peck, 76–8, 113).
   cracked The previous line suggests a bawdy quibble – 'deflowered' (Williams, *Dictionary*, 1.327–8).
4 **China dish** at this date still referring to porcelain imported from China. 'China houses' were becoming an important feature of the London luxury market (Peck, 47–51, 65, 115). In addition to the denunciations of Puritans like Philip Stubbes (*The Anatomy of Abuses*, 1583), contemporary mercantile theory regularly inveighed against the deleterious economic effects of importing of 'vain toys', 'trifles' and 'baubles', especially from the Mediterranean and the East, so there was probably a gratifying irony in the spectacle of Venetians purveying such commodities in an Ottoman market. Although Williams's earliest citation is from Brome's *Sparagus Garden* (1635) – 'You now keep a china-house, and deal in brittle commodities' (2.2) – *China* probably continues the bawdy innuendo, standing for 'maidenhead' (Williams, *Dictionary*, 1.236–7).
   soldering mending (*OED v.* 4), but also 'restoring cracked maidenhead' (Williams, *Dictionary*, 3.1270–1). The Q spelling 'sodring' points to the necessary elision of the second syllable.
4–11 **choice   pictures . . . princess** The tight restrictions applied to

representation in Islamic art made European portraiture, with its more realistic conventions, attractive in courtly Ottoman circles, where a number of sultans commissioned European painters to execute their portraits. However, Massinger's reference is probably more local: under James I, the burgeoning English traffic in luxury goods included a 'fevered search for sixteenth-century Italian pictures', for which Venice was an important source; and collectors also favoured portraits of the great and powerful (Peck, 162–83). Vitelli, in his guise as a Venetian merchant, pretends to carry this elite trade into the marketplace, whilst actually offering something close to pornography.
5 **workman** craftsman, artist
6 **studied** learned by heart – an actor's expression (*OED v.* 9b)
7 **thrifty tone** respectable style of oratory – with a play on *thrifty* = prosperous (*OED a.* 1)
8 **by . . . Termagant** the usual oath attributed to Moors and Saracens in medieval and Renaissance romance (cf. *Faerie Queene*, 6.7.47). *Termagant* was the 'name of an imaginary deity held in medieval Christendom to be worshipped by Muslims' (*OED n.* 1). In popular belief Mahomet and Termagant were supposed Mahometan idols: just as Mahomet, Maumet or Mammet became the archetypal instance of a false idol (from which the term came to apply to any kind of puppet or doll), so Termagant appeared in medieval plays as a violent, overbearing spirit (from which the word became a hyperbolical term for a roistering bully

4 soldering] *(sod'ring)*

That this is mistress to the great Duke of Florence,
That niece to old King Pippin, and a third 10
An Austrian princess by her Roman lip –
Howe'er my conscience tells me they are figures
Of bawds and common courtesans in Venice.

VITELLI
You make no scruple of an oath, then?

and, ultimately, for unruly, shrewish women). Gazet's use of the oath only indicates his ignorance of the Islamic world, about which Massinger's documentary sources, with their detailed, if often libellous, accounts of the Prophet's life, had made him relatively well informed (see 4.3.125–31).
Mahomet with the stress on the first syllable. I preserve this spelling throughout the edition partly as a reminder of the necessary pronunciation, and partly to distinguish the often fantastic bugbear of early modern imagination from the historical Prophet of Islam.

9 **this** i.e. the figure in this portrait
great . . . Florence Cf. the title of Massinger's 1636 tragicomedy *The Great Duke of Florence*. Here presumably Ferdinando II de' Medici, Duke of Florence, and Grand Duke of Tuscany (1621–70). Italy was divided between a number of city-states, of which Florence and Venice were among the most powerful.

10 **Pippin** probably King Pepin III, father of Charlemagne, the founder of the Holy Roman Empire. Massinger's spelling is probably a sign of Gazet's ignorant pronunciation, a 'pippin' being a name for certain types of apple.

11 **Roman lip** Conjecturing that Q's 'Roman nose' was the product of censorship responding to sensitivity over negotiations leading up to the Spanish treaty of 1630, Greg (74–5) proposed that the original reading (only partly restored by Massinger's MS correction in the Folger Harbord copy) was 'German lip' – a phrase

significantly censored in the 1631 MS of *Believe*, where 'German' was struck out and replaced with 'very'. However, Massinger may well have thought that *Roman lip* would give him sufficient cover while making his satiric jab clear to perceptive readers, since the rulers of the Austrian branch of the Habsburgs (which shared the family propensity for exaggeratedly full nether lips) were designated 'Holy Roman Emperors' or 'Kings of the Romans'.

12 **conscience** Gazet echoes the language of popular Protestantism which placed particular emphasis on the promptings of individual conscience as a guide to conduct. Underlying his commercial rationale may be St Paul's advice: 'Whatsoever is sold in the shambles, that eat, asking no question for conscience sake' (1 Corinthians, 10.25).

13 **courtesans in Venice** Venice was notorious throughout Europe for the number and conspicuous display of its prostitutes. Technically a courtesan was a woman who sold her favours at a high price to a small number of admirers, or sometimes only to a single lover; but Gazet's use of the term *common* suggests that he does not distinguish them from ordinary whores. The vending of these erotically charged portraits highlights the interplay between commercial and sexual exchange in the ensuing action.

14 **scruple** thought or circumstance that troubles the conscience (*OED n.*[2] 1); in this mercantile context it may be relevant that the original meaning – a small unit of weight, equivalent to 1/24 of an ounce – was still current.

11 Roman] German *(conj. Greg)* lip] *MS ADD;* nose *Q*

89

GAZET   Fie, sir,
'Tis out of my indentures! I am bound there   15
To swear for my master's profit as securely
As your intelligencer must for his prince
That sends him forth an honourable spy
To serve his purposes. And if it be lawful
In a Christian shopkeeper to cheat his father,   20
I cannot find but to abuse a Turk
In the sale of our commodities must be thought
A meritorious work.
VITELLI   I wonder, sirrah,
What's your religion?
GAZET   Troth, to answer truly,
I would not be of one that should command me   25

15 out . . . indentures 'included among
the formal terms of my service' (*is out
of* = comes from). Indentures were the
formal contracts between masters and
apprentices.
   bound legally compelled
17 **intelligencer** spy
18 **honourable spy** The seeming oxymoron is not necessarily ironic.
Massinger may be quoting Jonson's
Catiline, where Sempronia attributes
the phrase (incorrectly) to Thucydides,
but it seems to have had widespread
currency. Sir Henry Wotton, the
former English ambassador to Venice,
described the members of his profession as 'but honourable espies' (*State of
Christendom*, 1657, 104), citing Philippe
de Commines as its author; later it
would be adapted by Voltaire (see
Herford and Simpson, note on *Catiline*,
4.718). However, Gazet's invocation
of 'honour' in this crassly commercial
context is (unintentionally) ironic.
19–20 **if . . . father** a quasi-proverbial
formulation; cf. Tilley, F88: 'I would
cheat my own father at cards.'
19 **lawful** probably used in the loose (and
now obsolete) sense of 'permissible,
justifiable' (*OED a.* 1b) – unless Gazet
is referring to some now forgotten scan-

dal of the sort that commonly fed the
plots of city comedy.
21 **cannot find but** can only conclude that
   Turk The word could be used to apply
to Muslims generally (*OED n.* 3a) as
well as to ethnic Turks; it could also
refer to anyone exhibiting the tyrannical, barbarous, savage or intemperate
behaviour popularly ascribed to Turks.
22 **commodities** frequently used with a
sexual innuendo, especially in relation
to women (Williams, *Glossary*, 88). The
commercial setting of *The Renegado*
allows for extensive play on such terms;
see e.g. 1.1.41.
23 **meritorious work** i.e. one that could
help to earn salvation. Gazet plays
with the language of Catholic theology,
whose doctrine of salvation by works
had been rejected by Protestant reformers, but which proto-Arminians like
Richard Montagu in *A New Gagg for an
Old Goose* (1624; see p. 39) were beginning to rehabilitate (Milton, 210–15).
25–8 **one . . . The other** Although
the doctrinal references are clear,
Massinger's avoidance of names may
be a device to avoid censorship.
25–7 **one . . . table** Roman Catholic and
orthodox Anglican doctrine required
abstinence from red meat on Fridays,

To feed upon poor-john when I see pheasants
And partridges on the table; nor do I like
The other that allows us to eat flesh
In the Lent, though it be rotten, rather than be
Thought superstitious, as your zealous cobbler   30
And learned botcher preach at Amsterdam
Over a hotchpotch. I would not be confined
In my belief: when all your sects and sectaries
Are grown of one opinion, if I like it
I will profess myself; in the meantime,   35
Live I in England, Spain, France, Rome, Geneva,
I am of that country's faith.

VITELLI   And what in Tunis?
Will you turn Turk here?

during Lent and on other days of penitential observation.

26 **poor-john** salted hake – Lenten fare
and food for the poor

28–30 **The   other . . . superstitious**
Gazet also wants to dissociate himself
from those extreme Protestants who,
he says, would prefer to eat rotten meat
in Lent (despite the official prohibition
of meat-eating in that season) rather
than risk being seen as superstitious
Catholics by eating fish.

29 **the Lent** i.e. the season of Lent, the 40
days of fasting and penitence, between
Ash Wednesday and Easter eve, when
Christians commemorate Jesus's 40
days in the wilderness

30–1 **cobbler . . . Amsterdam** recalling
the former tailor John of Leyden and
other tradesmen who emerged as lead-
ers of the 1534 Anabaptist rising in
Munster

31 **botcher** mending tailor
Amsterdam a city notorious for its tol-
eration of Anabaptists and other radical
Protestant sects

32 **hotchpotch** meat stew – typically
mutton broth thickened with stewed

vegetables, eaten in Holland as *hutspot.*
Satirists (following Jonson's caricature
of Zeal-of-the-land Busy's depraved
lust for roast pig in *Bartholomew Fair*)
often mocked Puritans for fleshly appe-
tites that contradicted their professed
asceticism.

33–4 **when . . . opinion** a quasi-proverbial
formula for impossibility

33 **sectaries** members of nonconformist
sects

35 **profess myself** subscribe to that faith

36 **Live I** whether I live
Rome, Geneva respectively, the seat
of the papacy and the city principally
associated with Calvinist doctrine. John
Calvin (1509–64) was the Protestant the-
ologian whose predestinarian theology
not only commended itself to Puritan
sectaries but also largely governed the
Church of England through the reigns
of Elizabeth and James I. Calvin lived
and taught in Geneva, where his followers arranged the printing of the one of
the earliest and most influential English
translations of the Bible (1560).

38 **turn Turk** convert to Islam, become a
renegado

36 Geneva,] *Coxeter;* Geneva. *Q*

GAZET   No! – so I should lose
A collop of that part my Doll enjoined me
To bring home as she left it. 'Tis her venture,   40
Nor dare I barter that commodity
Without her special warrant.
VITELLI   You are a knave, sir!
Leaving your roguery, think upon my business:
It is no time to fool now.
Remember where you are, too: though this mart
    time   45
We are allowed free trading and with safety,
Temper your tongue and meddle not with the
    Turks,
Their manners nor religion.
GAZET   Take you heed, sir,
What colours you wear. Not two hours since, there
    landed
An English pirate's whore with a green apron;   50

38–40 **so . . . left it** i.e. undergo circumcision – but since this was often confused in the popular imagination with castration as a likely fate for anyone who turned Turk, Gazet may be fearing the same fate. Ironically, however, he will later develop an ambition to achieve the post of court eunuch – apparently unaware of the word's meaning (see 3.4.43–58).

39 **collop** slice of flesh
Doll abbreviation of Dorothy, but often used as a type-name for a whore (cf. Doll Tearsheet in *2H4* and *H5* and Doll Common in Jonson's *Alchemist*)

40 **venture** Doll has an investment in Gazet's voyage, in the form of his manhood; but just as Doll was a familiar name for a prostitute, so 'venturer' was a cant term for the same profession (*OED n.* 3). The implication may be that Gazet's merchant enterprise is an extension of Doll's other business interests.

41 **commodity** playfully extends the theme of sexual merchandizing introduced by Vitelli's sale of lascivious portraits. On the play's exploitation of the erotic associations of such terms as 'commodity' and 'commerce', see Robinson, 'Turks', 219–23.

45 **mart** market

46 **free trading** Licence to trade was carefully restricted by the authorities in most countries (including England).

47–8 **meddle . . . religion** Against a marginal gloss advertising '*A note for travellers*', Biddulph advises that 'whosoever will live in quiet amongst them, must neither meddle with their Law, their Women, nor their slaves' (sig. K5ʳ).

49 **colours** Given Vitelli's disguise, the metaphoric sense of 'fair pretence' or 'cloak' (*OED n.* 12a) may also be involved.

50 **English pirate** Many Englishmen were to be found amongst the privateering corsairs who harried Mediterranean

And, as she walked the streets, one of their muftis –
We call them priests at Venice – with a razor
Cuts it off, petticoat, smock and all, and leaves her
As naked as my nail – the young fry wondering
What strange beast it should be. I scaped a scouring: 55
My mistress' busk-point of that forbidden colour
Then tied my codpiece; had it been discovered,
I had been caponed.

VITELLI   And had been well served.
Haste to the shop and set my wares in order;
I will not long be absent.

---

shipping from the cities of the Barbary Coast.

apron Aprons without bibs, generally made of transparent material and edged with lace, were worn (usually indoors) as fashionable accessories over the dress. They were favoured by prostitutes, for whom green was a preferred colour (see Williams, *Dictionary*, 1.32, 2.620).

51 **muftis** priests; 'The *Turkes* honour their *Muftie* (which is their chiefe rule in Ecclesiasticall matters, next under the Grand Signor) as an Angell' (Biddulph, sig. L1ᵛ).

52–4 **with a razor … naked** This 'comic revelation of everything the religion seeks to conceal with its strict codes of public morality and dress … portrays Islam as … hypocritically strict' (D'Amico, 123).

53 **petticoat** an ornamented skirt worn sometimes externally, sometimes beneath a gown, frock or overskirt, which would often be bunched up to show the petticoat beneath

smock shift or chemise (*OED n.* 1a)

54 **As … nail** proverbial (Tilley, N4). The bawdy *nail* = penis (Williams, *Dictionary*, 2.932–3) is probably also involved here.

fry children (*OED n.*¹ 1)

55 **scouring** being put in fetters or the stocks (*OED* scour *v.*² 1f); but also 'scour' = coit with (Williams, *Dictionary*, 3.1205)

56 **busk-point** corset lace (often given as a favour to a lover)

forbidden colour Biddulph notes that Mahometan 'Churchmen' and descendants of the Prophet wore green: 'For greene, they account *Mahomets* colour, and if they see any Christian wearing a garment of that colour, they will cut it from his backe, and beate him, and ask him how he dare presume to wear *Mahomets* colour, and whether he bee kin to God or not? … one for having but greene shoestrings, had his shooes taken away. Another wearing greene breeches under his Gowne (being espied) had his breeches cut off, and he reviled and beaten' (sig. L2ᵛ); see also Sandys (sig. G2ᵛ), and Moryson (sig. 3T2ᵛ). Associated with paradise in Islamic symbology, the colour still appears on the flags of many Muslim nations. Its association in 17th-century England with prostitutes (Williams, *Dictionary*, 3.1205–7) makes its use by the pirate's whore doubly offensive.

57 **codpiece** laced appendage worn on front of male breeches, often prominent and ornamented

58 **caponed** castrated (like a capon, or emasculated rooster)

served treated; but, as Vitelli's following lines, together with Gazet's dutiful promise at 63, suggest, also a punning reminder of Gazet's servile status

GAZET   Though I strive, sir,   60
To put off melancholy, to which you are ever
Too much inclined, it shall not hinder me
With my best care to serve you.   *Exit.*
VITELLI   I believe thee.

Enter FRANCISCO.

O welcome, sir, stay of my steps in this life
And guide to all my blessed hopes hereafter.   65
What comforts, sir? Have your endeavours
    prospered?
Have we tired Fortune's malice with our sufferings?
Is she at length, after so many frowns,
Pleased to vouchsafe one cheerful look upon us?
FRANCISCO
You give too much to Fortune and your passions –   70
O'er which a wise man, if religious, triumphs.
That name fools worship; and those tyrants which
We arm against our better part, our reason,
May add but never take from our afflictions.
VITELLI
Sir, as I am a sinful man, I cannot   75

---

61 **melancholy** According to the psycho-
physiological theories governing early
modern medicine, the health of the
human body was determined by the
balance of four 'humours': melancholy, choler, blood and phlegm. The
symptoms of melancholy (as described
in Burton's *Anatomy of Melancholy*)
were extraordinarily various, extending from mere dejection to cover most
forms of mental illness, as well as the
symptoms of romantic love.

63 **I believe thee** The placing of Gazet's
exit in Q, if precise, may suggest that
this line is spoken with ironic amusement after the servant's departure.

64 **stay** support
65 **blessed** blessèd
67 **Fortune's malice** Represented as a
blind, capricious goddess, Fortune was
proverbially hostile to human beings.
70 **give** allow, yield
72 **That name** i.e. Fortune
those tyrants i.e. the *passions.*
Francisco speaks the language of
Renaissance neo-Stoicism, with its
stress on the need to overcome the
vicissitudes of Fortune by subjugat-
ing the intemperate passions to the
governance of reason.
74 **add** add to, increase
take from reduce, ameliorate

63 SD1] *(Exit Gazet)*   SD2] *after* serve you

But like one suffer.

FRANCISCO   I exact not from you

A fortitude insensible of calamity,

To which the saints themselves have bowed, and
        shown

They are made of flesh and blood; all that I
        challenge

Is manly patience. Will you – that were trained up   80

In a religious school, where divine maxims,

Scorning comparison with moral precepts,

Were daily taught you – bear your constancy's trial

Not like Vitelli, but a village nurse

With curses in your mouth, tears in your eyes?   85

How poorly it shows in you!

VITELLI   I am schooled, sir,

And will hereafter to my utmost strength

Study to be myself.

FRANCISCO   So shall you find me

Most ready to assist you. Neither have I

Slept in your great occasions since I left you: 90

I have been at the Viceroy's court and pressed

76–80 **I . . . patience** 'It is not that I expect you to be brave to the point of ignoring anguish so extreme that it has made even the saints confess their human frailty; all I ask is the kind of patient endurance to be expected of a man' (see 80n.).

77 **insensible of** incapable of being affected by (*OED a.* 4a)

79 **challenge** demand, insist on

80 **manly patience** Renaissance notions of masculinity were strongly marked by the Roman idea of *virtus* (manly virtue, courage, from Latin *vir* = man), and particularly by the Stoic ideal of passive endurance as a way of overcoming the trials of Fate and Fortune.

82 'which excel any mere moral injunctions'

84 **village nurse** a stereotype of especially coarse and ignorant femininity

90 **Slept . . . occasions** neglected your important business (*OED* occasion *n.*[1] 6a)

91–2 **pressed . . . entrance** presumably recalling Sandys's description of the sultan's seraglio (palace), where Christians were not 'ordinarily' permitted to go beyond the second of three courtyards (sig. D5ʳ)

90 occasions . . . you:] *Coxeter;* occasions . . . you *Q;* occasions; since . . . you, *Rawl.;* occasions: since . . . you *Oxf*

As far as they allow a Christian entrance,
And something I have learned that may concern
The purpose of this journey.

VITELLI   Dear sir, what is it?

FRANCISCO
By the command of Asambeg, the Viceroy,   95
The city swells with barbarous pomp and pride
For the entertainment of stout Mustapha,
The Pasha of Aleppo, who in person
Comes to receive the niece of Amurath,
The fair Donusa, for his bride.

VITELLI   I find not   100
How this may profit us.

FRANCISCO   Pray you give me leave:
Among the rest that wait upon the Viceroy –
Such as have under him command in Tunis,
Who as you have often heard are all false pirates –
I saw the shame of Venice and the scorn   105
Of all good men, the perjured renegado,
Antonio Grimaldi.

VITELLI   Ha! His name
Is poison to me.

FRANCISCO   Yet again?

VITELLI   I have done, sir.

FRANCISCO
This debauched villain, whom we ever thought –
After his impious scorn done in St Mark's   110
To me, as I stood at the holy altar –

---

96 **barbarous** playing on the designation
   of Tunis as part of 'Barbary'
97 **entertainment** festive reception, welcome (*OED n.*11a)
109 **debauched** The metre of the line
   requires stress on the first syllable
   or that the word be treated as trisyllabic (in which case *we ever* will be

elided).
110–11 The full extent of Grimaldi's
   blasphemy will not be revealed until
   4.1.26–33.
110 **St Mark's** the basilica of St Mark,
   the principal church of Venice, whose
   magnificence is celebrated in *Faustus*
   (3.1.16–19)

107 Antonio] *MS ADD; Antono Q*

The thief that ravished your fair sister from you,
The virtuous Paulina, not long since,
As I am truly given to understand,
Sold to the Viceroy a fair Christian virgin   115
On whom, maugre his fierce and cruel nature,
Asambeg dotes extremely.

VITELLI   'Tis my sister!
It must be she: my better angel tells me
'Tis poor Paulina. Farewell, all disguises!
I'll show in my revenge that I am noble.   120

FRANCISCO
You are not mad?

VITELLI   No, sir – my virtuous anger
Makes every vein an artery: I feel in me
The strength of twenty men; and, being armed
With my good cause, to wreak wronged innocence
I dare alone run to the Viceroy's court   125
And, with this poniard,   [*flourishing his dagger*]
                              before his face
Dig out Grimaldi's heart.

FRANCISCO   Is this religious?

---

112 **ravished** stole by violence. Like 'rape' (and Latin *rapio*, from which both derive), 'ravish' can also mean 'violate sexually'; cf. 1.3.74.
116 **maugre** in spite of
118 **better angel** guardian angel; Vitelli again appeals to his 'good angel' at 1.3.33. Cf. *Faustus*, where a Good and Bad Angel struggle for the possession of the protagonist's soul.
119–20 **Farewell . . . noble** the first hint that beneath his merchant guise Vitelli is in fact a gentleman: the code of honour required that a man of rank carry out his revenge openly.

122 **Makes . . . artery** Such is the force of passion in Vitelli's heart that it starts to pump the 'vital spirits', supposed to be conveyed by the arteries, through the veins as well. For the physiology underlying this remark, see Paster, esp. 64–6.
124 **wreak** avenge
126 **poniard** dagger
   before his face Massinger assumes that, as at the English court, even to unsheathe a weapon in the sovereign's presence would be a capital offence.
127 **religious** i.e. the behaviour to be expected from a pious Christian

113 Paulina,] *this edn;* Paulina *Q*   126 SD] *this edn*

VITELLI

> Would you have me tame now? Can I know my
>   sister
> Mewed up in his seraglio and in danger
> Not alone to lose her honour but her soul –   130
> The hell-bred villain by, too, that has sold both
> To black destruction – and not haste to send him
> To the Devil, his tutor? To be patient now
> Were in another name to play the pander
> To the Viceroy's loose embraces and cry 'aim!',   135
> While he by force or flattery compels her
> To yield her fair name up to his foul lust
> And after turn apostata to the faith
> That she was bred in.

FRANCISCO   Do but give me hearing,
> And you shall soon grant how ridiculous   140
> This childish fury is. A wise man never
> Attempts impossibilities; 'tis as easy
> For any single arm to quell an army
> As to effect your wishes. We come hither

---

129 **Mewed up** cooped up, imprisoned (originally 'to put a hawk in a "mew" or cage at moulting time', *OED v.*[2] 1) **seraglio** Italian: 'place of enclosure'; by association with Turkish *serāī* (lodging, palace) it came to mean the sultan's palace in Constantinople, but was often used to apply more specifically to the harem quarters.

130 Paulina's soul would be imperilled not merely by the loss of her chastity, but by the forced conversion imposed on members of the harem. **alone** only **honour** virginity

135 **cry 'aim!'** '"To encourage the archers by crying out "*Aim!*" when they were about to shoot." . . . Hence, To encourage, applaud, abet' (*OED n.* 3c)

136 **by . . . flattery** a stock phrase; cf. Heywood, *1 Edward IV*, 8.31: "Ere force or flattery shall mine honour stain'. Vitelli's jealous suspicion will attract a rebuke from Francisco (152–3). Ironically it will be Vitelli himself who falls victim when a Turkish princess decides to 'flatter' him (2.1.43), while his immaculate sister 'despise[s the] flatteries' of Asambeg (2.5.124).

138 **apostata** one who abjures his religious faith; a renegade; this Latin form of the noun remained more common than the English 'apostate' until the mid-17th century (*OED* apostate *n.* 1, 2).

141–2 **A wise . . . impossibilities** Cf. Tilley, I44: 'No man is tied to impossibilities.'

To learn Paulina's faith and to redeem her: 145
Leave your revenge to heaven. I oft have told you
Of a relic that I gave her, which has power –
If we may credit holy men's traditions –
To keep the owner free from violence.
This on her breast she wears, and does preserve   150
The virtue of it by her daily prayers.
So, if she fall not by her own consent –
Which it were sin to think – I fear no force.
Be therefore patient: keep this borrowed shape *disguise*
Till time and opportunity present us   155
With some fit means to see her – which performed,
I'll join with you in any desperate course
For her delivery.

VITELLI   You have charmed me, sir,
And I obey in all things. Pray you, pardon
The weakness of my passion.

---

145 *faith Most editors have accepted
Mason's emendation, but it is unneces-
sary, since Francisco and Vitelli already
know Paulina's fate – that she has been
sold into slavery in Asambeg's seraglio;
what is still to be determined is whether
her faith has been strong enough to
defend her against the Pasha's lust and
to save her from apostasy (136–9), i.e.
becoming a female renegade.
redeem her plays on two senses:
ransom her from bondage (*OED v.*
3), and deliver from sin, save her soul
(*OED v.* 6)
146 **Leave . . . heaven** Cf. Romans,
12.19, 'Vengeance is mine, I will repay,
saith the Lord', famously cited in
Kyd's *Spanish Tragedy* (3.13.1–2).
148 The magical efficacy attributed to
relics by the Catholic Church was
anathema to good Protestants; but
Massinger's caveat was no doubt a
protective stratagem designed to signal
that a key element in his plot was, after

all, to be taken only as a convenient
fictional device – a romantic fantasy.
154 **borrowed shape** standard phrase
for disguise. This is the first hint that
Vitelli may be something more than
the mere merchant he seems, though
his true identity is withheld until very
late in the play (5.5.12–13).
157 **desperate** reckless (*OED n.* 4); perhaps with an unconscious ironic ambi-
guity, given the play's preoccupation
with Grimaldi's theological despair
158 **delivery** escape (from the seraglio)
charmed persuaded. Vitelli speaks metaphorically, but the word takes an additional charge from a context in which
Francisco's relic is described as operating
like a magical charm. Although the word
may well play on Protestant suspicion
of Jesuits, the transformatory power of
religious magic – as opposed to the false
magics of Mahometan superstition and
sexual desire – will become a major
theme of the play (see pp. 38, 41–4, 53).

145 faith] fate *Rawl.*, *Mason*

FRANCISCO   And excuse it.   160
    Be cheerful, man, for know that good intents
    Are in the end crowned with as fair events.   *Exeunt.*

1.2   *Enter* DONUSA, MANTO [*and*] CARAZIE.

DONUSA

    Have you seen the Christian captive the great Pasha
    Is so enamoured of?

MANTO   Yes, an't please your excellency,
    I took a full view of her when she was
    Presented to him.

DONUSA   And is she such a wonder
    As 'tis reported?

MANTO   She was drowned in tears then,   5
    Which took much from her beauty; yet, in spite
    Of sorrow, she appeared the mistress of
    Most rare perfections; and, though low of stature,
    Her well-proportioned limbs invite affection;
    And when she speaks, each syllable is music   10
    That does enchant the hearers. But your highness,

---

162 **events** outcomes

1.2 Location: Donusa's chamber in the palace

1–2 Christian ... enamoured of Massinger would have read in Cervantes that Moors preferred to take renegade Christians 'as their lawful wives and are glad to do so because they value them more highly than those of their own nation' (*Captive's Tale*, 83).

1 **Pasha** here presumably Asambeg; Massinger may have read in 'The Liberall Lover' that '*Bashaw* [is] the usuall stile or title which the *Turks* give their *Viceroy's*' (113).

2 **an't** and it (i.e. 'if it')

3 **full view** Paulina has been sold to the Viceroy as a slave (1.1.115); according to Sandys, such women were immediately 'carried aside into a roome. And as those, "*Who horses cheapen, search them, and make proofe, / Lest a good shape, propt by tender hoofe, / Cheate him that should uncircumspectly buy . . .*" So, "*T'assure you of deceitless wares, they shew / All that they sell: nor boast they of the best, / Nor hide the bad, but give all to the test:*" even to the search of her mouth, and assurance (if so she be said to be) of virginitie' (sig. G5ᵛ).

8 **low of stature** Shortness was considered a defect in feminine beauty (see e.g. *MND*, 3.2.290–5, and cf. *AYL*, 1.3.112). Presumably Massinger had the relative heights of Bourne and Robins in mind.

1.2] *(Actus primus. Scena secunda.)* 1–3] *Oxf*; *Q lines* captive, / of? / excellency / 10 speaks] spoke *Vitkus*

That are not to be paralleled, I yet never
Beheld her equal.
DONUSA   Come, you flatter me –
But I forgive it: we that are born great
Seldom distaste our servants, though they give us   15
More than we can pretend to. I have heard
That Christian ladies live with much more freedom
Than such as are born here. Our jealous Turks
Never permit their fair wives to be seen
But at the public bagnios or the mosques –   20
And even then veiled and guarded. Thou, Carazie,
Wert born in England: what's the custom there
Among your women? Come, be free and merry:
I am no severe mistress, nor hast thou met with

---

11 **enchant** Continues the motif of virtuous magic from the previous scene. **But** with the exception of

12 **That are** who is

15 **distaste** regard with displeasure (*OED n.* 2)

15, 24, 26 **servants, mistress, serve** As the references to Mustapha's 'service' at 54, 81–3, 107–9, 119 and 123 remind us, the language of domestic service in this play is often charged with teasing erotic suggestiveness.

15–16 **give . . . to** 'attribute more beauty to us than we can properly claim'

16–28 **I have . . . queens** The superior liberty enjoyed by European (and especially English) women when compared with their Turkish sisters is a recurrent theme in 17th-century writing. Theophilus Lavender's 'Preface to the Reader' of Biddulph's *Travels* urges the value of the book as a reminder to wives that they should 'learne to love their husbands, when they read in what slavery women live in other Contries, and in what awe and subjection to their husbands, and what libertie and freedome they themselves enjoy' (sig. A2ʳ); cf. Dent, E147, 'England is the paradise of women, the hell of horses,

and the purgatory of servants'; see also *2 Honest Whore*, 4.1.168–9).

18–21 **jealous . . . guarded** According to Biddulph, Turkish wives live to serve their husbands and 'never goe abroad without [their] leaue . . . which is very seldome, except it be either to the *Bannio* or hot Bath, or once a weeke to weepe at the graves of the dead' (sig. K2ʳ), while Sandys similarly observes that they 'give [husbands] the reverence of a Maister . . . They receive chastisement from him . . . and so strictly are they guarded, as seldome seene to looke out at their doores . . . They never stirre forth, but (and then alwaies in troupes) to pray at the graves, and to the publike *Bannias*' (sigs G4ʳ, G5ʳ).

20 **bagnios** bath-houses

21 **even** ev'n

22 **born in England** Apart from prisoners taken by corsairs from Mediterranean shipping, significant numbers of English were captured in raids along the Atlantic coasts of the British Isles (Matar, *Turks*, 71–81).

23, 30 **free** frank, unreserved, but with the secondary sense of 'loose, licentious', esp. at 30, where the meaning 'unfettered, open' is also involved

A heavy bondage.

CARAZIE   Heavy? I was made lighter   25
By two stone weight at least to be fit to serve you.
But to your question, madam. Women in England
For the most part live like queens. Your country
   ladies
Have liberty to hawk, to hunt, to feast,
To give free entertainment to all comers,   30
To talk, to kiss – there's no such thing known there
As an Italian girdle. Your city dame
Without leave wears the breeches, has her husband
At as much command as her prentice, and if need be
Can make him cuckold by her father's copy.   35

DONUSA

But your court lady?

CARAZIE   She, I assure you, madam,

24–5 **I . . . bondage** Lavender (see 16–28n.) also reminds English servants of the habitual tyranny attributed to Turkish masters: 'Here servants may bee taught to be faithfull and dutifull to their Masters, when they shall read of the brutish and barbarous immantie [savagery] in other Countries of masters towards their servants; who not only beat them like dogs, but sell them at their pleasure, and sometimes kill them for small offences' (Biddulph, sig. A2ʳ).

26 **stone** The eunuch puns on the measure of weight (14 lbs) and the colloquialism for testicle.

28 **queens . . . country** Familiar puns on 'queans' (whores) and 'cunt' are probably intended.

30 **entertainment . . . comers** bawdy innuendo

31 **kiss** Cf. Puttenham, bk 3, ch. 24, 239: 'With us the wemen give their mouth to be kissed, in other places their cheek, in many places their hand.' The custom, as Oxf notes, was much remarked upon by foreign visitors.

32 **Italian girdle** chastity belt
   city dame merchant's wife

33 **wears the breeches** proverbial (Tilley, B645). For possible bawdy senses of *breeches* (buttocks; women's genitals) see Williams, *Dictionary*, 1.148–9.

34 **prentice** obsolete aphetic form of 'apprentice' (*OED*)

35 **by . . . copy** just as her father was cuckolded by her mother (*copy* = example). Biddulph, noting the extreme deference of Turkish wives to their lords, conjectures that 'If the like order were in England, women would be more dutifull and faithfull to their husbands than many of them are; and especially, if there were like punishment for whores, there would be lesse whoredome: for there, if a man have an hundred women, if any one of them prostitute herselfe to any man but her owne husband, he hath authoritie to bind her, hands and feete, and cast her into the river with a stone about her necke, and drowne her' (sig. K2ʳ⁻ᵛ).

Knows nothing but her will, must be allowed
Her footmen, her caroche, her ushers, her pages,
Her doctor, chaplains; and, as I have heard,
They are grown of late so learned that they maintain   40
A strange position, which their lords with all
Their wit cannot confute.

DONUSA   What's that, I prithee?

CARAZIE

Marry, that it is not only fit but lawful
Your madam there – her much rest and high feeding
Duly considered – should, to ease her husband,   45
Be allowed a private friend. They have drawn a bill   46
To this good purpose, and the next assembly   47
Doubt not to pass it.   48

DONUSA   We enjoy no more   49
That are of the Ottoman race, though our religion   50

---

37 **will** playing on the sense of 'carnal desire'

38–9 **footmen . . . chaplains** a retinue of household officers more appropriate to an aristocratic than a bourgeois household; literature of the period is full of satiric innuendo about the sexual role played by such upper servants.

38 **caroche** luxurious coach for town use **ushers** The gentleman usher's principal role was to hand his mistress to her coach and to walk bareheaded before her on formal occasions.

40 This line can be scanned either as a hexameter (treating 'learned' as disyllabic) or as a pentameter (eliding *They are* to a single syllable).

41 **position** proposition, thesis, tenet (*OED n.* 2); but perhaps also 'sexual posture' – as in the notoriously pornographic sonnet sequence *Sonetti lussuriosi* (widely known in English as 'Aretine's Postures'), by the early 16th-century Italian poet Pietro Aretino. Contemporary satire frequently implicates upper servants in this fashion – see e.g. the bawdy gibe at a household

doctor who 'ministers phisicke to her [Ladyship], on her backe' in *Bondman*, 1.2.9–14.

42 **wit** intelligence, acumen (*OED n.* 5a)

44 **rest . . . feeding** Idleness and rich diet were thought to stimulate lechery. Cf. *Revenger's*, 1.2.179–81, 2.1.194–6.

45 **ease** (1) put his mind at ease (*OED v.* 2); (2) relieve him of burdensome physical duties (*OED v.* 3); (3) give him sexual relief (Williams, *Dictionary*, 1.429–30)

46 **private friend** secret lover (*OED friend n.* 4). Oxf suggests a possible gibe at the vogue for platonic love; but although a translation of its foundational text, Honoré D'Urfé's *Astrée*, had been translated as early as 1620, this courtly affectation did not take proper hold until the 1630s, under the patronage of Queen Henrietta Maria. **drawn** drawn up, drafted

49 **race** i.e. the royal dynasty

49–50 **though . . . pleasure** Europeans credited the Mahometan religion with a very indulgent attitude towards the pleasures of the flesh (see pp. 12, 18–22).

Allows all pleasure. I am dull – some music! –   50
Take my chopines off – so, a lusty strain!
>   *A galliard [plays. Knocking within]*
Who knocks there?   *[Manto goes to the door and opens it.]*
MANTO   'Tis the Pasha of Aleppo,
Who humbly makes request he may present
His service to you.
DONUSA   Reach a chair. We must
Receive him like ourself, and not depart with   55
One piece of ceremony, state and greatness
That may beget respect and reverence
In one that's born our vassal. Now admit him.

> *Enter* MUSTAPHA [, *who*] *puts off his yellow pantofles*
> *[and falls to his knees].*

MUSTAPHA

The place is sacred; and I am to enter
The room where she abides with such devotion   60

---

51 **chopines** fashionable shoes, especially favoured in Venice, where their high cork soles were exaggeratedly enlarged
lusty merry (*OED a.* 1b) – but the sexual connotations of 'lust' cannot be excluded, given the power of erotic arousal with which music was credited (see e.g. *TN*, 1.1.1–3).
51 SD *galliard* lively dance in triple time
55 **like ourself** royal plural; in a fashion fitted to the dignity of my royal station
depart dispense (*OED v.* 12b)
58.1 *puts . . . pantofles* Cf. Sandys, who notes that, in contrast to the servitude experienced by ordinary wives, women in the sultan's family are given their high-ranking husbands to use like slaves: 'for his

daughters, sisters, and aunts, they have the *Bassas* giuen them for their husband . . . Their husbands come not unto them untill they be called: if but for speech onely, their shooes which they put off at the doore are there suffered to remaine: but if to lie with them, they are laid over the bed by an Eunuch: a signe for them to approch' (sigs H1v–H2r); see also 93–7n.
yellow As in the case of Malvolio's yellow stockings (*TN*, 2.5.149), the colour advertised a wooer's ambition to marry (see Linthicum, 48).
pantofles slippers
59–62 **The place . . . Prophet** Mustapha's extravagantly blasphemous comparison confuses the two greatest pilgrimage sites of Islam, the Ka'ba in Mecca and the Tomb of the Prophet

---

51 SD *plays] this edn   Knocking within] Vitkus   52 SD] Vitkus   58 SD and . . . knees] this edn

As pilgrims pay at Mecca when they visit
The tomb of our great Prophet.

DONUSA   Rise. [*to Carazie*] The sign
That we vouchsafe his presence.

([Carazie] takes up the pantofles.)

MUSTAPHA   May those powers
That raised the Ottoman empire and still guard it
Reward your highness for this gracious favour   65
You throw upon your servant. It hath pleased
The most invincible, mightiest Amurath –
To speak his other titles would take from him
That in himself does comprehend all greatness –
To make me the unworthy instrument   70
Of his command. Receive, divinest lady,

(Delivers a letter.)

This letter, signed by his victorious hand
And made authentic by the imperial seal.
There when you find me mentioned, far be it from
   you
To think it my ambition to presume   75

---

in Medina. Perhaps Mustapha is intended to demonstrate his adoration and humility by walking on his knees (cf. *R2*, 5.3.92).

63 **those powers** It is possible that this phrase reflects the widespread belief (apparent in Fletcher's *Island Princess*, for example) that Islam was polytheistic; but it is more likely to represent the kind of habitual vagueness apparent in Christian references to the 'heavenly powers' or 'powers above'.

68 **his other titles** Sandys, like numerous writers of the time, exercises his irony on this point: 'Thus great at this day is the *Ottoman* empire: but too great for it are their assumed titles: as, God on earth, shadow of God; sole Monarch of the world, King of Kings, Commander of all that can be commanded, Soveraigne of the most noble families of *Persia* and *Armenia*, Possessor of the holy cities of *Mecha* and *Jerusalem* . . . and so proceeding with a repitition of their severall kingdomes' (sig. E6ʳ).

62 SD] *this edn*   63 SD] *Rawl.; after 62 Q   Carazie] Vitkus; The Eunuch Q*   67–9 Amurath – / To . . . him / That . . . greatnesse –] *this edn; Amurath / (To . . . him) / That . . . greatness, Q; Amurath / (To . . . him / That . . . greatness) Rawl., Mason*   74 from you] *MS ADD (*from you,*); from yo Q*

At such a happiness, which his powerful will
From his great mind's magnificence, not my merit,
Hath showered upon me. But, if your consent
Join with his good opinion and allowance
To perfect what his favours have begun,   80
I shall, in my obsequiousness and duty,
Endeavour to prevent all just complaints
Which want of will to serve you may call on me.

DONUSA

His sacred majesty writes here that your valour
Against the Persian hath so won upon him   85
That there's no grace or honour in his gift
Of which he can imagine you unworthy.
And, what's the greatest you can hope or aim at,
It is his pleasure you should be received
Into his royal family, provided –   90
For so far I am unconfined – that I
Affect and like your person. I expect not

76–8 **which . . . me** Mustapha's language
makes the Sultan appear godlike.
80 **perfect** bring to completion (*OED v.* 1a)
81 **obsequiousness** dutiful service,
eagerness to please and obey (*OED
n.* a); not always negatively used at
this time, but given English attitudes
towards the manners of the Turkish
court, audiences are likely to have
registered the word's more disdainful
connotations, even though Mustapha
intends only a hyperbolical assertion of his role as Donusa's *cavaliere
servente*.
82 **prevent** forestall by precautionary
measures (*OED v.* 5)
85 **Against the Persian** In the 16th and
17th centuries numerous wars were
fought between Ottoman Turkey and
the Persian Empire. A recent phase
of this protracted struggle had been
staged by John Day, William Rowley
and George Wilkins in *The Travels of
the Three English Brothers* (1607).
won upon him won his good opinion
(*OED v.*[1] 10b)
86 **in his gift** within his power to give
88 **what's the greatest** which is the
greatest honour
90 ***family, provided** The syntax is
clearly continuous here; Q's full stop
after 'family' may be intended to signal
a pause while Donusa absorbs the
information that she is expected to
marry Mustapha; an actor could use
the pause dictated by the line break
and the parenthesis after *provided* to
similar effect.
91 **unconfined** have liberty to choose
92 **Affect** am drawn to, love (*OED v.*[1] 2a)

90–1 family, provided – / For . . . unconfined – that] *this edn;* familie. Prouided / For . . . vnconfind,
that *Q;* Family – provided / For . . . vnconfind) that *Rawl.;* family – provided, / For . . . unconfined,
that *Vitkus*

The ceremony which he uses in
Bestowing of his daughters and his nieces –
As that he should present you for my slave,   95
To love you, if you pleased me, or deliver
A poniard, on my least dislike to kill you.
Such tyranny and pride agree not with
My softer disposition. Let it suffice
For my first answer that thus far I grace you.   100
(Gives him her hand to kiss.)
Hereafter, some time spent to make inquire
Of the good parts and faculties of your mind,
You shall hear further from me.

MUSTAPHA   Though all torments
Really suffered, or in hell imagined
By curious fiction, in one hour's delay   105
Are wholly comprehended, I confess
That I stand bound in duty not to check at
Whatever you command or please to impose

93–7 Like Sandys, Biddulph observes that 'the daughters and sisters of the great Turke are more free than all other men and women . . . their father . . . will give unto them, for their husbands, the greatest *Bashawes* or *Viziers* whom they shall affect, and say unto them, Daughter, or sister, I give thee this man to be thy slave and bedfellow: and if he be not loving, dutifull, and obedient unto thee, heere, I give thee a *Canzhare* (that is a dagger) to cut off his head. And alwaies after, [they] weare a broade and sharpe dagger: and whensoeuer their husbands . . . displease them, they may and doe cut off their heads' (sig. K2ᵛ); see also 58n.

99 **softer** In contrast to the tyrannical hardness attributed to Turkish princesses, Donusa claims the 'softness' deemed appropriate to European women.

101 **inquire** inquiry (obsolete form)
102 **parts** personal qualities, talents (*OED n.* 12)
103–4 **all . . . imagined** all the torments of hell, whether real or imagined
105 **curious** ingenious; recondite (*OED n.* 4, 10c). In the context of speculation about hell, however, it may also suggest 'desirous of knowing what one has no right to know', i.e. guilty of the sin of curiosity (*OED n.* 5a).
fiction invention, fantasy (*OED n.* 3b)
106 **comprehended** included
106–9 **I confess . . . patience** Mustapha employs the pseudo-religious language of the courtly love tradition, according to which a knight in a lady's service was bound to obey whatever tasks she laid upon him in order to prove his love by his willingness to suffer for her sake.
107 **check** take offence

101 inquire] Enquiry *Rawl., Coxeter*

For trial of my patience.

DONUSA   Let us find
Some other subject: too much of one theme cloys me.   110
Is't a full mart?

MUSTAPHA   A confluence of all nations
Are met together. There's variety too
Of all that merchants traffic for.

DONUSA   I know not –
I feel a virgin's longing to descend
So far from mine own greatness as to be,   115
Though not a buyer, yet a looker on
Their strange commodities.

MUSTAPHA   If without a train
You dare be seen abroad, I'll dismiss mine
And wait upon you as a common man
And satisfy your wishes.

DONUSA   I embrace it.   120
[*to Carazie*] Provide my veil, and at the postern gate
Convey us out unseen. [*to Mustapha*] I trouble you.

109–10 **Let . . . me** Embarrassed by the intensity of Mustapha's courtship, Donusa is anxious to change the subject.

111 **confluence** 'a numerous concourse or assemblage'; literally 'a flowing together' (*OED n.* 5)

113 **traffic** trade (*OED v.* 1); the usual term for merchant activity in this period

113–14 **I . . . feel** The sense is 'I don't know why, but I find myself feeling'.

114 **virgin's longing** the kind of longing characteristic of someone who has never known such pleasures (as a virgin might long for sexual experience). Cf. 1.1.41n., and Robinson: 'In the erotically charged space of the Tunisian market, the promise of "strange commodities" incites "a Virgins longing"' ('Turks', 220); sex and commerce, Robinson suggests, become virtually

indistinguishable in Tunis.

117 **strange** unfamiliar, exotic, wonderful (*OED a.* 6–8, 10a)
train retinue

119 an indication that when Mustapha accompanies the veiled Donusa to the market-place in 1.3 he is meant to do so in the guise of a servant (*common man* = ordinary manservant), thereby literalizing the erotic 'service' he proffers (cf. 1.2.54, 81–3)

120 **satisfy your wishes** erotic innuendo

121 **veil** See Fig. 14.
postern rear entrance to a castle – often associated with illicit goings-on

122 **trouble you** put you to too much trouble; perhaps responding to some sign of irritation on Mustapha's part that his role as her *cavaliere servente* will reduce him to performing the literal service proper to a *common man*.

121, 122 SDD] *this edn*

MUSTAPHA

It is my happiness you deign to command me.   *Exeunt.*

1.3   *A shop [is] discovered, [with]* GAZET *in it,*
             FRANCISCO *and* VITELLI *walking by.*

GAZET What do you lack? Your choice China dishes, our
      pure Venetian crystal of all sorts, of all neat and new
      fashions from the mirror of the madam to the private
      utensil of her chambermaid, and curious pictures of the
      rarest beauties of Europa – what do you lack, gentlemen?   5
FRANCISCO [*to Vitelli*]

      Take heed, I say. Howe'er it may appear
      Impertinent, I must express my love
      In my advice and counsel: you are young
      And may be tempted, and these Turkish dames –
      Like English mastiffs that increase their fierceness   10
      By being chained up – from the restraint of freedom,

1.3.0.1 *shop* perhaps located in the discovery space; or possibly represented
by a small curtained booth brought
onto the stage. Vitelli's reference to a
space *above* at 143 may indicate that
the former is more likely, but Oxf
notes eight uses of a 'shop' in plays
written for the Phoenix theatre, which
might seem to suggest the existence of
a specially designed property.
1 **What . . . lack?** London vendor's cry
2–4 **new . . . chambermaid** The idea
of *new fashions* in something like our
contemporary sense was very much
a product of early modern consumer
culture, the *OED*'s first recorded use of
the phrase being from 1596. Massinger
mocks the luxury trade by singling
out mirrors (conventional symbols of
female vanity) as fashion items, as well
as by suggesting the ludicrous and
debasing notion of a fashion in cham-

ber pots (*private utensil[s]*) – and ones
designed for chambermaids at that.
The grotesque juxtaposition of high
and low is a traditional satiric device.
4 **curious** exquisitely wrought (*OED a.*
7a)
5 **Europa** Gazet's pretentious use of
the Latin form deliberately recalls
the idiom of geographers and carto-
graphers, and symbolic representations of the four continents as female
figures, in which Europa's elegant
attire (in contrast to the nakedness of
America and Africa and the luxurious
excess of Asia) represents the epitome
of civilization.
10–11 **Like . . . up** proverbial (Tilley,
M742). Cf. *Malfi*, 4.1.13 ('Like
English mastiffs, that grow feirce
with tying'), and Harrison, *Description
of England* (cited in Oxf, 143), who
writes of 'the mastiff, tiedog, or ban-

1.3] *(Actus primus. Scena tertia.)* 6 SD] *this edn* 7 love] *MS ADD (*loue,*);* loue: *Q* 8 In my] *MS
ADD (*in My*);* My *Q*

If lust once fire their blood from a fair object,
Will run a course the fiends themselves would shake at
To enjoy their wanton ends.

VITELLI   Sir, you mistake me.
I am too full of woe to entertain   15
One thought of pleasure, though all Europe's queens
Knelt at my feet and courted me, much less
To mix with such whose difference of faith
Must of necessity – or I must grant
Myself forgetful of all you have taught me –   20
Strangle such base desires.

FRANCISCO   Be constant in
That resolution. I'll abroad again
And learn as far as it is possible
What may concern Paulina. Some two hours
Shall bring me back.   *Exit.*

VITELLI   All blessings wait upon you.   25

GAZET

Cold doings, sir. A mart do you call this? 'Slight!
A pudding-wife, or a witch with a thrum cap

---

dog, so called because so many of them are tied up in chains or strong bonds in the daytime, for doing hurt abroad, which is an huge dog . . . terrible and fearful to behold, and oftentimes more fierce and fell than any Arcadian or Corsican cur'. In this context, Francisco's mention of *English* dogs is bound to recall the contrasts drawn by Carazie between the liberty enjoyed by English women and the oppressive confinement inflicted on their Turkish counterparts (1.2.16–28).

13 **course** race (*OED n.* 3); but in the context of *mastiffs* and the idea of erotic pursuit, the sense 'pursuing game with hounds' (*OED n.* 7a) is also present.

16 **all Europe's queens** The presence of Gazet's fraudulent portraits of

'the rarest beauties of Europa' (4–5) may undercut Vitelli's hyperbole here, especially given the unavoidable pun on 'queans' (whores).

22 **abroad** out of the house – so here, around the city

27 **pudding-wife** woman who sells puddings (stuffed animal entrails; sausages)

27–9 **a witch . . . fortunes** Glances mockingly at popular plays, such as *Macbeth* (1606; rev. 1616), Heywood's *Wise Woman of Hoxton* (1604), Middleton's *Witch* (1616) and Dekker, Ford and Rowley's *Witch of Edmonton* (1621), in which superstitious encounters with witches feature prominently.

27 **thrum cap** cheap cap made from waste ends of woollen yarn

18 such whose] *Vitkus;* such; whose *Q;* such, whose *MS ADD*   25 SD] *(Exit Francisco.)*

That sells ale underground to such as come
To know their fortunes in a dead vacation,
Have ten-to-one more stirring.

VITELLI   We must be patient.   30

GAZET

Your seller by retail ought to be angry
But when he's fingering money.

        Enter GRIMALDI, MASTER, BOATSWAIN,
        Sailors *and [after them two]* TURKS.

VITELLI   Here are company –
    [*aside*] Defend me, my good angel! I behold
A basilisk.

GAZET   What do you lack? What do you lack? Pure China   35
dishes? Clear crystal glasses? A dumb mistress to make
love to? What do you lack, gentlemen?

GRIMALDI

Thy mother for a bawd – or, if thou hast
A handsome one, thy sister for a whore!
Without these, do not tell me of your trash   40
Or I shall spoil your market.

VITELLI [*aside*]   Old Grimaldi?

28 **underground** i.e. 'in a cellar, or in some wretched room below ground level' (Oxf); or 'secretly' (*OED adv.* 2a, 1632). The metre requires a strong stress on *ground*.

29 **dead vacation** the period when the law courts were closed and London was emptied of lawyers and their clients – a notoriously slack time for commerce

30***Have . . . stirring** The Q punctuation (followed here) suggests that Gazet means 'have ten times as much business'; but it may be that 'ten-to-one' is parenthetic and represents the familiar proverbial wager: 'I'll bet you ten-to-one they have more business.'

32 **But** except

   Here are company Plural verbs with collective nouns are not infrequent in the period.

34 **basilisk** monstrous serpent, able to kill with a single glance; cf. *Combat*, 2.1.183–6, 4.1.134–5; *Bashful Lover*, 4.1.111–13; *Believe*, 3.3.187–8.

36 **dumb mistress** i.e. one of the portraits advertised at 1.1.4–13 and 1.3.4–5

36–7 **make love to** woo, court

41 **Old Grimaldi** If this is not simply colloquial disparagement, it may be a pointer to Grimaldi's age, perhaps designed to prepare the way for his moral and emotional collapse in Act 3.

30 Have ten-to-one] Have, ten, to-one *(conj. McMullan)*   32 SD *after them two*] *this edn*   33 SD] *Vitkus*
41 SD] *Vitkus; dash before* Old *in Q may indicate aside*

GRIMALDI

    'Swounds! Wherefore do we put to sea, or stand
    The raging winds aloft, or piss upon
    The foamy waves when they rage most, deride
    The thunder of the enemy's shot, board boldly   45
    A merchant's ship for prize, though we behold
    The desperate gunner ready to give fire
    And blow the deck up? Wherefore shake we off
    Those scrupulous rags of charity and conscience,
    Invented only to keep churchmen warm,   50
    Or feed the hungry mouths of famished beggars,
    But, when we touch the shore, to wallow in
    All sensual pleasures?

MASTER   Ay. But, noble captain,
    To spare a little for an afterclap
    Were not improvidence.

GRIMALDI.   Hang consideration!   55
    When this is spent, is not our ship the same?
    Our courage too the same to fetch in more?
    The earth where it is fertilest returns not
    More than three harvests, whilst the glorious sun
    Posts through the zodiac and makes up the year;   60
    But the sea, which is our mother that embraceth

42, 84 **'Swounds . . . 'Slight** God's wounds . . . God's light. The renegado's castaway condition is underlined by his repeated blasphemies.

43 **aloft** up in the rigging

46 **prize** ship captured at sea (*OED n.*³ 2b)

49 **scrupulous** over nice or meticulous in matters of right and wrong; prone to hesitations or doubt; cavilling (*OED a.* 1a, b)

54 **afterclap** unexpected subsequent misfortune (probably with a bawdy pun on 'clap' = gonorrhoea)

55 **consideration** (1) reflection, second thoughts (*OED n.* 2); (2) financial reward (*OED n.* 5)

59–60 **sun . . . year** In the old Ptolemaic universe (already outmoded in Massinger's time, but still invoked by astrologers today), the sun was imagined to travel through twelve 'houses' (marked by their zodiacal signs) in the course of the year.

60 **Posts** hurries (*OED v.*¹ 2)
    makes up renders complete (*OED v.* 95c)

Both the rich Indies in her outstretched arms,
Yields every day a crop, if we dare reap it.
No, no, my mates, let tradesmen think of thrift
And usurers hoard up; let our expense   65
Be, as our comings-in are, without bounds.
We are the Neptunes of the ocean,
And such as traffic shall pay sacrifice
Of their best lading. I'll have this canvas
Your boy wears lined with tissue, and the cates   70
You taste served up in gold. Though we carouse
The tears of orphans in our Greekish wines,
The sighs of undone widows paying for
The music bought to cheer us, ravished virgins
To slavery sold for coin to feed our riots,   75
We will have no compunction.

GAZET   Do you hear, sir?
We have paid for our ground.

GRIMALDI   Huh!

---

62 **Both . . . Indies** both the East and West Indies (including India and the Americas); cf. *Picture*, 1.1.51–2.

64–9 **let . . . lading** a pointed gibe at Vitelli, Gazet and others who traffic in the market-place – hence the resentful tone of Gazet's challenge at 76–81

66 **comings-in** takings

68–9 **such . . . lading** we shall make these merchants surrender their best cargo to us; *lading* = freight, cargo (*OED n.* 2)

69–70 **canvas . . . tissue** Sailors' clothes were often stitched from *canvas* (also used as sailcloth); *tissue*, on the other hand, was a rich kind of cloth, frequently interwoven with gold or silver thread (*OED n.* 2a).

70 **cates** provisions, dainties

71 **gold** i.e. gold dishes
carouse drink freely and repeatedly; swill (*OED v.* 1; 2)

72–3 **tears . . . widows** Cf. *New Way*, 4.1.126–7: 'Nay, when my eares are pierc'd with Widdowes cries, / And

undon Orphants wash with teares my threshold'.

72 **Greekish wines** The adjective did not (as is sometimes supposed) have any particularly derogatory implication. The Greeks are criticized by Sandys for their 'vice of immoderate drinking' (sig. H4ʳ); but Greek wines were associated with luxury in the period, partly because of their classical associations; thus in Marlowe's *Jew of Malta*, Ithamore promises the courtesan Bellamira, 'We will leave this paltry land / And sail from hence to Greece, to lovely Greece . . . Where . . . Bacchus' vineyards overspread the world' (4.2.83–7); cf. *New Way*, 3.2.169.

73 **undone** financially (and perhaps sexually) ruined

74 **ravished** raped; cf. 1.1.112n.

77 **paid . . . ground** Cf. 1.1.1n. Gazet implies that the presence of Grimaldi and his crew is interfering with their trade.

GAZET　　　　　　　　　　　　　　And huh, too,
　　For all your big words! Get you further off,
　　And hinder not the prospect of our shop
　　Or –
GRIMALDI　　What will you do?
GAZET　　　　　　　　　　　　　Nothing, sir, but pray　　　80
　　Your worship to give me handsel.
GRIMALDI　　　　　　　　　　　　By the ears,
　　Thus, sir, by the ears.　　[*Wrings Gazet's ears.*]
MASTER　　　　　　　　　　Hold, hold!
VITELLI [*to Gazet*]　　　　　　　　You'll still be prating.
GRIMALDI [*to his men*]
　　Come, let's be drunk – then each man to his whore!
　　'Slight, how do you look! You had best go find a corner
　　To pray in and repent. Do, do, and cry –　　　85
　　It will show fine in pirates.　　　　　　　*Exit.*
MASTER　　　　　　　　　　　We must follow,
　　Or he will spend our shares.
BOATSWAIN　　　　　　　　　I fought for mine.
MASTER
　　Nor am I so precise but I can drab too:
　　We will not sit out for our parts.
BOATSWAIN　　　　　　　　　　Agreed.
　　　　　Exeunt Master, Boatswain [and] Sailors.

---

79 **hinder ... prospect** don't block the view
81 **handsel** first money taken by a tradesman in the day (considered a token of good luck)
82 **prating** chattering, blabbing on (*OED n.* 1). Vitelli reproves Gazet for provoking Grimaldi.
86 **show fine** look good (ironic); see *OED* show *v.* 30. Such adverbial use of

an adjective is not uncommon in the period.
88 **precise** strict, scrupulous, fastidious, puritanical (members of Puritan sects were often described as 'precisians') **drab** go whoring
89 **sit ... parts** either 'as far as we are concerned we shall not abstain', or 'we shall not hold back from claiming our share'

82 SD1] *Vitkus subst.*　SD2] *this edn*　83 SD] *this edn*　84 look!] *MS ADD (*looke?*); looke, Q
86 SD] *(Exit Grimaldi)*

GAZET

> The Devil gnaw off his fingers! If he were   90
> In London among the clubs, up went his heels
> For striking of a prentice. – What do you lack?
> What do you lack, gentlemen?

1 TURK [*aside to 2 Turk*]

> I wonder how the Viceroy can endure
> The insolence of this fellow.

2 TURK [*aside to 1 Turk*]   He receives profit   95

> From the prizes he brings in, and that excuses
> Whatever he commits. Ha! What are these?

Enter MUSTAPHA, *and* DONUSA *veiled.*

1 TURK [*aside to 2 Turk*]

> They seem of rank and quality: observe 'em.

GAZET

> What do you lack? See what you please to buy!
> Wares of all sorts, most honourable madonna.   100

VITELLI [*aside to Gazet*]

> Peace, sirrah, make no noise! These are not people
> To be jested with.

DONUSA   Is this the Christians' custom

> In the venting their commodities?

MUSTAPHA   Yes, best madam.

> But you may please to keep your way: here's nothing

90–2 **If . . . prentice** 'London tradesmen kept staves in their shops, and
on the cry of "clubs!" they or their
apprentices went to quell any distur-
bance in the streets' (Oxf).

91 **up . . . heels** he'd be knocked to the
ground – or, possibly, hanged

95 **He receives profit** The fact that
the Viceroy claims a proportion of
Grimaldi's booty undercuts the renegade's boastful claim that the pirates'

revenue is *without bounds* (66).

96 **prizes** Cf. 46n.

98 **They . . . quality** perhaps suggesting
that Mustapha's servant guise is less
than effective

103 **venting** selling; equivalent to modern 'vending' but separately derived
(*OED* vent *v.*[3]), and here perhaps given
a slightly disdainful edge by association with 'vent' = discharge; get rid of
(*OED v.*[2] 2; 7).

94, 95, 98, 101 SDD] *this edn*

But toys and trifles not worth your observing.   105
[*Mustapha steps aside.*]

DONUSA

Yes, for variety's sake. – Pray you show us, friends,
The chiefest of your wares.

VITELLI   Your ladyship's servant;
And if in worth or title you are more,
My ignorance plead my pardon.

DONUSA [*aside*]   He speaks well.

VITELLI [*to Gazet*]

Take down the looking-glass.
        [*to Donusa*]   Here is a mirror   110
Steeled so exactly, neither taking from
Nor flattering the object it returns
To the beholder, that Narcissus might –
And never grow enamoured of himself –
View his fair feature in't.

DONUSA [*aside*]   Poetical, too!   115

VITELLI

Here China dishes to serve in a banquet,

---

105 perhaps reflecting the negative responses often encountered by English merchants seeking to vend their goods in the Orient. On *trifles*, see Knapp, 117–25, and Korda.
  toys and trifles frivolous knickknacks and trumpery
107 **chiefest** finest, best
  Your ladyship's servant What appears a merely routine courtesy anticipates Vitelli's usurpation of Mustapha's role as Donusa's amatory *servant*.
108 **more** deserving of an even loftier address than 'lady'
111–13 **Steeled . . . beholder** The mirror is backed with polished steel, so perfectly finished that it reflects without the slightest distortion. In Renaissance iconography a woman gazing into a mirror was typically an emblem of vanity.
111–12 **neither . . . returns** 'neither detracting from nor exaggerating the beauty of the image it reflects'
113 **Narcissus** beautiful youth in Greek myth who, catching sight of his own reflection in a pool, fell fatally in love with it. The story was well known from Ovid's *Metamorphoses* (3.428–642), and thus (like the other classical allusions below) represents a suspiciously poetical flourish on the part of the supposed merchant. The various recollections of Ovid serve to highlight Massinger's theme of erotic and religious transformation or 'turning'.

105 SD] *this edn*   109 SD] *this edn*   110 SD1, 2] *Vitkus*   115 SD] *this edn*

Though the voluptuous Persian sat a guest.
Here crystal glasses such as Ganymede
Did fill with nectar to the Thunderer
When he drank to Alcides and received him   120
In the fellowship of the gods. True to the owners,
Corinthian plate studded with diamonds
Concealed oft deadly poison; this pure metal
So innocent is and faithful to the mistress
Or master that possesses it that, rather   125
Than hold one drop that's venomous, of itself
It flies in pieces and deludes the traitor.

DONUSA [*aside*]

How movingly could this fellow treat upon
A worthy subject, that finds such discourse
To grace a trifle!

VITELLI   Here's a picture, madam,   130
The masterpiece of Michelangelo,
Our great Italian workman; here's another
So perfect at all parts that, had Pygmalion

---

117 **Though** even if
   voluptuous Persian Since classical
   times Persia (like the Orient generally) had been a byword for sensual
   indulgence.
118 **Ganymede** beautiful youth who
   became cup-bearer to the Greek gods,
   and with whom Zeus (Jupiter) fell in
   love (Ovid, *Metamorphoses*, 10.157–
   67); often used as a cant term for a boy
   lover (*OED n.* 2)
119 **the Thunderer** i.e. Zeus
120 **Alcides** Hercules, whose apotheosis
   is described by Ovid (*Metamorphoses*,
   9.290–328)
121 **True . . . owners** i.e. unlike the
   treacherous Corinthian plate he goes
   on to describe
122–3 **Corinthian . . . poison** Cf.
   Roman Actor, 1.3.103 ('*Corinthian
   poysons*'). The association of poison

with Corinth 'may be due to the story
of Medea, Queen of Corinth, who
killed Creusa, Jason's bride, by means
of a poisoned robe and diadem' (Oxf,
5.185). Cf. also Juvenal, *Satire* 10,
25–7: 'But you won't drink poison
from earthenware; that you need only
fear when you are handed a golden
bowl studded with jewels' (Gifford).
123–7 **this . . . traitor** As Oxf notes,
the belief that crystal would shatter
upon contact with poison is ridiculed
by the sceptical Sir Thomas Browne
(*Pseudodoxia*, bk 7, ch. 17, 3B^v).
132 **workman** See 1.1.5n.
133–6 **Pygmalion . . . remembered**
According to classical myth, the sculp-
tor Pygmalion fell in love with one of
his own creations, which the goddess of
love Aphrodite (Venus) then brought to
life (Ovid, *Metamorphoses*, 10.261–324).

123 Concealed] *Qb (*Concealed*)*; Conceale *Qa*   128 SD] *this edn*

Seen this, his prayers had been made to Venus
To have given it life, and his carved ivory image   135
By poets ne'er remembered. They are indeed
The rarest beauties of the Christian world
And nowhere to be equalled.

DONUSA   You are partial
In the cause of those you favour, I believe:
I instantly could show you one to theirs   140
Not much inferior.

VITELLI   With your pardon, madam,
I am incredulous.

DONUSA   Can you match me this?
                                        (*Unveils herself.*)

VITELLI
What wonder look I on! I'll search above
And suddenly attend you.   *Exit.*

DONUSA   Are you amazed?
I'll bring you to yourself.   (*Breaks the glasses.*)

MUSTAPHA   Ha! What's the matter?   145

142 **match me** ethic dative (used to imply that a person other than the subject or the object has an interest in the fact)

142 **SD** modelled on the episode in Act 2 of Cervantes's *Los Baños*, where Zara removes her veil to reveal her beauty and identity to Don Lope (see Appendix). Biddulph notes that when Turkish women 'come abroad, they are alwayes masked; for it is accounted a shame for a woman to be seene bare-faced' (sig. L4ʳ); Sandys similarly observes that 'their heads and their faces [are] so mabled [muffled] in fine linnen, that nor more is to be seene of them then their eyes: not that of some, who looke as through the sight of a Bever. For they are forbidden by the Alcoran to disclose their beauties unto any, but unto their fathers and husbands' (sig. G5ʳ).

143 **What . . . on** Overwhelmed by the sight of Donusa's face, Vitelli hastily leaves – ostensibly to search for a portrait to outdo her beauty, but clearly in order to compose himself.

above upstairs; perhaps an indication that Vitelli's shop was represented by the discovery space below the gallery, rather than by an onstage booth (see 1.3.0.1n.)

144 **amazed** (1) stunned, stupefied, infatuated, crazed; (2) overcome with panic or consternation; (3) filled with wonder (*OED n.* 1; 3; 4). Donusa's breaking of the glasses, which she passes off as a display of anger at Vitelli's extortionate prices, is actually a ruse to lure him to the palace and thereby teach him to recognize the infatuation that underlies his panic ('bring you to yourself', 145).

145 **Ha . . . matter** Mustapha's reaction shows that he has not overheard the exchange between Donusa and Vitelli;

GAZET [*aside*]

   My master's ware? We are undone! Oh, strange!
   A lady to turn roarer and break glasses?
   'Tis time to shut up shop, then.

MUSTAPHA [*to Donusa, stepping forward*]

                     You seem moved.
   If any language of these Christian dogs
   Have called your anger on, in a frown show it   150
   And they are dead already.

DONUSA
                   The offence
   Looks not so far. The foolish, paltry fellow
   Showed me some trifles and demanded of me,
   For what I valued at so many aspers,
   A thousand ducats. I confess he moved me;   155
   Yet I should wrong myself should such a beggar
   Receive the least loss from me.

MUSTAPHA
                 Is it no more?

DONUSA

   No, I assure you. [*to Gazet*] Bid him bring his bill

---

presumably he steps contemptuously aside after expressing his disdain for Vitelli's *toys and trifles* (105).

147 **roarer** wild bully or roisterer. Male roarers are stock characters in city comedy, but contemporary anxieties about aggressive masculinized women, represented in such misogynist pamphlets as *Haec Vir* and *Hic Mulier* (i.e. 'The womanish man' and 'The mannish woman'; both 1620) led to the staging of female roarers such as Moll (Frith) Cutpurse, the heroine of *Roaring Girl* (1611).

148, 155 **moved** angered (*OED v.* 9b). But the audience are probably meant to detect a *double entendre*, since Vitelli has stirred softer emotions in her: the alternative sense of 'sexually aroused'

(*OED v.* 26), on which Wycherley plays in his dedicatory epistle to *The Plain Dealer* (1677), may also be present.

152 **Looks . . . far** is not so serious; does not require such an extreme response

154 **aspers** An asper was a small Turkish coin valued at a little under a half-penny.

155 **ducats** A number of European countries issued gold ducats, valued at a little over nine shillings; but in Italy the term normally referred to a silver coin worth between three and four shillings. The Venetian ducat, according to Coryat's *Crudities* (1611), was worth 'six livers and two gazets' (sig. x9ʳ).

158 **bill** account (for the damage caused)

---

146 SD] *this edn*   148 SD] *this edn*   157 the least] *this edn (conj. Greg);* least *Q;* least the *MS ADD;* the Least Loss *Rawl.*   158 SD] *Vitkus*

119

Tomorrow to the palace and inquire
For one 'Donusa': that word gives him passage   160
Through all the guard. Say there he shall receive
Full satisfaction.   [*to Mustapha*]
                    Now, when you please.

MUSTAPHA   I wait you.

1 TURK [*aside to 2 Turk*]

    We must not know them: let's shift off and vanish.

                    Exeunt [*at one door*] *Mustapha, Donusa,*
                    [*and at the other*] *1* [*and*] *2 Turk.*

GAZET

    The swine's pox overtake you! – There's a curse
    For a Turk that eats no hog's flesh!

                  [*Enter* VITELLI.]

VITELLI   Is she gone?   165

GAZET

    Yes – you may see her handiwork.

VITELLI   No matter.

    Said she aught else?

GAZET   That you should wait upon her
And there receive court payment; and, to pass

---

162 **satisfaction** the full payment of
a debt (*OED n.* 1a); in the context a
sexual invitation is clearly implied,
since the word can also refer to the
gratification of desire (*OED n.* 5a).
wait await; attend, escort (*OED v.*
10a). Mustapha is playing the role of
dutiful servant, but imagines himself
'serving' Donusa as her lover; see
1.2.119.

163 **We ... them** Evidently the Turks,
having seen the unveiled Donusa, recognize her and Mustapha, but think it
prudent to conceal the fact.

shift off remove ourselves (*OED* shift
v. 19a)
164 **swine's pox** alternative name for
chickenpox – especially insulting, as
Gazet emphasizes, when used to a
Muslim
167 **wait upon her** be in attendance as
a servant (i.e. courtly lover); cf. 162.
168 **court payment** princely reward;
however, the negligence and profligacy
of the court world make it capable of
an opposite interpretation; cf. *White
Devil* (1612), 1.1.3–4, on 'courtly
reward, / And punishment'.

160–2 For . . . please.] *Coxeter; Q lines Donusa:* / guard; / satisfaction. /you.   162 SD] *Vitkus*   163
SD1] *this edn*   SD2] *Gifford subst.; after 162 Q*   *at one door, at the other*] *this edn*   165 SD] *Gifford*

The guards, she bids you only say you come
To one 'Donusa.'
VITELLI   How! Remove the wares –   170
Do it without reply. The Sultan's niece!
I have heard among the Turks for any lady
To show her face bare argues love, or speaks
Her deadly hatred. What should I fear? My fortune
Is sunk so low, there cannot fall upon me   175
Aught worth my shunning. I will run the hazard:
She may be a means to free distressed Paulina;
Or, if offended, at the worst to die
Is a full period to calamity.   [*Exeunt.*]

The end of the first act

2.1   *Enter* CARAZIE [*and*] MANTO.

CARAZIE
In the name of wonder, Manto, what hath my lady
Done with herself since yesterday?
MANTO   I know not.
Malicious men report we are all guided
In our affections by a wandering planet;
But such a sudden change in such a person   5
May stand for an example to confirm
Their false assertion.
CARAZIE   She's now pettish, froward –

170–1 **wares – / Do** Gazet presumably
    attempts to protest, but is cut off by
    Vitelli.
178 **if offended** if it offends her (i.e.
    Donusa)
178–9 **to die . . . calamity** proverbial
    (Tilley, D141; Dent, D141.1); cf. *Duke
    of Milan*, 4.3.186.
2.1 Location: a room in the palace
3 **we** i.e. women

4 **wandering planet** i.e. the moon, pro-
    verbially associated with inconstancy;
    the female menstrual cycle was alleged
    to demonstrate that women were gov-
    erned by the moon.
6–7 **to . . . assertion** to prove their false
    libels true
7 **pettish** petulant, peevish
    froward perverse, ill-humoured

179 SD1] *Vitkus*   **2.1**] *(Actus Secundus Scena prima.)*

121

> Music, discourse, observance tedious to her.

MANTO

> She slept not the last night, and yet prevented
> The rising sun in being up before him;   10
> Called for a costly bath, then willed the rooms
> Should be perfumed; ransacked her cabinets
> For her choice and richest jewels; and appears now
> Like Cynthia in full glory, waited on
> By the fairest of the stars.

CARAZIE   Can you guess the reason   15

> Why the Aga of the Janizaries and he
> That guards the entrance of the inmost port
> Were called before her?

MANTO   They are both her creatures

> And by her grace preferred; but I am ignorant
> To what purpose they were sent for.

Enter DONUSA.

CARAZIE   Here she comes,   20

---

8 **observance** customary ceremonial; observation of due deference (*OED n.* 2; 3)

9 **prevented** anticipated, outstripped

11–12 **rooms ... perfumed** The perfuming of rooms, usually by burning incense, was a common practice (see e.g. *New Way*, 3.2.6–7, and *Guardian*, 3.6.74–5). Manto's line may involve a direction to the actors to perfume the stage in order to increase the sensual effect of the seduction scene (2.4).

12–14 **ransacked ... glory** Zoraida, in Cervantes's *Captive's Tale*, appears to the narrator covered in jewels: 'more pearls hung from her lovely neck, her ears and hair than she had hairs on her head. On her ankles ... she wore two ... anklets of the purest gold, set with so many diamonds which ... her father valued at ten thousand *doblas* ... of all this she was

mistress, she who now is mine' (101).

14 **Cynthia** the moon (another name for Artemis or Diana, it had been a poetic sobriquet for Queen Elizabeth)

16 **Aga ... Janizaries** See LR 10n., 18n.

17 **inmost port** gate controlling admittance to the innermost part of the palace; but Massinger may also be remembering 'the Sublime Porte', the official title of the central office of Ottoman government (named after the Sultan's Gate, the original place of audience): in Sandys the sultan refers to his court as '*Our most happy and shining Port, a port of refuge for the world*' (sig. E6ʳ), while the 'Viz[i]ers of the Port' are described as being among the most powerful pashas in the court (E6ᵛ).

18 **creatures** instruments, abject dependants

19 **by ... preferred** promoted as a result of her patronage

Full of sad thoughts: we must stand further off.
What a frown was that! [*Carazie and Manto stand aside.*]

MANTO   Forbear.

CARAZIE   I pity her.

DONUSA

What magic hath transformed me from myself?
Where is my virgin pride? How have I lost
My boasted freedom? What new fire burns up   25
My scorched entrails? What unknown desires *passion*
Invade and take possession of my soul,
All virtuous objects vanished? Have I stood
The shock of fierce temptations, stopped mine ears
Against all siren notes lust ever sung   30
To draw my bark of chastity – that, with wonder,
Hath kept a constant and an honoured course –
Into the gulf of a deserved ill fame?
Now fall unpitied? And, in a moment,
With mine own hands dig up a grave to bury   35

23 **magic** As the action unfolds, Massinger develops a contrast between the superstitious 'magic' associated with the followers of Mahomet and the 'miracles' attributed to Christian piety (ultimately including Donusa's own conversion). For a discussion of early modern fears of the 'dark magic of Islam', see the introduction to William Percy's eccentric 1601 closet drama *Mahomet and his Heaven* (Percy, 35–46).
25 **fire** i.e. of passion
26 **scorched** scorchèd
28 **objects** i.e. of desire (*OED n.* 3b, 5a)
29–31 **stopped . . . chastity** In classical mythology the sirens were fabulous monsters, half woman, half bird, who lured sailors to their doom with their enchanting songs. In Book 12 of the *Odyssey*, Odysseus (Ulysses) succeeds in navigating past them by ordering his sailors to block their ears with wax; determined to hear their singing, he has himself lashed to the mast so that he will not be tempted to throw himself into the sea. Cf. 3.5.20–8n.
31 **draw** attract (*OED v.* 25, 26)
   bark ship
   with wonder astoundingly
33 **gulf** whirlpool (*OED n.* 3). Another of the perils avoided by Odysseus when he manages to sail his ship past the deadly whirlpool of Charybdis, though only at the cost of losing six of his men in his effort to avoid the dangerous rock Scylla.
34 **unpitied** unpitièd
35–7 **dig . . . actions** Donusa imagines her past record of noble actions as a grand funeral monument, now reduced to rubble and buried in the

22 SD] *this edn*   28 Have I stood] I that have stood *Gifford*   33–4 fame . . . unpitied] fame, / Now fall unpittied *Gifford;* fame, / Now to fall vnpittied *Oxf*

The monumental heap of all my years
Employed in noble actions? Oh, my fate!
But there is no resisting: I obey thee,
Imperious god of love, and willingly
Put mine own fetters on to grace thy triumph;   40
'Twere therefore more than cruelty in thee
To use me like a tyrant. What poor means
Must I make use of now, and flatter such
To whom, till I betrayed my liberty,
One gracious look of mine would have erected   45
An altar to my service! – How now, Manto,
My ever-careful woman! And Carazie –
Thou hast been faithful too.

CARAZIE   I dare not call
My life mine own, since it is yours, but gladly
Will part with it whene'er you shall command me,   50
And think I fall a martyr, so my death
May give life to your pleasures.

MANTO   But vouchsafe
To let me understand what you desire
Should be effected: I will undertake it,
And curse myself for cowardice if I pause   55
To ask a reason why.

DONUSA   I am comforted

common earth as a result of her degrading passion for a merchant.

39–40 **The Triumph of Love** (*Amor* or *Cupid*), originally described in Petrarch's *Trionfi*, was a favourite theme in Renaissance poetry, graphic art and street pageantry; its iconography derived from the ritual triumphs in which Roman generals, accompanied by chained prisoners and displays of spoils, celebrated their victories.

43–6 **flatter . . . service** The syntax here is somewhat contorted, but the general sense is clear enough: 'flatter those who, in exchange for just one kind look, would gladly have erected an altar to worship me – until I betrayed my freedom (by falling in love)'.

49 **My life . . . yours** Carazie uses the rhetoric of courtly love, but as a slave he is literally Donusa's property.

51–2 **And . . . pleasures** The juxtaposition of *martyr*, *death* and *pleasures* recalls the eroticized language of love's martyrdom, and the 'little death' of erotic rapture – ironically, given that Carazie is a eunuch.

51 **think** will believe that

52 **But vouchsafe** merely condescend

In the tender of your service, but shall be
Confirmed in my full joys in the performance.
Yet trust me: I will not impose upon you
But what you stand engaged for to a mistress 60
Such as I have been to you. All I ask
Is faith and secrecy.

CARAZIE   Say but you doubt me,
And, to secure you, I'll cut out my tongue –
I am libbed in the breech already.

MANTO   Do not hinder
Yourself by these delays.

DONUSA   Thus then I whisper 65
Mine own shame to you.   [*Whispers to Manto.*] –
                              Oh, that I should blush
To speak what I so much desire to do!
And further –
        (*Whispers [again], and uses vehement actions.*)

MANTO   Is this all?

DONUSA   Think it not base –
Although I know the office undergoes
A coarse construction.

CARAZIE   Coarse? 'Tis but procuring 70
A smock-employment, which has made more knights
In a country I could name than twenty years
Of service in the field.

DONUSA   You have my ends.

60–1 **But . . . you** 'any more than you are
    obliged to do for a mistress who has
    treated you as I have done'
62 **Say but** 'if you so much as say that'
64 **libbed** castrated
    breech crotch
69–70 **the office . . . construction** 'the
    task is liable to bawdy misunderstand-
    ing'
71 **smock-employment** sexual services
    (*OED* smock *n.* 3b)

72 **In . . . name** In the mouth of the
    English-born Carazie, a pointed gibe
    at the mores of James I's court:
    the King was notorious for sell-
    ing knighthoods, as well as for the
    honours he heaped on his male
    favourites. Here the suggestion is
    that ambitious courtiers could rise
    by engaging in affairs with powerful
    noblewomen.
73 **have my ends** grasp my purposes

66 SD] *this edn*   68 SD *again*] *this edn*

MANTO

Which say you have arrived at. Be not wanting
To yourself, and fear not us.

CARAZIE   I know my burden –   75
I'll bear it with delight.

MANTO   Talk not, but do.

Exeunt Carazie [and] Manto.

DONUSA

O love, what poor shifts thou dost force us to!   *Exit.*

2.2   *Enter* AGA, KAPIAGA *[and]* Janizaries.

AGA

She was ever our good mistress and our maker;
And should we check at a little hazard for her,
We were unthankful.

KAPIAGA   I dare pawn my head
'Tis some disguised minion of the court,
Sent from great Amurath to learn from her   5
The Viceroy's actions.

AGA   That concerns not us –
His fall may be our rise: whate'er he be,
He passes through my guards.

KAPIAGA   And mine – provided
He give the word.

Enter VITELLI.

VITELLI *[aside]*   To faint now, being thus far,
Would argue me of cowardice.

74–5 **Be . . . yourself** don't let yourself
    down
77 **shifts** expedients, subterfuges
2.2 Location: a palace gate
1 **our maker** the one who advanced our
    interests
2 **check . . . hazard** hold back because

    of a little danger
4–6 **some . . . actions** 'some disguised
    royal favourite sent by the Sultan to
    spy on Asambeg by sounding out
    Donusa'
4 **disguised** disguisèd
9 **give the word** supply the password

2.2] *(Actus Secundus, Scena Secunda.)*   9 SD] *this edn*

AGA   Stand! The word?   10

    Or, being a Christian, to press thus far

    Forfeits thy life.

VITELLI   'Donusa.'

AGA   Pass in peace.

Exeunt Aga and Janizaries.

VITELLI [*aside*]

    What a privilege her name bears! 'Tis wondrous

      strange!

    The Captain of the Janizaries! If the great officer,

    The guardian of the inner port, deny not –   15

KAPIAGA

    Thy warrant? Speak, or thou art dead.

VITELLI   'Donusa.'

KAPIAGA

    That protects thee: without fear, enter.

    So – [*calling offstage*] discharge the watch.

Exeunt [by opposite doors].

2.3   *Enter* CARAZIE [*and*] MANTO.

CARAZIE

    Though he hath passed the Aga and Chief Porter,

    This cannot be the man.

MANTO   By her description

    I am sure it is.

CARAZIE   O women, women,

    What are you? A great lady dote upon

11 **press thus far** intrude so far (into the palace)

15 **inner port** innermost door or gateway (with a sexual innuendo)

17 **fear** The scansion requires that the word be treated as disyllabic.

2.3 Location: an ante-chamber

1 **Aga** i.e. the Kapiaga

13 SD] *this edn* bears! 'Tis] *(conj. McIlwraith);* beares. / Tis *Qa;* beares? / Tis *Qb* 16 Thy . . . dead] *Gifford; Q lines* Speake, / dead. / *Donusa.* / 18 SD1] *this edn* SD2 *by opposite doors*] *this edn* 2.3] *(A Secundus Scena tertia.)* 2–3 By . . . is] *Gifford; one line Q*

A haberdasher of small wares!

MANTO   Pish! Thou hast none.   5

CARAZIE

No; if I had, I might have served the turn:
This 'tis to want munition when a man
Should make a breach and enter!

Enter VITELLI.

MANTO   Sir, you are welcome.
Think what 'tis to be happy and possess it.

CARAZIE

Perfume the rooms there and make way! Let music   10
With choice notes entertain the man the princess
Now purposes to honour.

VITELLI   I am ravished.   *Exeunt.*

2.4   *A table* [*with chairs*] *set forth, jewels and bags*
            upon it. Loud music. Enter DONUSA [, *finely*
            dressed and adorned with jewels]; [*she*] *takes a chair*
            [*and sits in state*]. [*Enter*] *to her* CARAZIE,
                        VITELLI [*and*] MANTO.

5 **haberdasher . . . wares** milliner;
   OED cites Minsheu, *Ductor* (1617): 'An
   Habberdasher of small wares . . . in
   London also called a Millenier'.
   Strictly speaking, 'small ware' con-
   sisted of tapes, braids, cords, bindings,
   etc., made from various textiles.
   Thou hast none Manto pretends to
   understand *small wares* as 'testicles'.
6 **served the turn** served the purpose
   (with a bawdy play on sexual 'service' and on *turn* = copulation; see
   Williams, *Glossary*, 316).
7 **want munition** i.e. be an eunuch (cf.

'artillery', 2.4.12)
8 **make . . . enter** i.e. force himself
   upon a woman
12 **ravished** enraptured (but with an
   unwitting play on the meaning 'raped')
2.4 Location: Donusa's chamber
0.1–2 *table . . . it* i.e. presumably revealed
   behind the curtains of the 'discovery
   space' (at the centre of the tiring-house
   façade at the rear of the stage)
0.3 *adorned with jewels* See 2.1.12–14.
0.4 *to her* i.e. Carazie and Manto usher
   Vitelli into Donusa's presence from
   the other door.

10 way! Let] *Qb* (way. Let*); way. / Let *Qa*   11–12 man . . . Now] *Qb* (man, the *Princesse* / Now*); man, /
The *Princesse* now *Qa*   2.4] *(Actus Secundus Scena Quarta.)*   0.1 *with chairs*] *this edn*   0.2–3 *finely dressed*]
Rawl.   0.3 *and . . . jewels*] *this edn*   0.3–4 *she, and*] *this edn*   0.4 *sits in state*] *Rawl.* *(*sitting in state*)*

DONUSA

   Sing o'er the ditty that I last composed
   Upon my lovesick passions. Suit your voice
   To the music that's placed yonder: we shall hear you
   With more delight and pleasure.

CARAZIE   I obey you.   *Sings.*

VITELLI

   Is not this Tempe or the blessed shades   5
   Where innocent spirits reside? Or do I dream,
   And this a heavenly vision? Howsoever,
   It is a sight too glorious to behold
   For such a wretch as I am.   *(Stands amazed.)*

CARAZIE   He is daunted.

MANTO

   Speak to him, madam; cheer him up, or you   10
   Destroy what you have builded.

CARAZIE [*aside*]   Would I were furnished
   With his artillery; and if I stood
   Gaping as he does, hang me!

VITELLI

   That I might ever dream thus!   *(Kneels.)*

                 [*Carazie and Manto withdraw.*]

DONUSA   Banish amazement:
   You wake – your debtor tells you so, your debtor;   15
   And, to assure you that I am a substance
   And no aerial figure, thus I raise you.
   Why do you shake? My soft touch brings no ague,

---

3 **music . . . yonder** i.e. the small orchestra in the music room above the stage

5 **Tempe** paradisial valley in the pastoral domain of Arcadia

5–6 **blessed . . . reside** i.e. the Elysian fields in the classical underworld

9 **daunted** overcome by Donusa's splendour

10 **cheer him up** restore his courage

12 **artillery** sexual equipment

14 SD2 Although Q includes no direction for the servants to leave, it seems unlikely that they are intended to remain for the intimate scene that follows.

17 **aerial** aërial; made of air, ethereal

18 **ague** fever

2 passions. Suit] *MS ADD (*passions, sute*); passions sute,* Q   4 SD] *(Song.)*   11 SD] *Oxf*   14 SD2] *this edn* 15 You wake] *Coxeter;* You, wake Q

No biting frost is in this palm; nor are
My looks like to the Gorgon's head that turn   20
Men into statues; rather they have power
(Or I have been abused) where they bestow
Their influence – let me prove it truth in you –
To give to dead men motion.

VITELLI   Can this be?
May I believe my senses? Dare I think   25
I have a memory, or that you are
That excellent creature that of late disdained not
To look on my poor trifles?

DONUSA   I am she.

VITELLI

The owner of that blessed name 'Donusa',
Which, like a potent charm – although pronounced   30
By my profane but much unworthier tongue –
Hath brought me safe to this forbidden place
Where Christian yet ne'er trod?

DONUSA   I am the same.

VITELLI

And to what end – great lady, pardon me,
That I presume to ask – did your command   35
Command me hither? Or what am I to whom
You should vouchsafe your favours – nay, your
         angers?

20–1 **Gorgon's . . . statues** The snake-
   haired gorgon Medusa, according to
   Greek myth, had the power to turn
   men to stone at a single glance.
20 ***turn** The proposed emendations
   assume that the subject of the verb is
   Gorgon's head; the true subject, however, is probably *My looks*, so that *that*
   means something like 'of the kind that'.
21–4 **power . . . motion** Donusa claims
   that her looks, reversing the Gorgon's

magic, have the power to bring the
   dead back to life: the teasing resur-
   rection conceit picks up the subdued
   wordplay in *raise* (17); in the context
   of her *soft touch*, *motion* suggests sexual
   arousal (*dead* = detumescent).
22 **abused** deceived
28 **trifles** paltry trinkets (i.e. the dubious goods Vitelli was offering in the
   market)
30 **potent charm** Cf. 1.1.158n.

20 turn] *(turne);* turns *Mason;* turn'd *(conj. Oxf)*

If any wild or uncollected speech
Offensively delivered, or my doubt
Of your unknown perfections have displeased you,   40
You wrong your indignation to pronounce
Yourself my sentence. To have seen you only,
And to have touched that fortune-making hand,
Will with delight weigh down all tortures that
A flinty hangman's rage could execute   45
Or rigid tyranny command with pleasure.

DONUSA

How the abundance of good flowing to thee
Is wronged in this simplicity! And these bounties,
Which all our eastern kings have kneeled in vain for,
Do, by thy ignorance or wilful fear,   50
Meet with a false construction. Christian, know –
For, till thou art mine by a nearer name,
That title, though abhorred here, takes not from
Thy entertainment – that 'tis not the fashion,
Among the greatest and the fairest dames   55
This Turkish Empire gladly owes and bows to,
To punish where there's no offence, or nourish
Displeasures against those without whose mercy
They part with all felicity. Prithee, be wise,
And gently understand me. Do not force her   60

41–2 **You . . . sentence** 'You will be doing something quite inappropriate to your (unjustified) resentment against me if you choose to pass judgement on me yourself.'

45 **flinty** harsh; cf. *Virgin Martyr*, 1.1.185, 'the flinty hangman's whips'.

46 **rigid** severe, inflexible (*OED a.* 3; the earliest example of this sense)

47–8 **abundance of good . . . bounties** i.e. the kindnesses that she is now extending to him; but also hinting at the sexual and material rewards she is about to offer him

48 **simplicity** humility; naivety

56 **owes** owns; acknowledges as its own

57 **nourish** nurture

58 **mercy** the kindness shown by a lover (borrowed from the vocabulary of courtly love, where it was normally granted by a high-ranking lady to her abject and lower-ranking admirer); the original religious connotation of the word is reanimated by the juxtaposition with *felicity*.

60 **gently** generously, as befits one of gentle birth; but perhaps also implying that she should recognize the gentleman beneath his disguise

That ne'er knew aught but to command – nor e'er
  read
The elements of affection but from such
As gladly sued to her – in the infancy
Of her new-born desires to be at once
Importunate and immodest.

VITELLI   Did I know,   65

Great lady, your commands, or to what purpose
This personated passion tends – since 'twere
A crime in me deserving death to think
It is your own – I should, to make you sport,
Take any shape you please to impose upon me,   70
And with joy strive to serve you.

DONUSA   Sport? Thou art cruel

If that thou canst interpret my descent
From my high birth and greatness but to be
A part in which I truly act myself!
And I must hold thee for a dull spectator   75
If it stir not affection and invite
Compassion for my sufferings. Be thou taught
By my example to make satisfaction
For wrongs unjustly offered. Willingly
I do confess my fault: I injured thee   80
In some poor petty trifles. Thus I pay for

61–2 read . . . affection i.e. studied the rudiments or basic alphabet of love (*OED* element *n.* 14a)

67 personated passion acted pretence of love. The theatrical metaphors here and in Donusa's following speech are characteristic of the way in which the play imagines the transformations of apostasy and conversion.

69 make you sport entertain or amuse you

70 shape role

71 serve 'Service' was what a knight offered his lady in the courtly love tradition.

73 but to be to be anything less than

74–5 A part . . . spectator On the meta-theatrical motif in this play and others by Massinger, see Introduction, pp. 8–10, 44–53.

75 dull dim-witted, obtuse; lacking sensual responsiveness (*OED a.* 1; 2)

61 nor] *Coxeter;* not *Q*   67–9 – since . . . own –] *this edn;* (since . . . own: *Q;* (since . . . owne *MS ADD*   73 greatness] *MS ADD subst.* (greatnesse,), *Qb;* greatness? *Qa*   74 myself!] *MS ADD (*my selfe?*);* my selfe. *Q*

The trespass I did to thee: here receive
These bags stuffed full of our imperial coin –
   [*giving him bags of gold*]
Or, if this payment be too light, take here
These gems for which the slavish Indian dives   85
To the bottom of the main;
   [*giving him a casket of jewels*] or, if thou scorn
These as base dross which take but common minds,
But fancy any honour in my gift –
Which is unbounded as the Sultan's power –
And be possessed of 't.

VITELLI   I am overwhelmed   90
With the weight of happiness you throw upon me;
Nor can it fall in my imagination
What wrong I e'er have done you, and much less
How, like a royal merchant, to return
Your great magnificence.

DONUSA   They are degrees,   95

82–5 Zoraida in 'The Captive's Tale' and Zara in *Los Baños* both woo their Christian lovers with offers of wealth.

83–5 **These bags . . . These gems** perhaps recalling the 'small box full of gold *escudos*, so many that she could hardly carry it', which Zoraida gives the narrator in *The Captive's Tale* (109)

85–6 **gems . . . main** Like Adorni in *Maid of Honour* (3.3.20–1), Donusa probably has in mind the pearls harvested by divers in the Indian Ocean – though *slavish Indian* (a phrase which also occurs in *Duke of Milan*, 1.3.361) may also have New World resonances.

86–90 **or . . . of't** 'or, if you despise these jewels as being the sort of valueless stuff that only common minds would value, you only need to express your

desire for anything that it is in my power to give, and it shall at once be yours (since my power is as limitless as the Sultan's)'

87 **take** captivate, delight (*OED v.* 10)

92–5 **Nor . . . magnificence** 'nor can I begin to imagine what wrong I have ever done you, let alone how I can properly reciprocate – as only the most princely merchant could do – your enormous generosity'

94 **royal merchant** The oxymoron involves a significant quibble: *royal* = noble, munificent (*OED n.* 9a), but the phrase also plays on the idea of Vitelli's affair with a princess as a kind of *royal* trade.

95 **magnificence** the bounty expected of a prince
degrees steps (i.e. in the ladder of my favour)

83, 86 SDD] *this edn*

Not ends, of my intended favours to thee.
These seeds of bounty I yet scatter on
A glebe I have not tried; but be thou thankful –
The harvest is to come.

VITELLI   What can be added
To that which I already have received,   100
I cannot comprehend.

DONUSA   The tender of
Myself – why dost thou start? – and, in that gift,
Full restitution of that virgin freedom
Which thou hast robbed me of. Yet I profess
I so far prize the lovely thief that stole it   105
That, were it possible thou couldst restore
What thou unwittingly hast ravished from me,
I should refuse the present.

VITELLI   How I shake
In my constant resolution! And my flesh,
Rebellious to my better part, now tells me,   110
As if it were a strong defence of frailty,
A hermit in a desert trenched with prayers
Could not resist this battery.

---

98 **glebe** field
101 **tender** offer; continues the language
of erotic merchanting and exchange.
103 **Full restitution** Donusa appears to
mean that by giving herself fully to
Vitelli she can somehow regain the freedom of will that she surrendered when
she fell so slavishly in love with him.
103–4 **virgin . . . of** 'unsullied inde-
pendence that I enjoyed before you
stole my affections'. However, *freedom*
can also have the sense of 'licence',
suggesting that Donusa's maidenhood
was perhaps less innocent than she
pretends, which may account for the
sexual freedom she now claims.
107 **ravished** stolen by force, but picking
up the sexual suggestion in Vitelli's

use of the word at the end of the previous scene (2.3.12)
108 **shake** waver; but (as the next sentence
may suggest) perhaps also 'tremble'
110 **better part** i.e. reason
111 'as though such an argument could
serve as a justification of moral weakness'; the ironic association of *defence*
with the ensuing military metaphors
(*trenched . . . battery*) emphasizes the
implausibility of Vitelli's self-vindi-
cation.
112 **trenched** fortified
113 **battery** assault
113–16 **Thou . . . on** Italians in general, and Venetians in particular, had
a reputation as passionate lovers – see
e.g. *City Madam*, 3.1.26–7.

98 thankful –] *Coxeter subst. (*thankful,*)*; thankefull *Q*

DONUSA   Thou an Italian –
  Nay more, I know't, a natural Venetian,
  Such as are courtiers born to please fair ladies –   115
  Yet come thus slowly on?

VITELLI   Excuse me, madam:
  What imputation soe'er the world
  Is pleased to lay upon us, in myself
  I am so innocent that I know not what 'tis
  That I should offer.

DONUSA   By instinct I'll teach thee,   120
  And with such ease as love makes me to ask it.
  When a young lady wrings you by the hand thus,
  Or with an amorous touch presses your foot,
  Looks babies in your eyes, plays with your locks,
  Do not you find without a tutor's help   125
  What 'tis she looks for?

VITELLI   I am grown already
  Skilful in the mystery.

DONUSA   Or if thus she kiss you,
  Then tastes your lips again?

VITELLI   That latter blow
  Has beat all chaste thoughts from me.

DONUSA   Say she points to
  Some private room the sunbeams never enters,   130
  Provoking dishes passing by to heighten
  Declined appetite, active music ushering

---

114 **natural** native (cf. *OED a.* 10b, 11)

117 **imputation** five syllables

120 **instinct** instinct

122–4, 127 **When ... locks, Or ... you** dramatized stage directions

124 **Looks ... eyes** The tiny reflections lovers saw in one another's eyes when they stared into them were imagined as babies. Cf. *False*, 2.3.172.

127 **mystery** the secrets of the art of love (*OED n.* 8) – perhaps with a flattering hint of 'revealed religious truth' (*OED n.* 2)

131 **Provoking dishes** The use of aphrodisiac dishes is a standard trope in satirical denunciations of decadence and 'luxury' – cf. *Revenger's*, 1.2.179–80, 2.1.194–6. In *Sea Voyage*, the island castaways are tempted by 'provoking dishes, candid Eringoes, / And Potatoes' (5.2.50–1).
passing by i.e. carried by servants

132 The metre seems to require treating *Declined* as trisyllabic and eliding the second syllable in both *appetite* and *ushering*.
active lively, brisk (*OED a.* 5)

Your fainting steps, the waiters, too, as born dumb,
   Not daring to look on you?   *Exit, inviting him to follow.*
VITELLI   Though the Devil
   Stood by and roared, I follow! Now I find   135
   That virtue's but a word and no sure guard,
   If set upon by beauty and reward.   [*Exit.*]

2.5   *Enter* AGA, KAPIAGA, GRIMALDI, MASTER,
                BOATSWAIN [*and* Janizaries].

AGA
   The Devil's in him, I think!
GRIMALDI   Let him be damned, too!
   I'll look on him, though he stared as wild as hell;
   Nay, I'll go near to tell him to his teeth,
   If he mends not suddenly and proves more thankful,
   We do him too much service. Were't not for shame
      now,   5
   I could turn honest and forswear my trade,

---

133 **born dumb** Mutes, like eunuchs, were a well-known feature of Ottoman courts.

134–5 **Though . . . follow**   Vitelli's defiant blasphemy is reminiscent of Faustus's 'This night I'll conjure, though I die therefore' (*Faustus*, 1.1.168), just as his yielding to Donusa may recall Faustus's fatal seduction by the demonic Helen of Troy (5.1.90–109).

136 **virtue's . . . word** Cf. *Arden*, 1.436 ('Oaths are words, and words is wind'), and Tilley, W833 ('Words are but wind').

137 **reward** pronounced as a full rhyme with *guard*

2.5 Location: Asambeg's audience-chamber in the palace

1 **The Devil's . . . think** Cf. Vitelli at 2.4.134–5: 'Though the Devil / Stood

by and roared, I follow!' Although the Aga is referring to Asambeg, the continuous action on early modern stages, uninterrupted by scene divisions (which were a literary rather than a theatrical convention) will have made his line sound at first like a comment on the infatuated Vitelli.

damned In the light of the theatrically ambiguous reference of the Aga's line, an unconscious pun on 'dam' (as in 'the devil and his dam') may be involved.

3 **I'll go near** I'm almost prepared

4 **mends** improves
   suddenly immediately

5 **do . . . service** do too much for him, offer him too much duty and obedience

6 **trade** plays ironically on the play's concern with merchanting

137 SD] *Vitkus; Exeunt Q*   2.5] *(Actus Secundus, Scaena Quinta.)*   0.2 *and Janizaries*] *this edn; &c Q*

Which – next to being trussed up at the main-yard
By some Low Country butterbox – I hate
As deadly as I do fasting or long grace
When meat cools on the table.

KAPIAGA   But take heed: 10
You know his violent nature.

GRIMALDI   Let his whores
And catamites know't! I understand myself,
And how unmanly 'tis to sit at home
And rail at us that run abroad all hazards,
If every week we bring not home new pillage   15
For the fatting his seraglio.

Enter ASAMBEG [*and*] MUSTAPHA.

AGA   Here he comes.

7–8 **next . . . butterbox** Perhaps alludes to the notorious Massacre of Amboyna in the Moluccas (1623), when ten English factors were captured, tortured and executed (though not hanged) by the Dutch. On Massinger's interest in East Indian affairs, see pp. 9–10.

7 **trussed . . . main-yard** hanged from the yard-arm of the mainmast (*OED* truss *v.* 7)

8 **butterbox** insulting slang for Dutchmen; see Moryson, who explains that when 'passing in boates from City to City for trade, [they] carry with them cheese, and boxes of butter for their foode, whereupon . . . strangers call them Butter boxes' (sig. 3M6ʳ).

12 **catamites** boy lovers; allegations of sodomy, supposedly encouraged by Mahometan 'licence', were a recurrent feature of anti-Turkish propaganda. See, for example, the anonymous *Policy of the Turkish Empire* (1597):

'they are so polluted with the filth of uncleane lustes, that they are not contented with the abuse of women, for the satiating of their beastly humours; but they are so outragiously given over to the abominable sin of Sodomie, that it is impossible without horror to be uttered' (sig. N2ʳ). In *The Turk* (1607–8), Eunuchus, slave to Muleasses the Turk, boasts an Italian catamite named Signor Bordella (2.3.1ff.). Cf. Parker, 8, 11–13, 27. In *Maid of Honour*, Roberto, King of Sicily, is accused of possessing a 'state Catamite' (1.1.272).

14 **us** i.e. the corsairs
run . . . hazards 'expose ourselves to every imaginable risk in the world at large'

15–16 **pillage . . . seraglio** either choice luxuries for fattening up the women of the Viceroy's harem; or perhaps more captives to enlarge the harem itself

16 **fatting his** The construction is a '*His* genitive' – see Hope, 1.1.49 (p. 39).

KAPIAGA

How terrible he looks!

[*Aga and Kapiaga abase themselves.*]

GRIMALDI   To such as fear him.

The Viceroy Asambeg! Were he the Sultan's self,

He will let us know a reason for his fury,

Or we must take leave without his allowance   20

To be merry with our ignorance.

ASAMBEG   Mahomet's hell

Light on you all! You crouch and cringe now: where

Was the terror of my just frowns when you suffered

Those thieves of Malta, almost in our harbour,

To board a ship and bear her safely off,   25

While you stood idle lookers-on?

AGA   The odds

In the men and shipping, and the suddenness

Of their departure yielding us no leisure

To send forth others to relieve our own,

Deterred us, mighty sir.

ASAMBEG   Deterred you, cowards!   30

How durst you only entertain the knowledge

---

17 **terrible** inspiring terror

18–19 **Were . . . will** 'even if he were the Sultan himself, I'd force him to'

20 **must** will have to

21 **Mahomet's hell** presumably the opposite of 'Mahomet's paradise', which Christian lore interpreted as a place of unbridled sensual pleasure. Ironically, in Dante's *Inferno* and numerous medieval texts Mahomet had been accorded a prominent place in the Christian hell. Percy's *Mahomet and his Heaven* (see 2.1.23n.), in which Islam is presented as 'the "dark double" of Christianity', exploits the myth of the Mahometan heaven as a place of paradisial sensuality.

24 **thieves of Malta** the Knights of St

John (or Knights Hospitallers); a military order founded during the Crusades, famous for its resistance to the Turks at the sieges of Rhodes (1522) and Malta (1565), but by this time also notorious for piracy, sometimes against Christian as well as Turkish shipping (see Fuchs, 89). Massinger had collaborated with Fletcher and Field on a play dramatizing its exploits, *The Knight of Malta* (*c.* 1618).

30 **Deterred you** Asambeg pounces sarcastically on the Aga's self-exculpatory euphemism.

31 **only** so much as

31–3 **How . . . command?** 'How dare you fear anything at all except failing to obey my commands?'

17 SD] *this edn*   18 Asambeg!] *MS ADD; Asambeg Q*

Of what fear was but in the not performance
Of our command? In me great Amurath spake;
My voice did echo to your ears his thunder
And willed you like so many sea-born Tritons,   35
Armed only with the trumpets of your courage,
To swim up to her and, like remoras
Hanging upon her keel, to stay her flight
Till rescue, sent from us, had fetched you off.
You think you are safe now: who durst but dispute it,   40
Or make it questionable, if this moment
I charged you from yon hanging cliff that glasses
His rugged forehead in the neighbour lake
To throw yourselves down headlong, or like faggots
To fill the ditches of defended forts,   45
While on your backs we marched up to the breach?

GRIMALDI

    That would not I.

ASAMBEG   Ha?

GRIMALDI   Yet I dare as much

As any of the Sultan's boldest sons,
Whose heaven and hell hang on his frown or smile –
His warlike Janizaries.

ASAMBEG   Add one syllable more,   50

---

32 **but** except
33 **Amurath** See LR 5n.
34 **thunder** traditionally the sound of Zeus/Jupiter, the ruler of the gods
35 **Tritons** sea-gods – conventionally shown armed with shell-trumpets and tridents
37 **remoras** sucking fish, thought to be able to slow a down a ship by fastening themselves to its keel
38 **stay** check, hold back (*OED v.* 20)
39 **fetched you off** rescued you
40 **but** even, so much as

42 **glasses** sees the reflection of (*OED v.* 4a)
44–5 **faggots . . . forts** In siege warfare, bundles of wood were used by attackers to fill up defensive ditches. Sandys describes a category of humble Turkish foot-soldiers called *Azapis* being 'thrust forward rather to wearie then to vanquish the enemy; whose dead bodies do serve the Janizaries to fill up ditches, and to mount the walls of assaulted fortresses' (sig. F1ᵛ).
49 **hang** depend
50 **Janizaries** See LR 18n.

46 breach?] *MS ADD (*breache*);* bre a c *Qa;* breac *Qb*   47] *Coxeter; Q lines* Ha? / much /

Thou dost pronounce upon thyself a sentence
That earthquake-like will swallow thee!

GRIMALDI   Let it open,
   I'll stand the hazard. Those contemned thieves –
   Your fellow-pirates, sir, the bold Maltese,
   Whom with your looks you think to quell – at
      Rhodes   55
   Laughed at great Suleiman's anger; and, if treason
   Had not delivered them into his power,
   He had grown old in glory as in years
   At that so fatal siege, or risen with shame,
   His hopes and threats deluded.

ASAMBEG   Our great Prophet,   60
   How have I lost my anger and my power?

GRIMALDI
   Find it, and use it on thy flatterers
   And not upon thy friends that dare speak truth.
   These Knights of Malta – but a handful to
   Your armies that drink rivers up – have stood   65
   Your fury at the height, and with their crosses
   Struck pale your horned moons. These men of
      Malta,
   Since I took pay from you, I have met and fought
      with,
   Upon advantage too; yet, to speak truth –

---

53 **contemned** contemnèd; despicable
54 **fellow-pirates** i.e. the Knights of St John (see 24n.)
56 **treason** The heroic defence of Rhodes by the Knights of St John was ended in December 1522, when a mutiny by the citizens forced the surrender of the town to the armies of Suleiman the Magnificent.
60 **deluded** disappointed, mocked (*OED v.* 1, 2)
64–7 **Knights . . . moons** The Knights of St John, having retreated to Malta,

withstood a second siege by Suleiman's forces in 1565, when a garrison of 592 knights held off an army of perhaps thirty thousand Turks.
65 **drink rivers up** Oxf compares *1 Tamburlaine*, 2.3.15–17: 'The host of Xerxes, which by fame is said / To drink the mighty Parthian Araris, / Was but a handful to what we have.'
67 **horned moons** hornèd; i.e. the crescent moon displayed on the Turkish banners
69 **Upon advantage** in a favourable position (*OED n.* 1c)

52 thee] *Qa;* the *Qb*

By the soul of honour! – I have ever found them   70
As provident to direct and bold to do
As any trained up in your discipline,
Ravished from other nations.

MUSTAPHA [*aside*]   I perceive
The lightning in his fiery looks: the cloud
Is broke already.

GRIMALDI   Think not therefore, sir,   75
That you alone are giants, and such pygmies
You war upon.

ASAMBEG   Villain! I'll make thee know
Thou hast blasphemed the Ottoman power, and safer
At noonday might have given fire to St Mark's,
Your proud Venetian temple. Seize upon him!   80
I am not so near reconciled to him
To bid him die – that were a benefit
The dog's unworthy of. To our use confiscate
All that he stands possessed of: let him taste
The misery of want, and his vain riots,   85
Like to so many walking ghosts, affright him
Where'er he sets his desperate foot. Who is't

---

71 'as foresighted in leadership and brave in action'
72–3 any . . . nations i.e. the Janizaries (see LR 18n.)
72 discipline art of war (*OED n.* 3b)
73 Ravished stolen by force (*OED v.* 4)
76–7 and . . . upon 'and that those you make war upon are mere pygmies'
78 Ottoman power The Ottoman Empire (1299–1922) derived its name from that of its first sultan, Osman I (1258–1326), who established the dynasty that replaced the waning power of the Seljuk Turks and founded an empire that by this time embraced large parts of Eastern Europe and North Africa, as well as most of the Near and Middle East; see pp. 2, 11–12, and Fig. 1.
79 St Mark's See 1.1.110n.
87 his desperate foot i.e. the foot of a man suffering from despair. Asambeg has in mind only the wretched condition of a fugitive, but (as the metaphor of *walking ghosts* probably suggests) the word ironically anticipates the condition of theological despair into which Grimaldi will soon fall.
87–8 Who . . . you? presumably addressed to the janizary guards who have been slow to arrest the daunting Grimaldi, but perhaps to Grimaldi

73 SD] *this edn*

That does command you?
[*Aga and Kapiaga seize Grimaldi.*]
GRIMALDI   Is this the reward
For all my service and the rape I made
On fair Paulina?
ASAMBEG   Drag him hence – he dies   90
That dallies but a minute!
BOATSWAIN   What's become
Of our shares now, Master?

> *Grimaldi* [*is*] *dragged off* [*by the Aga, Kapiaga*
> *and their Janizaries*], *his head covered.*

MASTER   Would he had been born dumb!
The beggar's cure, patience, is all that's left us.

> *Exeunt Master and Boatswain.*

MUSTAPHA

'Twas but intemperance of speech: excuse him –
Let me prevail so far. Fame gives him out   95
For a deserving fellow.

---

himself as a reminder of his subordinate position

88–9 **Is . . . service** Cf. the renegade pirate Ward's protestations at the end of Daborne's *Christian Turned Turk* (*c*. 1610): 'Ungrateful curs, that have repaid me thus / For all the service that I have done for you' (16.297–8).

89 **rape** abduction; the sense 'sexual assault' is effectively excluded by the play's stress on Paulina's magically protected virginity.

92.1–2 *the Aga . . . Janizaries* Q prints no exit for these characters, but it is presumably they who are instructed to remove Grimaldi.

92.2 *his head covered* Since the Muslim practice of veiling women was widely known and commented upon (see

1.2.121–2, 1.3.142 and Fig. 14), a symbolic unmanning of Grimaldi, anticipating the near castration of Gazet, may be intended.

93 **The . . . patience** proverbial: 'Patience is a beggar's virtue' (Dent, P106.11); cf. *New Way*, 5.1.245.

94 **intemperance** In the literature of early imperial venturing, temperance (moderation) was the virtue regularly claimed by the English and linked to their temperate climate; in Fletcher's play of mercantile conquest, *The Island Princess*, temperance distinguishes the Portuguese hero, Armusia, from the hot-blooded East Indians.

96–7 **At Aleppo . . . far** Mustapha would exercise the same authority in Aleppo as Asambeg enjoys in Tunis.

88 SD] *this edn* 92.1–2] *after 91 by . . . Janizaries*] *this edn* 93 SD] *Coxeter; after 92.1–2* Q *Master*] *Coxeter; Must.* Q; *Mast.* | *Rawl.*

ASAMBEG   At Aleppo
   I durst not press you so far. Give me leave
   To use my own will and command in Tunis –
   And, if you please, my privacy.

MUSTAPHA   I will see you
   When this high wind's blown o'er.   *Exit.*

ASAMBEG   So shall you find me   100
   Ready to do you service. Rage, now leave me;
   Stern looks and all the ceremonious forms
   Attending on dread majesty fly from
   Transformed Asambeg!   (*Plucks out a gilt key.*)
                Why should I hug
   So near my heart what leads me to my prison,   105
   Where she that is enthralled commands her keeper
   And robs me of the fierceness I was born with?
   Stout men quake at my frowns, and in return
   I tremble at her softness. Base Grimaldi
   But only named Paulina, and the charm   110
   Had almost choked my fury ere I could
   Pronounce his sentence. Would, when first I saw her,
   Mine eyes had met with lightning, and, in place
   Of hearing her enchanting tongue, the shrieks

---

96 **Aleppo** See LR 9n.
99 **And ... privacy** a barely polite dismissal
100 **high wind** Asambeg's storm of passion
104 **Transformed** transformèd
106 **enthralled** held in thrall (as a prisoner)
107–9 **And robs ... softness** The Turk's fear of losing his masculine roughness and being feminized by Paulina's *softness* mirrors anxieties about the ways in which European manhood might be compromised either by submission to Turkish power or by surrender to oriental luxury.
110–14 **charm ... enchanting** The

familiar metaphors of infatuation are given an additional charge by the implicit contrast between the magic of Asambeg's erotic 'transformation', and the potential 'miracle' of religious conversion for which Paulina stands, but to which Asambeg remains *blind* (118). Cf. the ironies in his use of *miracles*, *magic* and *saint* at 150, 162, 164.
113 **eyes ... lightning** Asambeg literalizes the conventional erotic metaphor in which lightning blazes from a mistress's eyes.
114–15 **shrieks / Of mandrakes** When pulled from the ground, the mandrake, a root vegetable of supposedly

100 SD] *(Exit Mustapha)*   104 SD] *after* hug

Of mandrakes had made music to my slumbers!   115
For now I only walk a loving dream
And, but to my dishonour, never wake;
And yet am blind but when I see the object
And madly dote on it. Appear, bright spark
Of all perfection!

       [*Asambeg*] *opens a door;* PAULINA [*is*] *discovered*
                [*and*] *comes forth.*

           Any simile,   120
Borrowed from diamonds or the fairest stars
To help me to express how dear I prize
Thy unmatched graces, will rise up and chide me
For poor detraction.

PAULINA   I despise thy flatteries –

    [*She spits.*]

Thus spit at 'em and scorn 'em – and, being armed   125
In the assurance of my innocent virtue,
I stamp upon all doubts, all fears, all tortures
Thy barbarous cruelty – or, what's worse, thy dotage,
The worthy parent of thy jealousy –
Can shower upon me.

ASAMBEG   If these bitter taunts   130
Ravish me from myself, and make me think

---

humanoid form, was reputed to emit
a shriek so terrible that it would
madden or kill anyone who heard
it.
116 **only . . . dream** 'am only sleepwalk-
ing through a dream of love'
117 **but** except
118 **but when** It is not clear whether
Asambeg means that he is blind to
everything but Paulina (*but* = except),
or whether, despite his somnolent con-

dition, it is only when he catches sight
of her that he is actually struck blind
(*but* = only).
124 SD   *She spits* Paulina's words at
125 are an implied stage direction.
Her gesture anticipates Donusa's when
she repudiates her faith in Mahomet
(4.3.158).
128 **barbarous** particularly insulting
when directed at a Viceroy of Barbary
(cf. 1.1.96)

120 SD] *after 119* *Asambeg*] *gloss* 123 Thy] *Coxeter;* The *Q* 124 SD] *this edn*

My greedy ears receive angelical sounds,
How would this tongue, tuned to a loving note,
Invade and take possession of my soul,
Which then I durst not call mine own!

PAULINA   Thou art false,   135
Falser than thy religion. Do but think me
Something above a beast – nay more, a monster
Would fright the sun to look on – and then tell me
If this base usage can invite affection;
If to be mewed up and excluded from   140
Humane society, the use of pleasures,
The necessary, not superfluous, duties
Of servants to discharge those offices
I blush to name –

ASAMBEG   Of servants? Can you think
That I, that dare not trust the eye of heaven   145
To look upon your beauties, that deny
Myself the happiness to touch your pureness,
Will e'er consent a eunuch or bought handmaid
Shall once approach you? There is something in you
That can work miracles (or I am cozened),   150
Dispose and alter sexes: to my wrong,
In spite of nature, I will be your nurse,
Your woman, your physician and your fool,
Till with your free consent – which I have vowed

---

137 **Something above** little more than
   more 'even worse than that'
140 **mewed up** confined, hidden away
141 **Humane** human
142–4 **duties . . . name** i.e. the intimate
   services associated with the bed-
   chamber, washing and the close-stool
145 **eye of heaven** sun
150 **cozened** cheated, deceived
151–3 **Dispose . . . woman** Asambeg's
   claim that Paulina's magic has the
   power to effeminate him reverses the
   usual anxieties about the ways in which

contact with the Orient might femi-
nize European men, either through
capitulation to luxury, or through
the seductive magnetism of oriental
women, or (worst of all) through
the violence of castration – dangers
variously represented in this play by
the experiences of Vitelli, Gazet and
Carazie (see pp. 18–27).

151 **Dispose** control, manage (*OED v.* 2)
   sexes qualities of males and females
   my wrong my own discredit or dis-
   advantage

Never to force – you grace me with a name   155
That shall supply all these.

PAULINA   What is't?

ASAMBEG   Your husband.

PAULINA

My hangman, when thou pleasest!

ASAMBEG   Thus I guard me
Against your further angers.   [*Returns Paulina to her closet.*]

PAULINA   Which shall reach thee
Though I were in the centre.

                              [*Asambeg*] *puts to the door and locks it.*

ASAMBEG   Such a spirit
In such a small proportion I ne'er read of,   160
Which time must alter. Ravish her I dare not –
The magic that she wears about her neck
I think defends her. This devotion paid
To this sweet saint, mistress of my sour pain,   164
'Tis fit I take mine own rough shape again.   *Exit.*

2.6   *Enter* FRANCISCO [*and*] GAZET.

FRANCISCO

I think he's lost.

GAZET   'Tis ten to one of that:
I ne'er knew citizen turn courtier yet

---

159 **centre** centre of the earth
159 SD *puts to* closes
162 **magic** i.e. the relic given her by
    Francisco (1.1.146–51)
163–4 **devotion . . . saint** In the context
    of Paulina's relic, Asambeg's language,
    though it belongs to the standard
    rhetoric of courtly love, is made to
    sound like blasphemous idolatry.
165 **mine . . . shape** my usual harsh
    demeanour

2.6 Location: outside the palace
1 **I . . . lost** Cf. 2.5.1. Here the refer-
    ence is to Vitelli, but it will sound at
    first like a comment on the besotted
    Asambeg.
2–3 **citizen . . . credit** The disasters
    likely to befall social-climbing citizens
    were a standard theme of anti-middle-
    class satire. The word *credit* plays
    across the two senses of 'honour' and
    'credit-worthiness'.

158 SD] *this edn; Leads her to the door* | *Vitkus* 159 SD] *after* angers *158* 165 SD] *(Exit Asambeg)* **2.6**] *(Actus Secundus Scaena Sexta.)* 2 ne'er] *Qb;* neuer *Qa*

But he lost his credit, though he saved himself.
Why, look you, sir, there are so many lobbies,
Out-offices and dispartitions here   5
Behind these Turkish hangings, that a Christian
Hardly gets off but circumcised.
FRANCISCO   I am troubled,
Troubled exceedingly.

Enter VITELLI [, *dressed in fine clothes, with a casket*],
                CARAZIE [*and*] MANTO.

                        Ha! What are these?
GAZET
One by his rich suit should be some French ambassador;
For his train, I think they are Turks.
FRANCISCO   Peace – be not seen!   10
    [*Francisco and Gazet stand aside.*]
CARAZIE [*to Vitelli*]
You are now past all the guards, and undiscovered

---

3   **though** even if
4–6 **lobbies . . . hangings**   'Court
lobbies, the servants' quarters, and
the narrow spaces behind . . . wall-
hangings were notorious settings for
sexual encounters' (Oxf). See Gibson,
'Behind the arras'; and cf. below,
3.4.1–4; *Duke of Milan*, 3.2.41–3;
Combat, 3.2.95–9.
5   **Out-offices** offices set apart from a
main building
    *****dispartitions** a crux that evidently
caused the Q compositors some dif-
ficulty: Oxf glosses Q*b* 'disputations' as
'amorous conversations' (though *OED n*.
4 would seem to license only 'conversations'), which fits oddly with *lobbies* and
Out-offices. Davies's conjectured reading
dispartations (= partitions) seems more
persuasive (see Oxf); and although *OED*
cites no other support for this neologism,

it is a plausible derivative of 'dispart' (*v*.
1) = divide into parts; accordingly it is
accepted here, with the spelling altered
to fit its assumed etymology, as making
the best sense.
6   **Turkish hangings** probably gesturing at the curtains that closed off the
discovery space
7   **but circumcised** without being circumcised (i.e. turning Turk, becoming
a renegado). In the English mind,
circumcision was often confused with
castration.
8.1 *****with a casket** See 3.5.48 SD.
9   Apparently alludes to the visit to King
James's court by the French nobleman Cadenet in December–January
1620–1; the extravagance of Cadenet's
dress attracted 'many thousands' of
spectators, according to Sir Simonds
D'Ewes (Oxf, 2.1).

---

5 dispartitions] *this edn (conj. Davies* dispartations*); disputations *Qb;* dispute actions *Qa*   6 hangings]
Qb; hanging *Qa*   Christian] *Qa (*Cristian*), Qc;* Christians *Qb*   8 Troubled] *Qb (*Troublde*);* Trouble
Qa   SD] *after 7   dressed . . . clothes*] *Vitkus   with a casket*] *this edn*   10 SD] *this edn*   11 SD] *this edn*

You may return.

VITELLI [*Gives gold to Manto and Carazie.*]
                      There's for your pains – forget not
My humblest service to the best of ladies.

MANTO

Deserve her favour, sir, in making haste
For a second entertainment.

VITELLI   Do not doubt me;   15
I shall not live till then.   *Exeunt Carazie [and] Manto.*

GAZET [*to Francisco*]   The train is vanished.
They have done him some good office, he's so free
And liberal of his gold. Ha! do I dream,
Or is this mine own natural master?

FRANCISCO   'Tis he,
But strangely metamorphosed.

    [*to Vitelli*]   You have made, sir,   20
A prosperous voyage – heaven grant it be honest:
I shall rejoice then too.

GAZET [*to Francisco*]   You make him blush
To talk of honesty. [*to Vitelli*] You were but now
In the giving vein, and may think of Gazet,
Your worship's prentice.

VITELLI [*Gives Gazet gold.*] There's gold – be thou free, too,   25

---

15 **entertainment** In the light of Vitelli's courtly offer of *service*, a complex equivocation is involved: (1) service, employment; (2) the payment or reward due for such service; (3) amusement; (4) the action of receiving, or providing for the wants of, a guest; (5) a banquet (*OED n.* 2; 3; 8; 11; 12); (6) sexual diversion (Williams, *Glossary*, 115).

16 **train** i.e. Manto and Carazie

20 **metamorphosed** Vitelli's physical transformation from merchant to rich-ly attired royal favourite, like Gazet's subsequent transformation from humble apprentice to prosperous master, provides a satiric counterpoint to the spiritual transformations of Grimaldi and Donusa.

21 **honest** chaste

25–7 **be . . . Venice** Vitelli discharges Gazet from his term of service as an apprentice and installs him as a full member of the company of merchants and thus a master in his own right.

12 SD] *this edn*   16 SD1] *after 15*   SD2] *this edn*   20 SD] *this edn*   22, 23 SDD] *this edn*   25 SD] *this edn*

And master of my shop and all the wares
We brought from Venice.
GAZET   Rivo, then!
VITELLI [*to Francisco*]   Dear sir,
This place affords not privacy for discourse;
But I can tell you wonders: my rich habit
Deserves least admiration; there's nothing   30
That can fall in the compass of your wishes –
Though it were to redeem a thousand slaves
From the Turkish galleys, or at home to erect
Some pious work to shame all hospitals –
But I am master of the means.
FRANCISCO   'Tis strange.   35
VITELLI
As I walk, I'll tell you more.
GAZET [*to Vitelli*]   Pray you, a word, sir;
And then I will put on. I have one boon more.
VITELLI
What is't? Speak freely.
GAZET   Thus then: as I am master
Of your shop and wares, pray you help me to some
    trucking
With your last she-customer – though she crack my
    best piece,   40
I will endure it with patience.

---

27 **Rivo** exclamation of enthusiasm, normally associated with drinking bouts
– sometimes 'Rivo Castiliano!', and
perhaps from Spanish '*arriba*!' (*OED*),
though here presumably assumed to be
Italian
34 **shame** put to shame
hospitals charitable foundations
housing the needy or sick (*OED n.*
2, 3)
37 Gazet wants to beg one more favour

from Vitelli, before putting on the
hat he has deferentially doffed, and
thereby asserting his new-found equal-
ity of status.
39 **trucking** bargaining, trade, exchange
of commodities
40 **crack . . . piece** remembering
Donusa's destruction of the china and
crystal in 1.3, but with a bawdy *double
entendre*: 'give me venereal disease'
(*piece* = genitals)

27 SD] *this edn*   36 SD] *this edn*

VITELLI   Leave your prating.

GAZET

    I may. You have been doing; we will do, too.

FRANCISCO

    I am amazed, yet will nor blame nor chide you

    Till you inform me further; yet must say

    They steer not the right course, nor traffic well,   45

    That seek a passage to reach heaven through hell.   *Exeunt.*

3.1   *Enter* DONUSA [*and*] MANTO.

DONUSA

    When, said he, he would come again?

MANTO   He swore

    Short minutes should be tedious ages to him

    Until the tender of his second service,

    So much he seemed transported with the first.

DONUSA

    I am sure I was! I charge thee, Manto, tell me,   5

    By all my favours and my bounties, truly

    Whether thou art a virgin, or like me

    Hast forfeited that name.

MANTO   A virgin, madam,

    At my years, being a waiting-woman, and in court too?

    That were miraculous! I so long since lost   10

    That barren burden, I almost forget

---

42 **doing** (1) busy, engaged in business;
(2) fornicating

46 **hell** Cf. Lear's description of a woman's nether parts: 'there's hell, there's
darkness, there is the sulphurous pit,
burning, scalding, stench, consump-
tion' (*KL*, 4.6.123–5).

3.1 Location: Donusa's chamber

3 **service** the *service* offered by a courtly
lover to his lady; but here with a

bawdy quibble on *service* = sexual duty
(Williams, *Dictionary*, 3.1220–1)

8–9 **a virgin . . . years** echoing a famous
line from Beaumont and Fletcher,
Maid's Tragedy: 'A maidenhead
Amintor, / At my yeares' (2.1.193–4).
This ostensible satire of the Ottoman
court will (like its original) have
reminded audiences of the much
derided mores of the Jacobean court.

3.1] *(Actus Tertius. Scaena prima.)*

That ever I was one.

DONUSA   And could thy friends
Read in thy face, thy maidenhead gone, that thou
Hadst parted with it?

MANTO   No, indeed. I passed
For current many years after – till, by fortune,   15
Long and continued practice in the sport
Blew up my deck; a husband then was found out
By my indulgent father, and to the world
All was made whole again. What need you fear, then,
That at your pleasure may repair your honour,   20
Durst any envious, or malicious tongue
Presume to taint it?

Enter CARAZIE.

DONUSA   How now?

CARAZIE   Madam, the Pasha
Humbly desires access.

DONUSA   If it had been
My neat Italian, thou hadst met my wishes.
Tell him we would be private.

CARAZIE   So I did,   25
But he is much importunate.

MANTO   Best dispatch him:
His lingering here else will deter the other

14–15 **passed / For current** was accepted
   as genuine coinage (i.e. as a real virgin)
17 **Blew . . . deck** made me pregnant.
   The use of nautical metaphors to
   describe erotic encounters is commonplace – see Francisco's sardonic comment on Vitelli's 'prosperous voyage'
   (2.6.20–1); but there is also an echo
   of Grimaldi's 'desperate gunner ready
   to . . . blow the deck up' (1.3.47–8).

20 **honour** quibbling on 'reputation' and
   'virginity'
21 **Durst any** if any dared
23 **access** Donusa's reply creates a sexual
   innuendo.
24 **neat** elegantly dressed (*OED a.* 5a)
25 **we** Donusa is probably using the royal
   first person.
26 **much importunate** very insistent
   dispatch get rid of (*OED v.* 3)

22 SD] *after* How now?

From making his approach.

DONUSA His entertainment
Shall not invite a second visit. Go,
Say we are pleased.

Enter MUSTAPHA.

MUSTAPHA All happiness –
DONUSA Be sudden. 30
'Twas saucy rudeness in you, sir, to press
On my retirements, but ridiculous folly
To waste the time that might be better spent,
In complimental wishes.
CARAZIE [*aside*] There's a cooling
For his hot encounter.
DONUSA Come you here to stare? 35
If you have lost your tongue and use of speech,
Resign your government. There's a mute's place void
In my uncle's court, I hear; and you may work me
To write for your preferment.
MUSTAPHA This is strange!
I know not, madam, what neglect of mine 40
Has called this scorn upon me.
DONUSA To the purpose:
My will's a reason, and we stand not bound
To yield account to you.
MUSTAPHA Not of your angers;
But with erected ears I should hear from you
The story of your good opinion of me 45

28–9 **His . . . visit** 'The way I treat him will ensure he won't want to come a second time.'
37 **your government** i.e. your office as pasha (governor) of Aleppo
mute's place Deaf mutes were a regular part of the Ottoman sultan's retinue, often serving as unofficial executioners.
38 **work** work on, persuade (*OED v.* 14)
39 **preferment** promotion, appointment (*OED n.* 1, 3)
44 **with erected ears** '"attentively"; from the Latin "erectis auribus"' (Oxf)

34 SD] *Oxf*

Confirmed by love and favours.

DONUSA   How deserved?
I have considered you from head to foot,
And can find nothing in that wainscot face
That can teach me to dote; nor am I taken
With your grim aspect or tadpole-like complexion;   50
Those scars you glory in, I fear to look on,
And had much rather hear a merry tale
Than all your battles won with blood and sweat –
Though you belch forth the stink, too, in the service
And swear by your mustachios all is true.   55
You are yet too rough for me: purge and take physic,
Purchase perfumers, get me some French tailor
To new create you; the first shape you were made with
Is quite worn out. Let your barber wash your face, too:
You look yet like a bugbear to fright children.   60
Till when, I take my leave. Wait me, Carazie.

*Exeunt Donusa [and] Carazie. [Manto attempts
to follow them, but is halted by Mustapha.]*

48 **wainscot face** i.e. resembling the oak used for panelling: hard, dark and perhaps wrinkled or scarred (*OED n.* 5b)

50 **tadpole-like** i.e. black (suggesting that Mustapha was to be played as a 'black moor', in black-face makeup). Q's spelling, 'toadpoole-like', is ambiguous: a 'toadpool' (breeding-place of toads) was imagined as 'a mass of corrupt poisonous matter' (*OED*); cf. *Oth*, 4.2.62–3, where Othello imagines Desdemona's body as 'a cistern for foul toads / To knot and gender in', and Middleton and Rowley's *Changeling*, 2.1.58, where Beatrice-Joanna addresses the villain Deflores as 'Thou standing toad-pool'. But 'toadpole' was a common spelling of 'tadpole', and seems the more likely reading here – though

the original pronunciation probably allowed for a suggestive play on the two words.

55 **mustachios** moustache. Contemporary illustrations frequently show Turks sporting extravagant moustaches (see Figs 7, 9, 11 and 23); the word perhaps also marks Mustapha with the attributes of a braggart soldier.

56 **physic** medicine

57 **me** ethic dative – obsolescent form in which *me* is not the object of *get*; cf. Petruchio's comically misunderstood 'knock me here soundly' (*TS*, 1.2.8).
French tailor France was regarded by the provincial English as a centre of (often effeminate) fashion.

57–8 **tailor . . . you** Cf. Tilley, T17: 'The tailor makes the man.'

61 **Wait** attend, wait upon

61.1 *Donusa] Donu. Carazie] Car.* 61.1–2 *Manto . . . Mustapha] this edn*

MUSTAPHA

Stay you, my lady's cabinet key!

MANTO   How's this, sir?

MUSTAPHA

Stay! And stand quietly, or you shall fall else –
Not to firk your belly up flounder-like, but never
To rise again.   [*Threatens her with his dagger.*]
                        Offer but to unlock   65
These doors that stop your fugitive tongue –
    observe me! –
And, by my fury, I'll fix there this bolt
To bar thy speech forever. So, be safe now,
And but resolve me – not of what I doubt,
But bring assurance to a thing believed –   70
Thou mak'st thyself a fortune, not depending
On the uncertain favours of a mistress,
But art thyself one. I'll not so far question
My judgement and observance as to ask
Why I am slighted and contemned, but in   75
Whose favour it is done. I that have read
The copious volumes of all women's falsehood,

---

62 **my . . . key** Cf. *Changeling*, 2.2.6–7, where Alsemero remarks of the waiting woman Diaphanta, 'These women are their ladies' cabinets; / Things of most precious trust are locked into 'em'; and *Island Princess*, 3.1.139–45: 'For I presume you turne a key sweet beauty . . . You look as if you kept my Ladies secrets.'

64 **firk . . . flounder-like** 'expose your belly and thrust it up like an over-turned flounder' (i.e. inviting sexual intercourse)

65 SD *dagger* Presumably this is the 'bolt' with which Mustapha will 'bar [Manto's] speech forever' (67–8).

65–6 **unlock . . . tongue** i.e. open your lips

66 **fugitive** vagabond, uncontrolled (*OED a.* 3)

67 **bolt** i.e. his dagger (see 65 SDn.)

68 **bar** (1) make fast (as with a bar or bolt), confine (*OED v.* 1a, 2a); (2) prevent, suppress (*OED v.* 7)
safe (1) unharmed, free from danger (*OED a.*1, 6); (2) trustworthy (*OED a.* 11a)

69 **resolve me** make things clear to me (*OED v.* 11c), inform me (*OED v.* 17a). Mustapha denies the sense 'free me from doubt' (*OED v.* 15a).

71–3 **not . . . one** The bribe will be large enough to buy her discharge from service and establish her as mistress of her own household; cf. Vitelli's promotion of Gazet to be 'master' of his shop (2.6.26).

65 SD] *this edn*

Commented on by the heart-breaking groans
Of abused lovers – all the doubts washed off
With fruitless tears, the spider's cobweb-veil   80
Of arguments alleged in their defence
Blown off with sighs of desperate men, and they
Appearing in their full deformity –
Know that some other hath displanted me,
With her dishonour. Has she given it up?   85
Confirm it in two syllables.

MANTO   She has.

MUSTAPHA

I cherish thy confession thus, and thus –
   (*Gives her jewels.*)
Be mine. Again I court thee: thus, and thus –
Now prove but constant to my ends.

MANTO   By all –

MUSTAPHA

Enough! I dare not doubt thee. Oh, land crocodiles   90
Made of Egyptian slime, accursed women!
But 'tis no time to rail – come, my best Manto.   *Exeunt.*

3.2   *Enter* VITELLI [*and*] FRANCISCO.

VITELLI

Sir, as you are my confessor, you stand bound
Not to reveal whatever I discover

---

80 **fruitless** The tears are fruitless
because although they serve to expose
the falsehood of a woman they cannot
win her love.
spider's cobweb-veil The cobweb of
specious argument is imagined both as
a device to conceal falsehood and as a
trap for unwary men.
82 **they** i.e. women
85 **it** her 'honour', i.e. virginity
87 SD The gesture echoes Donusa's gift

of jewels to Vitelli (2.4.86 SD).
90–1 **land . . . slime** For the belief
that crocodiles emerged spontane-
ously from the action of the sun
on the mud of the Nile, see *AC*,
2.7.20–6. Because of their alleged
propensity to weep deceitful tears,
crocodiles were proverbial figures of
female treachery.
3.2 Location: a street in Tunis
2 **discover** reveal

81 alleged] *Coxeter;* alleadge *Q, Rawl. (*alledge*)* **3.2]** *(Actus tertius Scaena Secunda)*

In that religious way – nor dare I doubt you.
Let it suffice you have made me see my follies,
And wrought, perhaps, compunction; for I would not   5
Appear an hypocrite. But when you impose
A penance on me beyond flesh and blood
To undergo, you must instruct me how
To put off the condition of a man;
Or if not pardon, at the least excuse   10
My disobedience. Yet despair not, sir;
For though I take mine own way, I shall do
Something that may hereafter to my glory
Speak me your scholar.

FRANCISCO   I enjoin you not
To go, but send.

VITELLI   That were a petty trial   15
Not worth one so long taught and exercised
Under so grave a master. Reverend Francisco,
My friend, my father – in that word, my all –
Rest confident you shall hear something of me
That will redeem me in your good opinion,   20
Or judge me lost forever. Send Gazet –
She shall give order that he may have entrance –
To acquaint you with my fortunes.   *Exit.*

FRANCISCO   Go, and prosper.
Holy saints guide and strengthen thee! Howsoever
As my endeavours are, so may they find   25

---

7 **penance** The Roman Catholic rite of
   confession makes absolution contingent
   on the performance of penitential duties.
   Here, as so often in the play, Massinger's
   language seems calculated to draw attention to the Catholic basis of its theology.
14–15 **I . . . send** 'I urge you not to go
   to Donusa, but to send a message to
   her instead.'

16 **worth** worthy
18 **in . . . all** playing on Francisco's dual
   role as surrogate father and priestly
   father-confessor
20–1 These lines play on the spiritual
   and affective senses of *redeem* and *lost
   forever.*
25–6 **find / Gracious acceptance** be
   accepted by the grace of God

23 SD] *(Exit Vitelli)*

Gracious acceptance.

Enter GAZET, [*and*] GRIMALDI *in rags.*

GAZET   Now you do not roar, sir;
You speak not tempests, nor take ear-rent from
A poor shopkeeper. Do you remember that, sir?
I wear your marks here still.

FRANCISCO   Can this be possible?
All wonders are not ceased then!

GRIMALDI   Do: abuse me,   30
Spit on me, spurn me, pull me by the nose,
Thrust out these fiery eyes that yesterday
Would have looked thee dead.

GAZET [*to Francisco*]   Oh, save me, sir!

GRIMALDI   Fear nothing:
I am tame and quiet; there's no wrong can force me
To remember what I was. I have forgot   35
I e'er had ireful fierceness, a steeled heart,
Insensible of compassion to others.
Nor is it fit that I should think myself
Worth mine own pity – oh!

FRANCISCO   Grows this dejection
From his disgrace, do you say?

---

27 **ear-rent** literally ground-rent for his
market stall; but Jonson (*Alchemist*,
1.1.169) uses 'ear-rent' as a mocking
term for the loss of ears in a pil-
lory. Here Gazet refers to Grimaldi's
pulling of his ears at 1.3.81–2, and
quibbles on the idea of *ear-rent* as 'the
"tax" imposed on a listener's patience
by a profitless or noisy talker' (*OED*).
30 **wonders . . . ceased** referring to the
Protestant belief that the age of miracles had passed. Cf. *Custom*: 'charity
growing cold, and miracles ceasing'
(3.3.6); 'Wonders are ceas'd Sir, we

must worke by meanes' (5.4.14); see
also *H5*, 1.1.67, 'miracles are ceased'.
36 **ireful** angry
37 Scansion of the line is uncertain: some
elision may be intended (either of the
third syllable of *Insensible* or between
Insensible and *of*), with *compassion* pronounced as four syllables; or perhaps
compassion should be treated as three
syllables, with a stress on the first.
40 **disgrace** In the context of Grimaldi's
despair, play on the religious connotations of 'grace' seems inevitable; cf.
70.

28 sir?] sir,   33 SP1] *Qb (Gaz.); Graz. Qa*   SD] *this edn*   SP2] *Qb (Gri.); G i Qa*

GAZET   Why, he's cashiered, sir,   40
His ships, his goods, his livery-punks confiscate;
And there is such a punishment laid upon him,
The miserable rogue must steal no more,
Nor drink, nor drab. —*chase whores*
FRANCISCO   Does that torment him?
GAZET   Oh, sir!
Should the state take order to bar men of acres   45
From those two laudable recreations,
Drinking and whoring, how should panders purchase,
Or thrifty whores build hospitals? 'Slid! If I
That, since I am made free, may write myself
A city gallant, should forfeit two such charters,   50
I should be stoned to death, and ne'er be pitied
By the liveries of those companies.
FRANCISCO   You'll be whipped, sir,
If you bridle not your tongue. Haste to the palace:
Your master looks for you.
GAZET   My quondam master!
Rich sons forget they ever had poor fathers;   55
In servants 'tis more pardonable. As a companion

---

40 **cashiered** dismissed from his service to the state
41 **livery-punks** hired whores
44 **drab** chase whores
45 **take order** issue commands
men of acres wealthy country land-owners
48 **thrifty ... hospitals** Oxf suggests a possible allusion to the charitable work of Theodora, wife of the emperor Justinian and a former courtesan.
'Slid abbreviation of 'God's eyelid' – a common and relatively mild oath
49 **since ... free** Since Vitelli discharged him from his apprenticeship, Gazet is a freeman of his livery company (presumably the Haberdashers).
write designate (*OED v.* 11b)
51 **I ... death** with a bawdy *double entendre*: 'I might as well be castrated'

52 **liveries ... companies** Gazet imagines the whores and panders as forming their own livery companies; if he were to lose his charters to trade with them, he could expect no pity from their members. Vitkus suggests a pun on 'liver' as the supposed seat of love and violent passion, and – given Gazet's recurrent castration anxieties – a play on *stoned* also seems inevitable; cf. 3.4.52. For similar punning on 'stone', see *Law*, 4.1.146–8, and *Goose Chase*, 1.3.195, 4.1.139.
54 **quondam** sometime, former
55 Cf. Tilley, F91: 'A sparing father and a spending son'.
56 **In servants ... pardonable** The ambitious servant, who seeks to rise out of his 'place', is a recurrent figure

Or so, I may consent. But is there hope, sir,
He has got me a good chapwoman? Pray you, write
A word or two in my behalf.

FRANCISCO   Out, rascal!   59

GAZET

I feel some insurrections.

FRANCISCO   Hence.

GAZET   I vanish.   *Exit.*

GRIMALDI

Why should I study a defence or comfort,
In whom black guilt and misery, if balanced,
I know not which would turn the scale? Look upward
I dare not, for should it but be believed
That I – dyed deep in hell's most horrid colours –   65
Should dare to hope for mercy, it would leave
No check or feeling in men innocent
To catch at sins the Devil ne'er taught mankind yet.
No, I must downward, downward! Though repentance
Could borrow all the glorious wings of grace,   70
My mountainous weight of sins would crack their
    pinions

in drama of the period not only in tragedy (e.g. Iago in *Oth*, Deflores in *Changeling*), but also in comedy (Mosca in *Volpone*, Tapwell in *New Way*).

56–7 **As ... consent** 'I might agree to being termed his companion, or something of the sort.'

58 **chapwoman** a market-woman (to take over his own former role). It is, no doubt, Gazet's lechery that encourages him to hire a woman, rather than the more common chapman.

60 **insurrections** rebellious impulses; lascivious rebellion of the flesh ('risings' or erections)

61–98 Cf. the 'many tears and sighs of deep repentance' wept by Cervantes's renegade in *The Captive's Tale* (89).

66–8 **it ... yet** 'it would leave nothing to inhibit even innocent men from attempting sins so outrageous that the Devil hasn't even taught them to humanity yet'

69–72 **Though ... with me** a common emblematic image, represented for example by the printer's emblem on the title-page of the 1604 Quarto of *Faustus*. Grimaldi's despair, which suggests the utter impotence of repentance, seems tinged by the Calvinist predestinarianism repudiated by the growing Arminian faction in the Anglican Church. The fact that he will be rescued from his despair by a Jesuit priest is symptomatic of the play's ecumenical tendency.

60 SD] *(Exit Gazet)*

And sink them to hell with me.

FRANCISCO   Dreadful! Hear me,
Thou miserable man.

GRIMALDI   Good sir, deny not,
But that there is no punishment beyond
Damnation.

Enter MASTER [*and*] BOATSWAIN.

MASTER   Yonder he is. I pity him.   75
BOATSWAIN
Take comfort, captain, we live still to serve you.

GRIMALDI
Serve me? I am a devil already. Leave me!
Stand further off, you are blasted else! I have heard
Schoolmen affirm man's body is composed
Of the four elements; and, as in league together   80
They nourish life, so each of them affords
Liberty to the soul when it grows weary
Of this fleshy prison. Which shall I make choice of?
The fire? No – I shall feel that hereafter.
The earth will not receive me. Should some whirlwind   85
Snatch me into the air and I hang there,
Perpetual plagues would dwell upon the earth,
And those superior bodies that pour down
Their cheerful influence deny to pass it
Through those vast regions I have infected.   90
The sea? Aye, that is justice. There I ploughed up

77–98 lines modelled on the hero's
final despairing soliloquy in *Faustus*
(5.2.57–115)
79 **Schoolmen** academics – more especially adherents of medieval scholasticism
80 **four elements** earth, air, fire and water

– thought to be constituent of the four
humours which, in Galenic medicine,
determined the human constitution
88 **superior bodies** the stars and planets,
whose influence was thought to govern
the destinies of those on earth

91 The sea? . . . I] *this edn;* The (Sea) . . . iustice there, I *Q;* The sea, (aye that is Iustice there) I
Rawl.; The Sea . . . iustice; there I *Coxeter;* The Sea . . . iustice, there. I *Oxf;* The sea? . . . justice.
There I *Vitkus*

Mischief as deep as hell. There, there I'll hide
This cursed lump of clay. May it turn rocks
Where plummet's weight could never reach the sands,
And grind the ribs of all such barks as press   95
The ocean's breast in my unlawful course.
I haste then to thee: let thy ravenous womb,
Whom all things else deny, be now my tomb!   *Exit.*

MASTER

Follow him and restrain him.   [*Exit Boatswain.*]

FRANCISCO   Let this stand

For an example to you. I'll provide   100
A lodging for him, and apply such cures
To his wounded conscience as heaven hath lent me.
He's now my second care; and my profession
Binds me to teach the desperate to repent   104
As far as to confirm the innocent.   *Exeunt.*

3.3   *Enter* ASAMBEG, MUSTAPHA, AGA [*and*] KAPIAGA.

ASAMBEG

Your pleasure?

MUSTAPHA   'Twill exact your private ear;
And when you have received it, you will think
Too many know it.

---

93 **lump of clay** Cf. Genesis, 2.7: 'And the Lord God formed man of the dust of the ground.'
turn turn into
94 echoing *Tem*, 5.1.56 ('deeper than did ever plummet sound') and *1H4*, 1.3.204 ('Where fathom-line could never touch the ground')
96 **course** (1) path, ship's course (*OED n.* 11a, 12a); (2) conduct (*OED n.* 22b)
97 **thee** i.e. the sea
98 **Whom** refers to Grimaldi, who imagines himself rejected by all the elements but water
103 **profession** (1) calling as a priest (*OED n.* III 6); (2) religious vows (*OED n.* I 1a); (3) faith (*OED n.* II 5a)
104 **desperate** those suffering from the mortal sin of despair (i.e. the conviction that they are beyond salvation)
105 **confirm** strengthen spiritually (*OED v.* 4)
3.3 Location: a room in the palace
1 **exact** require (*OED v.* 3)

92 hell. There, there] *Q;* hell: there, there *Coxeter* 98 SD] *(Exit Grimaldi)* 99 SD] *Vitkus* 3.3] *(Actus tertius, Scaena tertia.)*

ASAMBEG [*to Aga and Kapiaga*]   Leave the room, but be
    Within our call.   *Exeunt Aga [and] Kapiaga.*
              Now sir, what burning secret
    Brings you – with which it seems you are turned
        cinders –   5
    To quench in my advice or power?
MUSTAPHA   The fire
    Will rather reach you.
ASAMBEG   Me?
MUSTAPHA   And consume both;
    For 'tis impossible to be put out
    But with the blood of those that kindle it –
    And yet one vial of it is so precious,   10
    It being borrowed from the Ottoman spring,
    That better 'tis, I think, both we should perish
    Than prove the desperate means that must restrain it
    From spreading further.
ASAMBEG   To the point, and quickly!
    These winding circumstances in relations   15
    Seldom environ truth.
MUSTAPHA   Truth, Asambeg?
ASAMBEG

    Truth, Mustapha! I said it, and add more:
    You touch upon a string that to my ear
    Does sound Donusa.
MUSTAPHA   You then understand
    Who 'tis I aim at.

---

7 **consume** cònsume
8–9 Mustapha is deliberately oblique at
  this point, since he is making the
  dangerous assertion that his passion
  can only be extinguished by killing the
  Sultan's niece, Donusa.
11 **Ottoman spring** the bloodline of the

Ottoman sultans
15 **winding circumstances** tortuous
  circumlocutions
  relations narrative accounts
16 **environ** encompass
18 **string** lute-string

3 SD] *this edn* 4 SD] *Gifford; after* know it *3 Q* 4–5 secret . . . with] *(conj. McIlwraith subst.);*
secret brings you / (With *Q* 5 Brings] Bring *Mason*

ASAMBEG   Take heed, Mustapha!   20
    Remember what she is, and whose we are.
    'Tis her neglect, perhaps, that you complain of;
    And should you practise to revenge her scorn
    With any plot to taint her in her honour –
MUSTAPHA
    Hear me!
ASAMBEG   I will be heard first. There's no tongue   25
    A subject owes that shall out-thunder mine.
MUSTAPHA
    Well, take your way.
ASAMBEG   I then again repeat it:
    If Mustapha dares, with malicious breath,
    On jealous suppositions, presume
    To blast the blossom of Donusa's fame   30
    Because he is denied a happiness
    Which men of equal, nay, of more desert,
    Have sued in vain for –
MUSTAPHA   More?
ASAMBEG   More! 'Twas I spake it.
    The Pasha of 'Natolia and myself
    Were rivals for her; either of us brought   35
    More victories, more trophies to plead for us
    To our great master than you dare lay claim to;
    Yet still by his allowance she was left
    To her election. Each of us owed nature
    As much for outward form and inward worth   40
    To make way for us to her grace and favour

---

26 **owes** owns
29 **suppositions** pronounced as five syllables
30 **blast** blight, wither (*OED v.* 8a)
34 **Pasha of 'Natolia** Knolles (sigs 6B6^r, 6C4^r) and Sandys (sig. E6^r) name the 'beglerbeg of Natolia' as one of the Ottoman sultan's principal viceroys; see below, 3.4.36n.
'Natolia modern Anatolia, the large peninsula that makes up the principal part of Asian Turkey; sometimes called Asia Minor
39 **To her election** to choose for herself

21 are.] *MS ADD;* are; *Q*

As you brought with you. We were heard, repulsed,
Yet thought it no dishonour to sit down
With the disgrace – if not to force affection
May merit such a name.

MUSTAPHA   Have you done yet?   45

ASAMBEG

Be therefore more than sure the ground on which
You raise your accusation may admit
No undermining of defence in her;
For if with pregnant and apparent proofs –
Such as may force a judge, more than inclined   50
Or partial in her cause, to swear her guilty –
You win not me to set off your belief,
Neither our ancient friendship, nor the rites
Of sacred hospitality – to which
I would not offer violence – shall protect you.   55
Now, when you please.

MUSTAPHA   I will not dwell upon
Much circumstance, yet cannot but profess,
With the assurance of a loyalty
Equal to yours, the reverence I owe
The Sultan and all such his blood makes sacred,   60
That there is not a vein of mine which yet is
Unemptied in his service but this moment
Should freely open, so it might wash off
The stains of her dishonour. Could you think

43–4 **sit down / With** put up with, rest
content with (*OED* sit *v.* 23d)
44–5 **if . . . name** 'if not trying to com-
pel someone to love against their will
deserves to be called disgraceful'
47–8 **admit . . . defence** 'is not likely
to be undercut by any excuse she can
offer in her own defence'
49 **pregnant** convincing (*OED a.*[1])
apparent clear, palpable (*OED a.* 3)

52 ***set off** praise, commend (*OED v.*
147g); the Q reading makes perfectly
good sense, although Oxf notes that, in
Massinger's hand, 'bee' might easily be
confused with 'set', so that McIlwraith's
emendation remains possible.
61–2 **vein . . . Unemptied** Shedding
blood in battle for one's sovereign was
imagined as the epitome of honourable
service.

52 set off] be of *(conj. McIlwraith)*

Or, though you saw it, credit your own eyes   65
That she, the wonder and amazement of
Her sex, the pride and glory of the empire,
That hath disdained you, slighted me, and boasted
A frozen coldness which no appetite
Or height of blood could thaw, should now so far   70
Be hurried with the violence of her lust
As, in it burying her high birth and fame,
Basely descend to fill a Christian's arms
And to him yield her virgin honour up –
Nay, sue to him to take't?

ASAMBEG   A Christian?

MUSTAPHA   Temper   75
Your admiration – and what Christian, think you?
No prince disguised, no man of mark nor honour,
No daring undertaker in our service,
But one whose lips her foot should scorn to touch:
A poor mechanic pedlar.

ASAMBEG   He?

MUSTAPHA   Nay, more,   80
Whom do you think she made her scout – nay, bawd –
To find him out, but me? What place makes choice of
To wallow in her foul and loathsome pleasures,
But in the palace? Who the instruments
Of close conveyance but the captain of   85
Your guard, the Aga, and that man of trust
The warden of the inmost port? I'll prove this;
And, though I fail to show her in the act,

---

77 **of mark** important, distinguished (*OED* mark *n.* 21)
78 **undertaker** one who is hired to undertake some task for another – in this case, a mercenary
80 **mechanic** menial
81 **scout** mean spy (*OED n.* 4)
   bawd The term meant either procuress

or procurer, though the latter is perhaps more often called a 'pander', so there may be an angry hint of emasculation in Mustapha's use of the word.
87–91 **I'll . . . on** Mustapha is made to echo Iago (*Oth*, 1.1.107–12, 3.3.400–11).
87 **warden . . . port** See 2.1.17n.
88 **though** even if

Glued like a neighing mare to her proud stallion,
Your incredulity shall be convinced 90
With proofs I blush to think on.

ASAMBEG   Never yet
This flesh felt such a fever. By the life
And fortune of great Amurath, should our Prophet –
Whose name I bow to – in a vision speak this,
'Twould make me doubtful of my faith! Lead on; 95
And when my eyes and ears are, like yours, guilty,
My rage shall then appear; for I will do
Something; but what, I am not yet determined.   *Exeunt.*

3.4   *Enter* CARAZIE, MANTO [*and*] GAZET [*, dressed
in Vitelli's clothes*].

CARAZIE
They are private to their wishes.

MANTO   Doubt it not.

GAZET
A pretty structure this! A court, do you call it?
Vaulted and arched – O, here has been old jumbling

---

89 **mare* Massinger's MS correction substitutes the sexually specific term for the indeterminate original, 'jennet' (a small Spanish horse), perhaps because he had come to think that the word referred only to the stallion – see *Very Woman*, 3.5.55–6.

94 *Whose . . . to* possibly a relic of the longstanding belief that Mahometans worshipped their Prophet; or perhaps representing Massinger's vague awareness of the reverential formula 'Peace be upon him', pronounced whenever the Prophet's name is mentioned

97–8 *for . . . determined* Asambeg becomes incoherent with rage. Cf. *KL*,

2.2.468–71: 'I will have such revenges on you both / That all the world shall – I will do such things – / What they are yet I know not, but they shall be / The terrors of the earth!'

3.4 Location: a room in Donusa's quarters

1 *private . . . wishes* as private as they could wish (referring to Donusa and Vitelli)

2 *court* great house, castle, or palace (*OED n.*[1] 2, 5)

3 *Vaulted and arched* For the bawdy pun here, see Williams, *Dictionary*: 'arches' = bawdy house; 'vault' = copulate (1.34–5; 3.1466). The etymology is explained by Harrington, who notes

89 mare . . . proud] *MS ADD;* Gennet to her *Q* 3.4] *(Actus Tertius, Scaena Quarta.)* 0 SD *dressed . . . clothes*] this edn

Behind this arras.

CARAZIE [*aside to Manto*]   Prithee, let's have some sport
With this fresh cod's head.

MANTO   I am out of tune –   5
But do as you please.

    [*aside*]   My conscience! Tush, the hope
Of liberty throws that burden off! I must
Go watch, and make discovery.   *Exit.*

CARAZIE [*aside*]   He's musing
And will talk to himself – he cannot hold:
The poor fool's ravished.

GAZET [*to himself*]   I am in my master's clothes.   10
They fit me to a hair, too: let but any
Indifferent gamester measure us inch by inch
Or weigh us by the standard, I may pass;
I have been proved and proved again true metal.

CARAZIE [*aside*]

How he surveys himself.

GAZET [*to himself*]   I have heard that some   15
Have fooled themselves at court into good fortunes

---

in *Metamorphosis of Ajax* (1596) that
his Latin dictionary glosses '*fornicare*'
as 'to make an arch or vault' (135).
jumbling fornicating (*OED v.* 6a)

4 **arras** tapestry wall-hanging (so named
from the town of Arras in modern
Belgium, a famous centre of weaving);
again probably gesturing at the curtains
of the discovery space (see 2.6.6n.)

5 **cod's head** blockhead
out of tune 'not in the mood for it'

6 **conscience! Tush** Cf. Gazet's equally
offhand dismissal of conscience in the
opening scene (1.1.12–15), and contrast Grimaldi's pangs of 'wounded
conscience' (3.2.102; 4.1.9, 89).

8 **make discovery** i.e. expose the secret
liaison of Donusa and Vitelli

9 **hold** contain himself

10 SD Unlike Carazie, whose asides are
directed at the audience, Gazet is talking to himself in soliloquy.

10 **I . . . clothes** Gazet's borrowed attire
allows him to assume Vitelli's merchant
persona, which was itself a disguise.

12 **Indifferent** impartial
gamester gambler; Gazet imagines
himself as coin paid down for a wager
which the suspicious gambler will
need to check for possible forgery.

13 **standard** 'the legal magnitude of a
unit of . . . weight' (*OED n.* 9b)

16 'have made themselves rich by playing
the fool's part at court'

16–18 **court . . . city . . . country** In
early modern England financial, as

---

4 SD] *Vitkus* 6 SD] *Oxf* 7–8] *Gifford; Q lines* off, / discovery. / 8 SD2] *Vitkus* 10 SD] *this
edn* 13 pass;] *MS ADD subst. (*passe.*);* pass *Q* 15 SD1] *Vitkus* SD2] *this edn*

That never hoped to thrive by wit in the city
Or honesty in the country. If I do not
Make the best laugh at me, I'll weep for myself –
If they give me hearing. 'Tis resolved: I'll try　　　　20
What may be done.

　　　[*to Carazie*]　　　By your favour sir, I pray you,
Were you born a courtier?

CARAZIE　　　　　　　　　　　No, sir. Why do you ask?

GAZET

Because I thought that none could be preferred
But such as were begot there.

CARAZIE　　　　　　　　　　Oh, sir, many!

And howsoe'er you are a citizen born,　　　　25
Yet, if your mother were a handsome woman
And ever longed to see a masque at court,
It is an even lay but that you had
A courtier to your father – and I think so,
You bear yourself so sprightly.

GAZET　　　　　　　　　　　It may be.　　　　30

But pray you, sir, had I such an itch upon me
To change my copy, is there hope a place

well as political, power was typically
triangulated in this fashion. Gazet
associates the *country* with *honesty* –
not simply in the sense of straight-
forwardness and simplicity, but also
in the sense of honour (deriving from
the 'honourable' wealth of landed
property); he identifies the *city* (the
centre of mercantile activity) with *wit*
(intelligence, ingenuity, and cunning)
and the *court* with abject and ingratiat-
ing foolery.

23 **preferred** promoted, advanced in
rank (*OED v.* 1)

26–9 **Yet . . . father** Oxf cites Sir Edward
Peyton, *The Divine Catastrophe of the
Kingly Family of the House of Stuarts*
(1652): 'The masks and playes at

Whitehall were used onely for incen-
tives of lust: therefore the courtiers
invited the citizens wives to those
shews, on purpose to defile them in
such sort. There is not a lobby nor
chamber (if it could speak) but would
verify this.'

28 **lay** bet; perhaps playing on *lay* = coit
with (Williams, *Dictionary*, 2.788–9)

32 **change my copy** change my behaviour
or course of action; assume another
character (*OED n.* 11a) – here a euphemism for 'turn Turk', but with a play on
the notion of a son as a *copy* of the father,
on *copy* as a model of penmanship to be
imitated by a pupil (*OED n.* 8b), on a
printer's use of *copy* (*OED n.* 9a) and on
his own 'copying' of Vitelli's guise

21 SD] *this edn*　24–5 Oh . . . born] *Coxeter; one line Q*

May be had here for money?

CARAZIE   Not without it,

That I dare warrant you.

GAZET   I have a pretty stock,

And would not have my good parts undiscovered.   35

What places of credit are there?

CARAZIE   There's your beglerbeg.

GAZET

By no means that! It comes too near the beggar –

And most prove so that come there.

CARAZIE   Or your sanjak.

GAZET

Sans-jack! Fie, none of that!

CARAZIE   Your chiaus.

GAZET   Nor that.

place office, position; the venal practice of selling offices was a stock subject of Jacobean anti-court satire.

34 **pretty** considerable (*OED n.* 5)
stock capital sum to trade with or invest (OED *n.*[1] VI 48a), but when combined with *good parts* (35) a bawdy *double entendre* may be involved (= supply of sexual ammunition)

35 **parts** qualities, talents (with a play on 'part' = vaginal area; Williams, *Dictionary*, 2.996–7)

36 **credit** honour; influence
beglerbeg governor. Sandys writes of 'the *Beglerbegs*, (the name signifieth a Lord of Lords) of whom there be only two, the one of *Greece*, and the other of *Natolia*' (sig. E6[r]); see also Knolles (sigs 6B6[r], 6C4[r]).

36, 38 **there** i.e. the court

37 **comes too near** sounds too much like

38 **sanjak** i.e. sanjakbeg, the governor of a province (or *sancak*). According to Sandys 'the *Sanziacks* [are] gouernors of Cities, for so the name signifies' (sig. E6v[r]); according to Knolles, who

places them under the immediate command of the beglerbegs, they 'are sent as governors into provinces during the princes pleasure. These are men of great experience' (sig. 6B6[r]).

39 **Sans-jack** without a penis
chiaus (chowse) messenger, herald, ambassador (Turkish *châwush* or *chaouch*). According to Sandys, 'the Chauses . . . go on Embassies, execute Commandements; and are Pursiuants, and under-Sherrifs, attending the imployment of the Emperour' (sig. E6[v]); while Knolles writes that they 'are as it were sergeants at armes. These men are well esteemed, and are often imployed in embassies to forreine princes: They also carrie letters and commendations from the prince of his cheife Visier, and they apprehend offendors' (sig. 6B7[r]). A Turkish confidence trickster had imposed himself on the English court in 1607, pretending to be the Sultan's *châwush*. His imposture gave rise to 'chouse' as a term for swindler – hence Gazet's indignation.

39 Sans-jack] *(conj. McIlwraith)*; Saus-iacke *Q*; Sauce-iacke *Gifford*

CARAZIE

Chief gardener.

GAZET   Out upon't!   40

'Twill put me in mind my mother was an herb-woman.

What is your place I pray you?

CARAZIE   Sir, an eunuch.

GAZET

An eunuch! Very fine, i'faith, an eunuch!

And what are your employments? Neat and easy?

CARAZIE

In the day I wait on my lady when she eats,   45

Carry her pantofles, bear up her train;

Sing her asleep at night, and when she pleases

I am her bedfellow.

41 **put . . . mind** remind me that
herb-woman literally a grower and vendor of herbs, but also a quibbling title for a bawd (Williams, *Glossary*, 156); cf. *Per*, 4.6.84: 'your herb-woman, she that sets seeds and roots of shame and iniquity'.

42 **eunuch** Despite his fear of becoming a *Sans-jack* and his reluctance to 'barter that commodity' which his Doll 'enjoined me / To bring home as she left it' (1.1.38–42), Gazet apparently regards *eunuch* simply as a lofty court title. The royal eunuchs were an important part of the sultan's retinue: 'He hath alwayes above one thousand Eunuches entertained in severall places, whereof some are in very great credit with him, and can prevaile much . . . many of them are imployed to attend his Concubines and Virgines in his Seraglio. They are not onely deprived of their genitors, but in their youth they have the whole of their privities smoothed off by their bellies, and in their turbants they beare short quills of silver, through which they make

water' (Knolles, sig. 6B5ʳ); cf. also Sandys (sig. G6ʳ): 'Many of the children that the *Turkes* do buy . . . they castrate, making all smooth as the backe of the hand, (whereof divers do die in the cutting), who supply the uses of nature with a silver quill, which they weare in their Turbants. In times past, they did onely but geld them: but being admitted to the free converse of women, it was observed by some, that they more then befittingly delighted in their societies . . . They are here in great repute with their maisters, trusted with their states, the government of their women and houses in their absence . . . in so much as not a few of them have come to sit at the sterne of state, (the second Viz[i]er of the Port being now an Eunuke:) and others to the government of armies.' Castration, as Sandys suggests, was a hazardous business, fewer than one in ten surviving the operation and its aftermath. Cf. 4.1.151–6.

44 **Neat** clean, dainty

46 **pantofles** Cf. 1.2.58.1.

41 in mind] *Coxeter;* mind Q   44 Neat and easy?] *MS ADD;* neate and easie. *Q; Car.* Neate and easie. *Gifford*

GAZET   How! her bedfellow?
And lie with her?

CARAZIE   Yes, and lie with her.

GAZET   Oh, rare!
I'll be an eunuch, though I sell my shop for't   50
And all my wares.

CARAZIE   It is but parting with
A precious stone or two. I know the price on't.

GAZET

I'll part with all my stones; and when I am
An eunuch, I'll so toss and touse the ladies!
Pray you, help me to a chapman.

CARAZIE   The court surgeon   55
Shall do you that favour.

GAZET   I am made! An eunuch!

                    Enter MANTO.

MANTO

Carazie, quit the room!

CARAZIE   Come, sir, we'll treat of
Your business further.

GAZET   Excellent! An eunuch!   *Exeunt.*

3.5   *Enter* DONUSA [*, and*] VITELLI [*bearing a casket*].

VITELLI

Leave me, or I am lost again: no prayers,
No penitence, can redeem me.

52 **precious . . . two** i.e. his testicles.
The punning on *precious stone[s]* as
the *price* of Gazet's promotion gives a
satiric colouring to the episode in the
next scene, where Vitelli returns to
Donusa the jewels that have been the
price of his preferment (3.5.48–9).
54 **touse** pull about rudely, tousle

55 **chapman** purchaser
56 **made** As an eunuch, Gazet will in fact
be 'unmade'.
57 **treat of** deal with, discuss (*OED v.* 2)
3.5 Location: Donusa's chamber
1–2 **no prayers . . . redeem me** Cf.
Grimaldi's despair in 3.2.

3.5] *(Actus Tertius. Scaena Quinta).*   0 SD *bearing a casket*] *this edn*

DONUSA   Am I grown
  Old or deformed since yesterday?
VITELLI   You are still –
  Although the sating of your lust hath sullied
  The immaculate whiteness of your virgin beauties –   5
  Too fair for me to look on; and, though pureness,
  The sword with which you ever fought and conquered,
  Is ravished from you by unchaste desires,
  You are too strong for flesh and blood to treat with,
  Though iron grates were interposed between us   10
  To warrant me from treason.
DONUSA   Whom do you fear?
VITELLI
  That human frailty I took from my mother,
  That, as my youth increased, grew stronger on me,
  That still pursues me, and, though once recovered,
  In scorn of reason and, what's more, religion,   15
  Again seeks to betray me.
DONUSA   If you mean, sir,
  To my embraces, you turn rebel to
  The laws of Nature, the great queen and mother
  Of all productions, and deny allegiance
  Where you stand bound to pay it.
VITELLI   I will stop   20
  Mine ears against these charms, which, if Ulysses
  Could live again and hear this second siren –
  Though bound with cables to his mast, his ship too

---

9   **treat with** negotiate with; handle
10 **grates** here apparently prison bars
    (though 'grate' could also mean the
    prison itself; see 4.2.11)
11 **warrant** protect
12 The frailty derives from his mother
    because of Eve's sin in Genesis. Vitelli
    implicitly identifies his temptress as a
    second Eve.

14 **though once recovered** although I
    had at one point recovered from it
19 **productions** effects (of which Nature
    is the grand cause), natural phenom-
    ena
20–8 **I . . . him** Vitelli compares
    Donusa's temptation to the song of the
    sirens in Book 12 of Homer's *Odyssey*;
    cf. 2.1.29–31n.

5 immaculate] *MS ADD;* imaculate *Q*

Fastened with all her anchors – this enchantment
Would force him, in despite of all resistance,   25
To leap into the sea and follow her,
Although destruction with outstretched arms,
Stood ready to receive him.

DONUSA   Gentle sir,
Though you deny to hear me, yet vouchsafe
To look upon me. Though I use no language,   30
The grief for this unkind repulse will print
Such a dumb eloquence upon my face
As will not only plead but prevail for me.

VITELLI

I am a coward. I will see and hear you –
The trial else is nothing, nor the conquest   35
My temperance shall crown me with hereafter,
Worthy to be remembered. Up, my virtue!
And holy thoughts and resolutions arm me
Against this fierce temptation! Give me voice
Tuned to a zealous anger to express   40
At what an overvalue I have purchased
The wanton treasure of your virgin bounties,
That in their false fruition heap upon me
Despair and horror. That I could with that ease
Redeem my forfeit innocence, or cast up   45
The poison I received into my entrails
From the alluring cup of your enticements
As now I do deliver back the price
          (*Returns the casket.*)

27 The metre requires scanning either
destruction as four syllables or *outstretched*
as three.
35 **else** otherwise
36 **temperance** Cf. 2.5.94 and n.
37 **Up** rise up (*OED adv.* 29a)
45 **cast up** vomit
47 **cup . . . enticements** recalling the
drugged cup with which the enchantress Circe turned Ulysses' followers

into swine in Book 10 of the *Odyssey*; in
this context the cup is clearly identified
with Donusa's vagina, so that 'The
poison I received into my entrails' (46)
will play on the fear of venereal disease.
48–9 **As . . . lust** See 3.4.52.
48 SD The definite article suggests that the
casket has already appeared: presumably
Vitelli is meant to carry it with him in
2.6, on his first return from Donusa's

And salary of your lust! Or thus unclothe me
Of sin's gay trappings, the proud livery   50
   (*Throws off his cloak and doublet.*)
Of wicked pleasure, which but worn and heated
With the fire of entertainment and consent,
Like to Alcides' fatal shirt, tears off
Our flesh and reputation both together,
Leaving our ulcerous follies bare and open   55
To all malicious censure.

DONUSA   You must grant,
If you hold that a loss to you, mine equals,
If not transcends it. If you then first tasted
That poison – as you call it – I brought with me
A palate unacquainted with the relish   60
Of those delights which most, as I have heard,
Greedily swallow; and then the offence,
If my opinion may be believed,
Is not so great – howe'er, the wrong no more
Than if Hippolytus and the Virgin Huntress   65
Should meet and kiss together.

VITELLI   What defences

---

chamber. Cf. Gazet's willingness to part with his 'precious stone[s]' 3.4.51–4.

50 **gay** brilliant, showy – but also suggesting the superficial happiness of sexual pleasure

52 **entertainment** sexual diversion (Williams, *Glossary*, 115)

53 **Alcides' fatal shirt** To revenge the attempted rape of his wife, Deianira, Hercules (Alcides) shot the centaur Nessus with a poisoned arrow. Nessus in turn presented Deianira with some of his blood, pretending it to be a love-charm. When Hercules donned a shirt which his jealous wife had soaked in the supposed charm, the poison began to burn him, and in his attempts to

rip off the shirt the maddened hero tore away pieces of his own flesh. Cf. *Combat*, 4.1.9–10.

64 **no more** is no more

65 **Hippolytus** Killed after rejecting the incestuous desires of his stepmother, Phaedra, Hippolytus was understood as a type of male chastity. Cf. *Roman Actor*, 4.2.69–71.
Virgin Huntress Diana (Artemis), goddess of chastity

66–9 **What . . . foot** 'what extraordinary defences lust can erect to preserve the dangerous precipice from which we tumble into the depths of lecherous abandon, when it does not even offer us the slightest step or foothold'

64 wrong] wrong's *Oxf (conj. McIlwraith)*

Can lust raise to maintain a precipice

    [*Enter*] ASAMBEG *and* MUSTAPHA *above.*

To the abyss of looseness, but affords not
The least stair or the fastening of one foot
To re-ascend that glorious height we fell from!   70

MUSTAPHA

  By Mahomet, she courts him.   ([*Donusa*] *kneels.*)

ASAMBEG   Nay, kneels to him.

  Observe: the scornful villain turns away too,
  As glorying in his conquest.

DONUSA [*to Vitelli*]   Are you marble?

  If Christians have mothers, sure they share in
  The tigress' fierceness; for if you were owner   75
  Of human pity, you could not endure
  A princess to kneel to you, or look on
  These falling tears which hardest rocks would soften,
  And yet remain unmoved. Did you but give me
  A taste of happiness in your embraces   80
  That the remembrance of the sweetness of it
  Might leave perpetual bitterness behind it,
  Or showed me what it was to be a wife,
  To live a widow ever?

ASAMBEG   She has confessed it.

    Enter KAPIAGA [*and*] AGA, *with* [GUARDS].

71–3 **By . . . conquest** The indignation of Mustapha and Asambeg is fuelled, like Donusa's sense of humiliation, by the role-reversal involved in the spectacle of a Turkish princess abasing herself before a common man (cf. 1.2.92–9).

75 **tigress' fierceness** Tigers were proverbially fierce, and the ferocity of the tigress made her the antitype of proper femininity; cf. the denunciation of Queen Margaret in *3H6*, 1.4.137: 'O, tiger's heart wrapped in a woman's hide.'

67 SD *Enter*] *Vitkus* 71 SD] *Vitkus; opp. 73 Q* *Donusa*] *Vitkus* 73 SD] *this edn* 84 SD GUARDS] *this edn; others Q*

Seize on him, villains! Oh, the furies!

DONUSA How! 85

Asambeg and Mustapha [exeunt to] descend.

Are we betrayed?

VITELLI The better – I expected
A Turkish faith.

DONUSA Who am I, that you dare this?
'Tis I that do command you to forbear
A touch of violence.

AGA We already, madam,
Have satisfied your pleasure further than 90
We know to answer it.

KAPIAGA Would we were well off!
We stand too far engaged, I fear.

DONUSA For us?
We'll bring you safe off. Who dares contradict
What is our pleasure?

Enter ASAMBEG [*and*] MUSTAPHA [*below*].

ASAMBEG Spurn the dog to prison!
[*to Donusa*] I'll answer you anon.

VITELLI What punishment 95
Soe'er I undergo, I am still a Christian.

Exeunt [some of the Guard] with VITELLI.

DONUSA

What bold presumption's this? Under what law
Am I to fall that set my foot upon

---

85 **villains** base, ignoble slaves (i.e. 'villeins'), but with the added suggestion of 'scoundrels'

87 **Turkish faith** regarded as an oxymoron, therefore 'treachery'

89–91 **We . . . answer it** 'We have already allowed you to indulge you desires more than we dare answer for (to the Sultan).'

91 **well off** well out of this

92 **too far engaged** too deeply involved
us Here, and elsewhere in the exchange that follows, Donusa deploys the royal plural as a haughty reminder of her rank.

---

85 SD] *this edn; after 84 SD Q exeunt to*] *this edn* 94 SD *below*] *this edn* 95 SD] *Vitkus* 96 SD *Exeunt . . . Guard*] *this edn; Exit Guard | Gifford; Ex. Q*

Your statutes and decrees?
MUSTAPHA   The crime committed
Our Alcoran calls death.
DONUSA   Tush! Who is here   100
That is not Amurath's slave – and so, unfit
To sit a judge upon his blood?
ASAMBEG   You have lost
And shamed the privilege of it, robbed me too
Of my soul, my understanding, to behold
Your base unworthy fall from your high virtue.   105
DONUSA
I do appeal to Amurath.
ASAMBEG   We will offer
No violence to your person till we know
His sacred pleasure – till when, under guard
You shall continue here.
DONUSA   Shall?
ASAMBEG   I have said it.
DONUSA
We shall remember this.   [*Other*] *Guards lead off Donusa.*
ASAMBEG   It ill becomes   110
Such as are guilty to deliver threats
Against the innocent. I could tear this flesh now,
But 'tis in vain; nor must I talk, but do.
Provide a well-manned galley for Constantinople.
Such sad news never came to our great master: 115

100 **Alcoran calls death** 'A Turke having had the use of a Christian woman, they are both condemned to die, unlesse she will abjure her faith; the like is observed betwixt a Christian and a Turkish woman, if they have bin found together' (Knolles, sig. 6B8ᵛ). **Alcoran** the Qur'an. The Muslim holy book had been accessible in Europe since Luther's sponsorship of a Latin translation as a way of countering the supposed 'lies and fables' of Islam in 1543.
103 **it her royal blood**
114 **Constantinople** (modern Istanbul) the seat of the Ottoman sultans, and former capital of the Byzantine Empire, captured by the Turks in 1453

101 Amurath's] *(Amurahs)*   106 Amurath] *(Amurah)*   110 SD] *Oxf*; *after 109 Q Other Guards lead*] *The Gard Leades Q*   114 well-manned] *MS ADD (*well man'd*)*; well made *Qa*; well mande *Qb*

As he directs, we must proceed, and know
No will but his, to whom what's ours we owe.   *Exeunt.*

4.1   *Enter* MASTER [*and*] BOATSWAIN.

MASTER

He does begin to eat?

BOATSWAIN   A little, master;

But our best hope for his recovery is that
His raving leaves him, and those dreadful words,
'Damnation' and 'despair', with which he ever
Ended all his discourses, are forgotten.   5

MASTER

This stranger is a most religious man, sure;
And I am doubtful whether his charity
In the relieving of our wants, or care
To cure the wounded conscience of Grimaldi
Deserves more admiration.

BOATSWAIN   Can you guess   10

What the reason should be that we never mention
The church or the high altar, but his melancholy
Grows and increases on him?

MASTER   I have heard him,

When he gloried to profess himself an atheist,

4.1 Location: Francisco's lodgings

4 'Damnation' and 'despair' The belief that one was damned and beyond salvation led to despair – itself, by the viciously circular logic of this doctrine, a mortal sin that would incur damnation.

7 charity In Massinger's time the word was not confined to the mere act of charitable giving, but still included its primary meaning of Christian love (*caritas*).

12 high altar the principal altar in a cathedral or church. In England,

high altars were removed during the Reformation and replaced by communion tables (no longer placed at the east end, but closer to the congregation); under Laud's arch-bishopric the tables were returned to the position of the high altars, though the 'table' nomenclature was still normally preferred.
melancholy depression

14 atheist The term did not necessarily imply systematic disbelief in a deity, but could be applied to any 'godless man' whose immorality constituted a

4.1] *(Actus Quartus, Scaena Prima.)*

Talk often, and with much delight and boasting   15
Of a rude prank he did ere he turned pirate –
The memory of which, as it appears,
Lies heavy on him.

BOATSWAIN   Pray you, let me understand it.

MASTER

Upon a solemn day when the whole city
Joined in devotion and with barefoot steps   20
Passed to St Mark's – the Duke and the whole
    Signory
Helping to perfect the religious pomp
With which they were received – when all men else
Were full of tears and groaned beneath the weight
Of past offences, of whose heavy burden   25
They came to be absolved and freed, our captain –
Whether in scorn of those so pious rites
He had no feeling of, or else drawn to it
Out of a wanton, irreligious madness,
I know not which – ran to the holy man   30

practical defiance of religion; nevertheless atheism, like blasphemy, was a serious offence; allegations of atheism against the dramatist Christopher Marlowe had resulted in the issue of a warrant for his arrest at the time of his death in 1593.

16 **rude** barbarous, violent (*OED a.* 3b, 5b)
  prank malicious or wicked trick (*OED n.*² a)
19 **solemn** devoted to religious rites and ceremonies (*OED n.* 1)
21 **St Mark's** See 2.5.79n.
  Duke i.e. the Doge (the elective head of state in the Venetian republic)
  Signory the *Signoria* or governing council of Venice
22–3 **Helping . . . received** 'serving by their mere presence to perfect

the elaborate ritual with which the church welcomed them' (thereby symbolizing an ideal alliance of ecclesiastical and political authority)
23–6 **when . . . freed** Massinger evidently has in mind the elaborate rites of public penitence still observed in some Catholic countries, especially during Easter Week.
30–3 **ran . . . pavement** In describing this outrage, and emphasizing the importance of the priest's *sacred vestments* (81), Massinger may have been remembering an episode described in Cervantes's *Los Baños*, where Ossorio describes a Mass performed at Algiers, in the course of which the Moors 'dragged the priest from the altar in his vestments, out of the place and through the streets'.

179

As he was doing of the work of grace,
And, snatching from his hands the sanctified means,
Dashed it upon the pavement.

BOATSWAIN   How escaped he –

It being a deed deserving death with torture?

MASTER

The general amazement of the people   35
Gave him leave to quit the temple, and a gondola –
Prepared, it seems, before – brought him aboard;
Since which he ne'er saw Venice. The remembrance
Of this, it seems, torments him – aggravated
With a strong belief he cannot receive pardon   40
For this foul fact but from his hands against whom
It was committed.

BOATSWAIN   And what course intends

His heavenly physician, reverend Francisco,
To beat down this opinion?

MASTER   He promised

To use some holy and religious finesse   45

---

31 **work of grace** sacrament of the Mass
(the instrument of divine grace which
mystically repeats Christ's sacrifice on
behalf of all sinners). Jane Degenhardt
argues that '[t]he particular moment
in the mass that Grimaldi chooses to
disrupt is the very moment of incarna-
tion, when God is embodied and body
and soul are joined' – the moment,
that is to say, of transubstantiation, in
which wine becomes the sacred blood
of Christ and bread his flesh, a moment
of mystical metamorphosis or 'turning'
(82).
32 **sanctified means** i.e. the sacramental bread and wine (the 'means of
grace' in theological discourse). From
a Catholic perspective, the doctrine
of transubstantiation implies that, in
dashing the chalice from the priest's

hand, Grimaldi literally spilled the
blood of Christ, thereby re-enacting
the blasphemy of Crucifixion.
sanctified sanctifièd
35 **amazement** stronger than now –
'stupefaction, bewilderment, consternation' (*OED n.* 1–3)
36 **gondola** light, flat-bottomed boat
used on Venetian canals
39 **aggravated** made more grievous and
burdensome (*OED v.* 6a)
41 **fact** crime (*OED n.* 1c)
from his hands The colloquial
expression is given a literal appro-
priateness by virtue of the fact that a
priest's sanctified hands are the con-
duits of divine grace.
43 **heavenly physician** spiritual healer
45 **religious** scanned as four syllables
finesse cunning stratagem (*OED n.* 7)

---

31 doing of] *Coxeter;* of doing *Q;* doing *Rawl.*

To this good end, and in the meantime charged me
To keep him dark and to admit no visitants –
But on no terms to cross him. Here he comes.

Enter GRIMALDI *with a book.*

GRIMALDI [*to himself*]
    For theft: he that restores treble the value
    Makes satisfaction; and, for want of means   50
    To do so, as a slave must serve it out
    Till he hath made full payment. There's hope left here.
    Oh, with what willingness would I give up
    My liberty to those that I have pillaged,
    And wish the numbers of my years, though wasted   55
    In the most sordid slavery, might equal
    The rapines I have made, till with one voice
    My patient sufferings might exact from my
    Most cruel creditors a full remission:
    An eye's loss with an eye, limb's with a limb –   60
    A sad account! Yet to find peace within here,
    Though all such as I have maimed and dismembered
    In drunken quarrels, or o'ercome with rage
    When they were given up to my power, stood here now
    And cried for restitution, to appease 'em   65
    I would do a bloody justice on myself,
    Pull out these eyes that guided me to ravish
    Their sight from others, lop these legs that bore me
    To barbarous violence, with this hand cut off

47 dark in the dark (i.e. ignorant of what we are planning)

48 SD *book* The Q SD is unspecific, to avoid censorship, but Grimaldi's ensuing soliloquy makes it plain that he is poring over the scriptures.

49–52 he . . . payment a paraphrase of Exodus, 22.1–3: 'If a man shall steal an ox or a sheep . . . he shall restore five oxen for an ox, and four sheep for a sheep . . . if he have nothing, then he shall be sold for his theft.'

57 rapines plunder, pillage

60 paraphrasing Exodus, 21.24: 'Eye for eye . . . hand for hand, foot for foot'

61 sad account heavy reckoning

49 SD] *this edn*

This instrument of wrong, till nought were left me 70
But this poor bleeding limbless trunk, which gladly
I would divide among them.

Enter FRANCISCO *in a cope like a bishop.*

Ha! What think I
Of petty forfeitures? In this reverend habit –
All that I am turned into eyes – I look on

---

70 **instrument of wrong** Grimaldi may intend sacrificing his own hand like the Roman hero Scaevola, or the Protestant martyr Cranmer (who on the execution pyre is said to have deliberately held the hand that had signed his recantation in the rising flames, so that it would be burned first); but a train of association in this speech (*rapines . . . ravish . . . legs . . . rapes*, 57–77), supported by the wider context of castration-anxiety typical of plays dealing with the Islamic world, suggests that it is self-castration he has in mind.

72 SD *It is evident that Grimaldi (and the audience) are meant to see Francisco at this point; but Q's placement of his entry may imply that he is first revealed standing in the discovery space and that he only steps forward at 80 when he begins to speak. Such a self-consciously theatrical tableau would be appropriate to the *finesse* which the Master has promised (45).
cope 'A vestment of silk or other material resembling a long cloak made of a semicircular piece of cloth, worn by ecclesiastics in processions, also at Vespers, and on some other occasions' (*OED n.* 2). The Anglican *Constitution and Canons Ecclesiastical* of 1603 had stipulated that 'Copes . . . be worn in Cathedral churches by those that administer the Communion' (no. 24); but many Protestants regarded such vestments as popish, and when King James sent two of his chaplains to Madrid in 1623 to persuade the Spanish of how much the Churches of England and Rome had in common, he felt bound to specify the use of 'surplices, copes, candlesticks, chalices, and patens' so that their services should appear 'as near the Roman form as can lawfully be done' (Patterson, 323–4); for further discussion of the controversy over vestments, see Collinson, 71–83, 92–7.
like a bishop Editors have puzzled over this detail, which has been taken to show Massinger's ignorance of Catholic practice, since Jesuits did not normally become bishops. However, the SD is probably meant only to instruct the company to dress Francisco in the most splendid liturgical costume they can produce: the sartorial display emphasizes that the ensuing action is designed as a piece of therapeutic play-acting on Francisco's part which (in a fashion reminiscent of some key episodes in *Roman Actor*) gives Grimaldi the opportunity to undo his original blasphemy. Francisco's reference to *these sacred vestments* (81) makes it plain that he is dressed in the same robes that he wore on the occasion of Grimaldi's assault in St Mark's.

73 **petty forfeitures** trivial penalties
habit priestly vestments (*OED n.* 2a)

74 **All . . . am** my entire being is

72 SD] *Coxeter; after* kneele to't *80 Q*

A deed of mine so fiendlike that repentance –   75
Though with my tears I taught the sea new tides –
Can never wash off. All my thefts, my rapes,
Are venial trespasses compared to what
I offered to that shape – and in a place, too,
Where I stood bound to kneel to't.   (*Kneels.*)
FRANCISCO   'Tis forgiven.   80
I – with his tongue whom, in these sacred vestments,
With impure hands thou didst offend – pronounce it.
I bring peace to thee: see that thou deserve it
In thy fair life hereafter.
GRIMALDI   Can it be?
Dare I believe this vision, or hope   85
A pardon e'er may find me?
FRANCISCO   Purchase it
By zealous undertakings and no more
'Twill be remembered.
GRIMALDI   What celestial balm
I feel now poured into my wounded conscience!
What penance is there I'll not undergo –   90
Though ne'er so sharp and rugged – with more
    pleasure

---

80 SD Grimaldi's gesture repeats Donusa's at 3.5.71; each marks a moment of confession (cf. 3.5.84), one signalling the first stage in the conversion of a Mahometan princess to Christianity, the other confirming the return of a renegade to the Church.

81–2 **with . . . offend** Although the wording here is ambiguous, Francisco's speech at 1.1.110–11 establishes that he himself was the priest whom the renegade offended. Grimaldi's failure to recognize Francisco at 3.2.73–5 is presumably a result of his distraction, but it underlines the theatrical magic of the Jesuit's change of costume and the transformatory drama of the 'vision' it produces (85).

81 **his tongue** Francisco's own tongue – but perhaps also referring to the enunciation of Christ's words in the Mass, since it was ultimately against Christ (and therefore God himself) that Grimaldi's blasphemous offence was committed

82 **impure hands** symbolically contrasted with the sanctified hands of the priest (cf. 41)

85 **vision** three syllables here

87–8 **no . . . remembered** i.e. his offence will be forgotten

88 **celestial balm** Soothing balms were an important part of the early modern pharmacopoeia, but the term also recalls the balm used in sacramental rituals of anointing.

Than flesh and blood e'er tasted? Show me true
   Sorrow,
Armed with an iron whip, and I will meet
The stripes she brings along with her as if
They were the gentle touches of a hand   95
That comes to cure me. Can good deeds redeem me?
I will rise up a wonder to the world,
When I have given strong proofs how I am altered:
I, that have sold such as professed the faith
That I was born in to captivity,   100
Will make their number equal that I shall
Deliver from the oar, and win as many,
By the clearness of my actions, to look on
Their misbelief and loathe it. I will be
A convoy for all merchants, and thought worthy   105
To be reported to the world hereafter
The child of your devotion, nursed up
And made strong by your charity to break through
All dangers hell can bring forth to oppose me.
Nor am I – though my fortunes were thought
   desperate –   110
Now you have reconciled me to myself,
So void of worldly means but, in despite
Of the proud Viceroy's wrongs, I can do something
To witness my good change. When you please, try me,

95–6 **gentle . . . cure me** See 41n. to *from his hands*; 82n.
96 **Can . . . me** a further reference to the contentious doctrine of salvation by works (see 1.1.23n.)
102 **the oar** i.e. enslavement in the Turkish galleys
103 **clearness** purity, innocence
105 **convoy** guide and escort
108 **charity** Christian love (see 7n.)

110 **desperate** extremely dangerous, beyond rescue (*OED a.* 2, 3); characterized by the recklessness of despair (*OED a.* 5)
114 ***To . . . change** The corrected Q reading ('prooue that I haue power') involves an even more substantive change than Massinger's later MS revision, indicating that the dramatist himself must have been involved

113 Viceroy's wrongs,] *Coxeter;* Viceroyes, wrongs *Q;* Vice-roys wrongs *Rawl.* 114 witness . . . change] *MS ADD;* witnesse of my change *Qa;* prooue that I haue power *Qb;* wittness my change *Rawl.*

And I will perfect what you shall enjoin me   115
Or fall a joyful martyr.

FRANCISCO   You will reap
The comfort of it. Live yet undiscovered,
And with your holy meditations strengthen
Your Christian resolution. Ere long
You shall hear further from me.

GRIMALDI   I'll attend   120
All your commands with patience.   *Exit Francisco.*

                                 Come, my mates,
I hitherto have lived an ill example
And, as your captain, led you on to mischief,
But now will truly labour that good men
May say hereafter of me to my glory –   125
Let but my power and means hand with my will –
His good endeavours did weigh down his ill.

                    Exeunt Grimaldi, Master [and] Boatswain.

                    Enter FRANCISCO *[in his usual attire].*

FRANCISCO

This penitence is not counterfeit. Howsoever
Good actions are in themselves rewarded,

---

in the process of printing-house
correction. Arguably the earlier
revision, by turning penitence into
a form of self-assertion, is more
consistent with Grimaldi's turbulent
personality.
115 **perfect** bring to completion, consummate (*OED n.* 1a)
117 **undiscovered** either 'in hiding',
or 'with the fact of your repentance
concealed'
126 **Let but** provided that

hand go hand in hand, concur (*OED
v.* 6)
128 **not counterfeit** i.e. unlike
Francisco's own performance that
induced it. Francisco's virtuous counterfeiting parallels Vitelli's rather more
ambiguous role-playing in his merchant guise.
129 proverbial (cf. Tilley, B81: 'Virtue is
its own reward', and *Duke of Milan*,
2.1.251–2), but again referring to justification by works

121 SD] *this edn; after 120 Q* 126 means hand] *Q (*meanes, hande*);* meanes stand *(conj.
McIlwraith)* 127 SD2 *in . . . attire*] *Vitkus* 128 counterfeit. Howsoever] *this edn;* counterfeit, how-
soeuer *Q;* counterfeit: howsoever, *Vitkus* 129 rewarded,] *this edn;* rewarded. *Q*

My travail's to meet with a double crown,   130
If that Vitelli come off safe and prove
Himself the master of his wild affections.

Enter GAZET.

Oh, I shall have intelligence: how now, Gazet?
Why these sad looks and tears?
GAZET   Tears, sir? I have lost
My worthy master. Your rich heir seems to mourn for   135
A miserable father, your young widow,
Following a bed-rid husband to his grave,
Would have her neighbours think she cries and roars
That she must part with such a Goodman Do-Nothing,
When 'tis because he stays so long above ground   140
And hinders a rich suitor. All is come out, sir:
We are smoked for being coney-catchers; my master
Is put in prison, his she-customer
Is under guard too – these are things to weep for.
But mine own loss considered, and what a fortune   145
I have, as they say, snatched out of my chops

---

130 'my labours will be crowned with twofold success', i.e. the salvation of both Grimaldi and Vitelli
131 **If that** if
133 **intelligence** information, news – perhaps punning on Gazet's name (*gazzette* = news-sheet)
135 **seems to mourn** gives the (false) impression of mourning
136–41 **your . . . suitor** The hypocrisy of young widows (especially those once married to older husbands) is a standard satiric motif, going back at least to the *Wife of Bath's Prologue* in Chaucer's *Canterbury Tales* (587–92); cf. *Picture*, 2.1.12–17.
139 **Goodman Do-Nothing** mocking

sobriquet for an impotent husband
142 **smoked** suspected (*OED v.* 8a); exposed (*OED v.* 6b)
coney-catchers swindlers, con-men (slang – literally 'rabbit-catchers'). The Q spelling 'cunnicatchers' points up the indecent pun: 'coney' could be used as an affectionate or (by association with 'cunny' = cunt) a contemptuous term for a woman.
143 **she-customer** whore (*OED* customer *n.* 4b); but also playing on the familiar commercial sense of the word, since Donusa first appeared to Vitelli and Gazet as a customer at their shop
146 'I have had snatched, as they say, out of my very jaws'

130 travail's] *Coxeter;* travailes *Q* 146 have . . . snatched] *Q;* have had . . . snatch'd *Mason;* haue . . . had snatched *(conj. McIlwraith)*

Would make a man run mad.

FRANCISCO   I scarce have leisure –

I am so wholly taken up with sorrow

For my loved pupil – to inquire thy fate;

Yet I will hear it.

GAZET   Why, sir, I had bought a place –   150

A place of credit, too – and had gone through with it.

I should have been made an eunuch – there was honour

For a late poor prentice! – when upon the sudden

There was such a hurly-burly in the court

That I was glad to run away and carry   155

The price of my office with me.

FRANCISCO   Is that all?

You have made a saving voyage! We must think now,

Though not to free, to comfort sad Vitelli.

My grieved soul suffers for him.

GAZET   I am sad, too.   159

But had I been an eunuch –

FRANCISCO   Think not on it.   *Exeunt.*

4.2   *Enter* ASAMBEG [*, who*] *unlocks the door* [*and*]
                              leads forth PAULINA.

ASAMBEG

Be your own guard: obsequiousness and service

151–6 Although he speaks of his determination to 'go through with' his plan to become an eunuch, and of being 'glad to run away', it is still unclear to what extent (if any) Gazet has any inkling of what it means to be an eunuch (see 3.4.42n.).

153 a . . . prentice someone who was until recently only a poor apprentice

156 price Gazet probably means only the bribe he expected to pay for his splendid position, but, even if he is unaware

of it, the audience will know that the real price was to be the surrender of his private parts.

157 saving thrifty; delivering yourself from hurt

158 'although not to free the wretched Vitelli, at least to bring him spiritual comfort'

4.2 Location: Asambeg's chamber in the palace

1 obsequiousness See 1.2.81n.

4.2] *(Actus Quartus, Scaena Secunda.)*

Shall win you to be mine. Of all restraint
Forever take your leave: no threats shall awe you,
No jealous doubts of mine disturb your freedom,
No fee'd spies wait upon your steps. Your virtue,   5
And due consideration in yourself
Of what is noble, are the faithful helps
I leave you as supporters to defend you
From falling basely.

PAULINA   This is wondrous strange.
Whence flows this alteration?

ASAMBEG   From true judgement   10
And strong assurance: neither grates of iron
Hemmed in with walls of brass, strict guards, high
    birth,
The forfeiture of honour nor the fear
Of infamy or punishment can stay
A woman, slave to appetite, from being   15
False and unworthy.

PAULINA   You are grown satirical
Against our sex. Why, sir, I durst produce
Myself in our defence, and from you challenge
A testimony not to be denied:
All fall not under this unequal censure.   20

---

10 **alteration** Paulina may wonder if Asambeg's sudden generosity is a first step to the more significant change of conversion.

11 **grates** prisons or cages (*OED n.* 6); cf. 3.5.10.

11–12 **iron ... brass** These metals are linked in numerous scriptural passages as metonyms for durability; see e.g. Numbers, 31.22: 'brass and iron which may abide the fire'. The figure *walls of brass* occurs several times in the Massinger canon: see *Bashful Lover* ('Innocence is a wall of Brasse', 5.1.18); and *Double Marriage* ('Walls of Brasse resist not / A noble undertaking',

1.1.135–6), and *Lawyer* ('compass'd with walls of brasse', 4.7.43). See also *Faustus* ('wall all Germany with brass', 1.1.86), *Jew of Malta* ('countermin'd with walls of brasse', 1.2.381) and *JC* ('Nor stony tower, nor walls of beaten brass, / Nor airless dungeon, nor strong links of iron, / Can be retentive to the strength of spirit', 1.3.93–5).

16–17 **satirical ... sex** Paulina correctly identifies Asambeg's sneer with the standard tropes of contemporary misogynist satire.

18 **challenge** demand, lay claim to (*OED v.* 5)

20 **unequal** biased

I, that have stood your flatteries, your threats,
Bore up against your fierce temptations, scorned
The cruel means you practised to supplant me –
Having no arms to help me to hold out
But love of piety and constant goodness –   25
If you are unconfirmed, dare again boldly
Enter into the lists and combat with
All opposites man's malice can bring forth
To shake me in my chastity, built upon
The rock of my religion.

ASAMBEG   I do wish   30
I could believe you, but when I shall show you
A most incredible example of
Your frailty in a princess sued and sought to
By men of worth, of rank, of eminence, courted
By happiness itself, and her cold temper   35
Approved by many years – yet she to fall,
Fall from herself, her glories, nay, her safety,
Into a gulf of shame and black despair –
I think you'll doubt yourself, or in beholding
Her punishment forever be deterred   40
From yielding basely.

PAULINA   I would see this wonder –
'Tis, sir, my first petition.

23 **supplant me** bring about my moral downfall (*OED v.* 2)
24 **arms** both armour and weaponry (*OED n.* 1, 2)
26 **unconfirmed** unconvinced
   dare The subject is still *I* (21).
28 **opposites** adversaries
30 **rock . . . religion** Cf. Matthew, 16.18: 'thou art Peter, and upon this rock I will build my church; and the gates of hell shall not prevail against it' – an important text for the Roman Catholic Church, since the popes derived their

authority from St Peter as the first bishop of Rome.
33 **Your frailty** i.e. the moral weakness and susceptibility of women in general
35 **happiness** good fortune (inverts the usual figure of the goddess Fortune courted by ambitious mortals)
   cold temper chaste temperament
36 **Approved** demonstrated
38 **shame . . . despair**   Asambeg's description of Donusa makes her condition resemble Grimaldi's.

25 goodness –] *this edn;* goodnesse. *Q*   37 safety,] *MS ADD (*safetie*);* safet, *Q*

189

ASAMBEG   And thus granted:
Above, you shall observe all.
          Exit Paulina [, who then re-enters on the gallery above].

          Enter MUSTAPHA.

MUSTAPHA   Sir, I sought you
And must relate a wonder: since I studied
And knew what man was, I was never witness   45
Of such invincible fortitude as this Christian
Shows in his sufferings; all the torments that
We could present him with to fright his constancy
Confirmed, not shook it; and those heavy chains
That eat into his flesh appeared to him   50
Like bracelets made of some loved mistress' hairs
We kiss in the remembrance of her favours.
I am strangely taken with it, and have lost
Much of my fury.
ASAMBEG   Had he suffered poorly
It had called on my contempt; but manly patience   55
And all-commanding virtue wins upon
An enemy. I shall think upon him.

          Enter AGA *with a black box.*

          Ha!
So soon returned? This speed pleads in excuse

---

43 SD1 **re-enters . . . above* The Q SD
('*Paul. steps aside*') is difficult to recon-
cile with the implied stage direction in
Asambeg's words *Above* and *Descend*
(43, 185). John Jowett (private communication) plausibly suggests that a
change of intention about the staging
of the scene may have been involved,
and that the abruptness of Asambeg's
commands indicates that they may have

been tacked on once it was decided that
it was preferable to have Paulina observe
the remainder of the scene from above
– perhaps in a deliberate recollection of
Asambeg's and Mustapha's eavesdrop-
ping from this position in 3.5.68ff.
51–2 For this practice see e.g. Donne's
Elegy 11, 'The Bracelet'.
55 **called on** invoked, demanded (*OED v.*
23)

43 SD1] *this edn; Paul. steps aside Q*   57 SD] *after* Ha!

Of your late fault, which I no more remember.
What's the Grand Signor's pleasure?

AGA   'Tis enclosed here.   60
The box, too, that contains it may inform you
How he stands affected. I am trusted with
Nothing but this: on forfeit of your head,
She must have a speedy trial.

ASAMBEG   Bring her in
In black as to her funeral –   [*Exit Aga.*]
                                    'tis the colour   65
Her fault wills her to wear, and which in justice
I dare not pity. Sit, and take your place.
However in her life she has degenerated,
May she die nobly, and in that confirm
Her greatness and high blood.

A solemn music. [Enter GUARDS,] *the* AGA *and*
KAPIAGA, *leading in* DONUSA *in black, her train*
borne up by CARAZIE *and* MANTO.

MUSTAPHA [*aside*]   I now could melt –   70

---

60 **Grand Signor** the Ottoman sultan or 'Great Turk'
61–2 **The box . . . affected** Cf. Biddulph (sig. N4ᵛ): 'if some great Vizier or Bashawe . . . fall into [the Sultan's] disfavour, if he send but a *Cappagie*, that is a Pursevant to him with his writing, with a black seale in a blacke box, none of them all dare withstand him, but suffer this base Cappagie to strangle him.' An ironic visual recollection of Donusa's casket of jewels is inevitable, and some playgoers might have recalled the scene in *Spanish Tragedy* where Pedringano's execution is ensured by the empty box that supposedly contains his pardon.

62 **affected** inclined (*OED ppl.a.* II 1)
65 **black** According to Biddulph, the denizens of Mahomet's paradise '*shall be clothed with all sorts of colours except blacke.* And therefore the *Turkes* to this day weare no blacke; but when they see a man clothed in blacke, many of them will go backe, and say they will fly from him who shall never enter into Paradise' (sig. L1ʳ); see also Lithgow: 'All *Turkes* do detest the colour of blacke, and thinke that those that weare it, shall never enter into Paradise' (sig. I1ʳ).
68 **degenerated** lost the virtues proper to her own 'race' or kind (*genus*)

65 SD] *Vitkus*   70.1 *Enter* GUARDS] *this edn; A Guard. Q*   SD2] *this edn*

But soft compassion leave me!

MANTO [*aside*]   I am affrighted
With this dismal preparation. Should the enjoying
Of loose desires find ever such conclusions,
All women would be vestals.

DONUSA   That you clothe me
In this sad livery of death assures me   75
Your sentence is gone out before, and I
Too late am called for in my guilty cause
To use qualification or excuse –
Yet must I not part so with mine own strengths,
But borrow from my modesty boldness to   80
Inquire by whose authority you sit
My judges, and whose warrant digs my grave
In the frowns you dart against my life?

ASAMBEG   See here
This fatal sign and warrant!   [*Points to the box.*]
                    This, brought to
A general fighting in the head of his   85
Victorious troops, ravishes from his hand
His even then conquering sword; this, shown unto
The Sultan's brothers, or his sons, delivers
His deadly anger, and, all hopes laid by,
Commands them to prepare themselves for heaven –   90
Which would stand with the quiet of your soul

---

72 **dismal** sinister, ill-omened (*OED a.* 2)
73 **find . . . conclusions** always come to such ends
74 **vestals** virgins (after the seven vestal virgins, priestesses who tended the temple of the city's tutelary goddess, Vesta, in ancient Rome)
75 **livery of death** i.e. the black costume specified in 70 SD; but, in a play much concerned with various kinds of 'service', *livery* is carefully chosen

to suggest the humiliating subjection that the princess experiences in her punishment.
76 **is . . . before** has already been pronounced
78 **qualification** mitigating circumstance (five syllables, stress on second and fourth)
85 **in** at
86 **ravishes** snatches (*OED v.* 4)
91 **stand** accord (*OED v.* 79e)

71 SP] *Coxeter; Fran. Q* 71 SD] *this edn* 84 SD] *this edn*

To think upon and imitate.

DONUSA   Give me leave

A little to complain: first, of the hard
Condition of my fortune, which may move you –
Though not to rise up intercessors for me,   95
Yet in remembrance of my former life,
This being the first spot tainting mine honour –
To be the means to bring me to his presence;
And then I doubt not but I could allege
Such reasons in mine own defence, or plead   100
So humbly – my tears helping – that it should
Awake his sleeping pity.

ASAMBEG   'Tis in vain.

If you have aught to say, you shall have hearing;
And in me think him present.

DONUSA   I would thus then

First kneel and kiss his feet, and after tell him   105
How long I had been his darling, what delight
My infant years afforded him, how dear
He prized his sister in both bloods, my mother –
That she, like him, had frailty that to me
Descends as an inheritance; then conjure him   110
By her blessed ashes and his father's soul,
The sword that rides upon his thigh, his right hand
Holding the sceptre and the Ottoman fortune,
To have compassion on me.

ASAMBEG   But suppose –

As I am sure – he would be deaf: what then   115

92–3 **Give . . . complain** The formality of Donusa's phrasing identifies her speech with the poetic genre of female 'complaint'; see e.g. Kerrigan.

97 **spot** blemish

104 **in . . . present** consider his authority to be embodied in me

105 **kneel . . . feet** an implied stage direction

108 **both bloods** Oxf glosses 'in line of descent, and in inherited sensuality (a common sense of "blood")'; but Donusa surely means that her mother was the Sultan's full sister (rather than one of the numerous half-siblings produced by other wives and concubines).

112 'By' is understood before *The sword* and *his right hand*.

Could you infer?

DONUSA   I then would thus rise up
And to his teeth tell him he was a tyrant,
A most voluptuous and insatiable epicure
In his own pleasures, which he hugs so dearly,
As proper and peculiar to himself,   120
That he denies a moderate lawful use
Of all delight to others. And to thee,
Unequal judge, I speak as much, and charge thee
But with impartial eyes to look into
Thyself, and then consider with what justice   125
Thou canst pronounce my sentence. Unkind nature,
To make weak women servants, proud men masters!
Indulgent Mahomet, do thy bloody laws
Call my embraces with a Christian, death –
Having my heat and May of youth to plead   130
In my excuse – and yet want power to punish
These that with scorn break through thy cobweb edicts
And laugh at thy decrees? To tame their lusts

116 **infer** allege (*OED v.* 2); bring about, make happen (*OED v.* 1)

118–19 **most . . . pleasures** Prurient speculation about the harem led English commentators to repeated tirades against the supposed licentiousness of the Turkish sultan and his subjects.

118 **epicure** one devoted to sensual pleasure, a voluptuary; deriving from a vulgarized notion of the teachings of the Greek philosopher Epicurus (341–270 BC)

120 'as his exclusive personal property'

123 **Unequal** unjust, biased (cf. 20)

126 **Unkind** unnatural, ungenerous, wicked; Donusa's oxymoron implicitly challenges the dispensation that appears to make *weak women* 'naturally' inferior to men.

127 **women . . . masters** English domestic theory repeatedly analogized the subordinate position of women

to that of servants. The defiant way in which Donusa points out the contrast between the liberties allowed to men and the fierce restraints imposed on women is probably calculated to appeal to the increasingly influential female audience in Jacobean theatres. However, the potential subversiveness of Donusa's protest is at least partially defused by its association with the *bloody laws* of *Indulgent Mahomet* (128).

130 **heat** According to contemporary humoral theory, young people were naturally hotter in blood and 'complexion' – hence their greater susceptibility to desire.

131 **want** lack

132 **cobweb** i.e. designed to entrap, but ultimately feeble

133–4 **To . . . bit** i.e. their religion offers nothing strong enough to restrain their desires in the way that a bit can

There's no religious bit: let her be fair
And pleasing to the eye, though Persian, Moor,   135
Idolatress, Turk or Christian, you are privileged
And freely may enjoy her. At this instant
I know, unjust man, thou hast in thy power
A lovely Christian virgin: thy offence
Equal, if not transcending, mine, why then –   140
We being both guilty – dost thou not descend
From that usurped tribunal and with me
Walk hand in hand to death?

ASAMBEG   She raves, and we
Lose time to hear her: read the law.

DONUSA   Do, do!
I stand resolved to suffer.   145

AGA [*Takes a paper from the box and reads.*] *If any virgin of*
what degree or quality soever, born a natural Turk, shall
be convicted of corporal looseness and incontinence with
any Christian, she is by the decree of our great prophet
Mahomet to lose her head –   150

ASAMBEG
Mark that – then tax our justice!

AGA *– ever provided that if she, the said offender, by any*
reasons, arguments or persuasion, can win and prevail with
the said Christian offending with her to alter his religion

tame a wild horse. Horses (especially stallions) were familiar emblems of untrammelled passion and desire; see e.g. *Oth*, 1.1.109–10 ('you'll have your daughter covered with a Barbary horse'), and Veronese's painting *Mars and Venus United by Love* (Metropolitan Museum, New York).

135–6 **Persian . . . Christian** The sultans notoriously filled their harems with wives and concubines drawn from all quarters of their empire, as well as from neighbouring states, such as Persia, and from among the captives

brought back by corsairs and Ottoman troops.

142 **usurped** wrongfully appropriated (since Donusa has denied the authority of both Asambeg and his tyrannical master, the Sultan, to judge her)

144 **to hear her** by listening to her plea

151 **tax** disparage (the sense is 'if you dare')

152–7 *if . . . whatsoever* Cf. Sandys (sig. F4ᵛ): 'they hold it a great grace, and an act of singular pietie, to draw many to their Religion; presenting them with money, change of rayments, and free-

and marry her, that then the winning of a soul to the 155
Mahometan sect shall acquit her from all shame, disgrace
and punishment whatsoever.

DONUSA

    I lay hold on that clause and challenge from you
    The privilege of the law.

MUSTAPHA   What will you do?

DONUSA

    Grant me access and means, I'll undertake 160
    To turn this Christian Turk and marry him.
    This trial you cannot deny.

MUSTAPHA   Oh, base!

    Can fear to die make you descend so low
    From your high birth, and brand the Ottoman line
    With such a mark of infamy?

ASAMBEG   This is worse 165
    Than the parting with your honour! Better suffer
    Ten thousand deaths, and without hope to have
    A place in our great Prophet's paradise,
    Than have an act to after-times remembered
    So foul as this is.

MUSTAPHA   Cheer your spirits, madam: 170
    To die is nothing, 'tis but parting with
    A mountain of vexations.

ASAMBEG   Think of your honour:
    In dying nobly you make satisfaction
    For your offence, and you shall live a story
    Of bold heroic courage.

DONUSA   You shall not fool me 175
    Out of my life: I claim the law and sue for

ing them from all tributes and taxes.
Insomuch that if a Christian have
deserved death by their law, if he will
convert, they will many times remit his
punishment.'

156 *sect* faith, religion (*OED n.* 4)

168 **our . . . paradise** Given that
'Mahomet's paradise' was a byword
for male sensual indulgence (see
2.5.21n., and cf. Donne, *Elegy* 19, 21),
this has a certain irony when directed
at Donusa.

A speedy trial. If I fail, you may
Determine of me as you please.

ASAMBEG   Base woman!
But use thy ways, and see thou prosper in 'em;
For, if thou fall again into my power,   180
Thou shalt in vain, after a thousand tortures,
Cry out for death – that death which now thou fliest
    from.
Unloose the prisoner's chains! Go, lead her on
To try the magic of her tongue – I follow.

> [*Exeunt Mustapha, Aga and Kapiaga, followed by
> Donusa, Manto, Carazie and Guards.*]

[*aside*] I am on the rack. – Descend, my best Paulina.   185

> [*Exeunt Paulina from above and Asambeg from below.*]

4.3   *Enter* FRANCISCO [*and*] GAOLER.

FRANCISCO

I come not empty-handed: I will purchase
Your favour at what rate you please. There's gold.

> [*Gives Gaoler gold.*]

GAOLER

'Tis the best oratory. I will hazard

---

178 **Determine of** pass sentence on
(*OED n.* 5) – perhaps with the additional implication of 'terminate'
184 **try** suggesting both that Donusa herself will test the magic of her tongue,
and that they in turn will subject its
efficacy to trial and judgement
magic . . . tongue The metaphor
takes on an additional charge from
the implicit contrast with the true
sacramental 'magic' of Christianity,
most conspicuously represented by
Francisco's sacred cope, by Paulina's
relic and, above all, by the baptismal water with which Vitelli per-

fects Donusa's transformation (see
5.3.123–33).
184, 185 SDD *Q's failure to print exit
directions here does not seem to have
been caused by compositorial difficulties (such as poor casting-off), and
presumably represents a careless omis-
sion in the manuscript.
185 **I am . . . rack** perhaps implying
that Donusa's gibes about Mahometan
double standards for men and women
(128–43) have hit home
4.3 Location: a prison
3 **oratory** eloquence (but perhaps playing on *oratory* = place of prayer)

184 SD] *this edn*   185 SD1] *this edn*   SD2] *this edn; Exeunt | Coxeter*   **4.3**] *(Actus Quartus. Scaena
Tertia)*   2 SD] *this edn*

A check for your content.   [*Opens the trapdoor.*]
                              Below there!
VITELLI (*under the stage*)   Welcome.
   Art thou the happy messenger that brings me   5
   News of my death?   [*Vitelli's head appears.*]
GAOLER   Your hand.

      VITELLI [*is*] *plucked up* [*by the Gaoler*].

FRANCISCO   Now, if you please,
   A little privacy.
GAOLER   You have bought it, sir:
   Enjoy it freely.   *Exit.*
FRANCISCO   O my dearest pupil,
   Witness these tears of joy, I never saw you
   Till now look lovely, nor durst I e'er glory   10
   In the mind of any man I had built up
   With the hands of virtuous and religious precepts
   Till this glad minute. Now you have made good
   My expectation of you. By my order,
   All Roman Caesars that led kings in chains   15
   Fast bound to their triumphant chariots, if
   Compared with that true glory and full lustre
   You now appear in, all their boasted honours,

3–4 **hazard / A check** risk a reprimand

4 SD Early modern stages were equipped with a trapdoor, and the area beneath the stage often represented hell, but could also be used, as here, to represent a prison.

5 **happy messenger** bearer of fortunate news

6 SD1 *The likelihood that the Rawlinson MS preserves the original stage business is increased by the episode in *Island Princess*, 2.1.34.1, where the similarly imprisoned King of Tidore '*appeares loden with chaines; his head, arms only above*'.

14 **By my order** Francisco swears by the Jesuit order.

15–16 **All . . . chariots** echoing *1 Tamburlaine*, whose oriental hero not only forces captive kings to draw his chariot, but threatens to 'triumph over all the world' and boasts of holding 'the Fates fast bound in iron chains' (1.2.173–4). Cf. also *Maid of Honour*, 4.4.3–5.

---

4 content. Below there!] *Coxeter subst.;* content below there? *Q*   SD1] *this edn*   SD2] *Vitkus; Vitelli under the Stage | after* Welcome. *Q*   6 SD1] *Rawl.*   SD2] *this edn; Vitelli pluck'd up Qb; Vitelli plack'd up Qa; Vitelli is plucked up | Vitkus*   8 SD] *(Exit Gaoler)*

Purchased with blood and wrong, would lose their
   names
And be no more remembered!

VITELLI   This applause   20
Confirmed in your allowance joys me more
Than if a thousand full-crammed theatres
Should clap their eager hands to witness that
The scene I act did please and they admire it.
But these are, father, but beginnings, not   25
The ends of my high aims. I grant to have mastered
The rebel appetite of flesh and blood
Was far above my strength, and still owe for it
To that great power that lent it. But when I
Shall make't apparent the grim looks of Death   30
Affright me not, and that I can put off
The fond desire of life that like a garment
Covers and clothes our frailty, hastening to
My martyrdom as to a heavenly banquet
To which I was a choice invited guest,   35
Then you may boldly say you did not plough
Or trust the barren and ungrateful sands
With the fruitful grain of your religious counsels.

FRANCISCO

You do instruct your teacher. Let the sun
Of your clear life, that lends to good men light,   40

20–4 **This . . . admire it** Vitelli's characterization of his impending martyrdom extends the metatheatrical theme opened by Francisco's virtuous 'counterfeiting' in 4.1.

21 **allowance** applause, praise (*OED n.* 1) – the usual term for the approval of a theatre audience

28–9 **owe . . . lent it** 'am indebted to God who lent me the strength of will (to master my fleshly desires)'

30 **grim . . . Death** Death is allegorized here, like one of the cadaverous summoners in the graphic tradition derived from medieval art.

32 **fond** foolish, infatuated

34 In contrast to denunciations of the sensual indulgence (including banqueting) routinely associated with 'Mahomet's paradise', this traditional image dresses martyrdom in the sacramental language of the communion feast.

36–8 Vitelli draws on Christ's parable of the sower as an allegory for the dissemination of religious truth (see Matthew, 13.3–8, Luke, 8.4–8).

But set as gloriously as it did rise –
Though sometimes clouded – you may write *nil ultra*
To human wishes.

VITELLI   I have almost gained
The end of the race, and will not faint or tire now.

Enter AGA *and* GAOLER.

AGA

Sir, by your leave – [*to Francisco*] Nay, stay not –
    [*to Vitelli*]   I bring comfort: 45
The Viceroy, taken with the constant bearing
Of your afflictions and presuming too
You will not change your temper, does command
Your irons should be ta'en off.

                The chain taken off [*by the Gaoler. Exit Gaoler.*]
                          Now arm yourself

With your old resolution: suddenly   50
You shall be visited.

    [*to Francisco*]   You must leave the room, too,
And do it without reply.

FRANCISCO   There's no contending.

    Be still thyself, my son.   *Exit Francisco.*

VITELLI   'Tis not in man

---

42 *nil ultra* nothing further

43–4 I . . . **now** The figure of Christian
life as a race, in which the prize is
heaven, is a favourite with St Paul
– see 2 Timothy, 4.7, 1 Corinthians,
12.24–6, and Hebrews, 12.1.

45 **Nay, stay not** Q brackets this injunc-
tion, probably indicating an aside to
Francisco, who nevertheless lingers
until the Aga orders him to leave a
second time at 51. However, it may be
that it is addressed to Vitelli and means
'no, don't hold back'.

49 SD **Exit* Oxf suggests that 'the Aga's
remark at 51 shows that someone has
preceded Francisco out of the room',
but it may simply mean that Francisco's
departure is another proviso, in which
case the Gaoler's exit may not be necessary.

50 **suddenly** very soon

53–4 '**Tis** . . . **alter me** Spoken as Donusa
re-enters with the express intention of
persuading him to 'turn Turk', Vitelli's
line focuses the audience's attention
once again on the issue of conversion.

45 SD1, 2] *this edn* stay] *Q;* stir *Rawl.;* stare *Coxeter;* start *Gifford*   49 SD] *this edn; opp.* 50
Q   by . . . Exit Gaoler] *this edn*   51 SD] *this edn*

To change or alter me.

Enter DONUSA, ASAMBEG, MUSTAPHA [*and*] PAULINA.

PAULINA [*aside*]   Whom do I look on?
My brother? 'Tis he! But no more, my tongue: 55
Thou wilt betray all.
ASAMBEG   Let us hear this temptress.
The fellow looks as he would stop his ears
Against her powerful spells.
PAULINA [*aside*]   He is undone else.
VITELLI
I'll stand th'encounter: charge me home.
DONUSA   I come, sir,   (*Bows herself.*)
A beggar to you, and doubt not to find   60
A good man's charity, which if you deny,
You are cruel to yourself – a crime a wise man
(And such I hold you) would not willingly
Be guilty of; nor let it find less welcome,
Though I – a creature you contemn – now show you   65
The way to certain happiness; nor think it
Imaginary or fantastical,
And so not worth th'acquiring, in respect
The passage to it is nor rough nor thorny,
No steep hills in the way which you must climb up,   70

56–8 temptress . . . spells Picks up the siren motif from 2.1.29–31 and 3.5.21–8; there may be an implied stage direction for Vitelli.

57 as as if

59 charge me drive your attack

59–66 I come . . . happiness Cf. *Virgin Martyr*, 3.1.74–7.

59 SD presumably = 'makes a full bow'

61 charity Cf. 4.1.7, 108.

64 it i.e. happiness

65 contemn disdain, treat with contempt

67 fantastical illusory (the product of 'fantasy', or 'fancy', even more delusive than imagination)

68 in respect considering that

69–73 The passage . . . it a parodic summary of the perils to be expected in the quests of chivalric romance, echoing the motif of love as dangerous enchantment

54 SD1] *after* 53   SD2] *Coxeter*   58 SD] *Vitkus*   59 SD] *(Bowes her selfe);* [Vitelli] Looks at Donusa and bows *Rawl.*

No monsters to be conquered, no enchantments
To be dissolved by counter-charms before
You take possession of it.

VITELLI   What strong poison
Is wrapped up in these sugared pills?

DONUSA   My suit is
That you would quit your shoulders of a burden,   75
Under whose ponderous weight you wilfully
Have too long groaned, to cast those fetters off
With which, with your own hands, you chain your
    freedom.
Forsake a severe – nay, imperious – mistress,
Whose service does exact perpetual cares,   80
Watchings and troubles; and give entertainment
To one that courts you, whose least favours are
Variety and choice of all delights
Mankind is capable of.

VITELLI   You speak in riddles.
What burden, or what mistress, or what fetters   85
Are those you point at?

DONUSA   Those which your religion,
The mistress you too long have served, compels you
To bear with slave-like patience.

VITELLI   Ha!

PAULINA [*aside*]   How bravely

73–4 **poison . . . pills** Cf. Tilley, P325 ('To sugar the pill'), S958 ('For fair sugar fair ratsbane)' and P58 ('Poison is hidden in golden cups').

79–88 **Forsake . . . patience** Donusa imagines Vitelli's Christian faith as a rival, the conventionally cruel mistress of courtly love, in whose slavish *service* he is kept in thrall.

81 **entertainment** favourable treatment (*OED n.* 5); but also inflected by its association with amorous *service* (80),

since *entertainment* was also the action of taking someone into service (*OED n.* 1). The language of courtly love is inverted here, since conventionally it was the lady who accepted a lover's service.

82 **favours** kindnesses, or formal tokens of favour (*OED n.* 2, 7) – again conventionally given by a lady to her knight in return for service. The sense 'physical charms' (*OED n.* 8) may also be present.

86 **point at** refer to (*OED v.* 9b)

88 SD] *Coxeter*

202

That virtuous anger shows!

DONUSA   Be wise, and weigh
The prosperous success of things: if blessings   90
Are donatives from heaven – which, you must grant,
Were blasphemy to question – and that
They are called down and poured on such as are
Most gracious with the great disposer of 'em,
Look on our flourishing empire – if the splendour,   95
The majesty and glory of it dim not
Your feeble sight – and then turn back and see
The narrow bounds of yours, yet that poor remnant
Rent in as many factions and opinions
As you have petty kingdoms; and then, if   100
You are not obstinate against truth and reason,
You must confess the deity you worship
Wants care or power to help you.

PAULINA [*aside*]   Hold out, now,
And then thou art victorious!

ASAMBEG [*to Mustapha*]   How he eyes her!

MUSTAPHA [*to Asambeg*]
As if he would look through her.

ASAMBEG [*to Mustapha*]   His eyes flame, too,   105
As threatening violence.

VITELLI   But that I know

90 **prosperous** auspicious (*OED a.* 2)
91 **donatives** gifts, bounty
94 **gracious** endowed with divine grace
    (*OED n.* 6)
    great disposer i.e. God
95–103 **Look . . . you** The power and
    extent of the Turkish sultanate, when
    contrasted with the relatively meagre
    domains of most Christian states and the
    fractious condition of Christendom as a
    whole, was a constant source of anxiety
    for European commentators, especially
    since the Ottoman Empire was built, as
    they were only too painfully aware, upon
    'the wofull ruines of the greater part of

the Christian Commonweale' (Knolles,
sig. 6C1^r), 'the wild beasts of mankind
having broken in upon them, and rooted
out all civilitie; and the pride of a sterne
and barbarous Tyrant possessing the
thrones of ancient and just dominion'
(Sandys, 'To the Prince', sig. A2^v). See
pp. 11–12.
98 **remnant** end of a piece of cloth
    (*OED n.* 5b)
106–17 **But . . . work** Cf. Dorothea's
    denunciation of the 'jugling myster-
    ies' of the persecutors whom she
    denounces as servants of the 'Divel' in
    Virgin Martyr, 3.1.111–12.

103 SD] *Gifford²*   104, 105 SDD] *this edn*

The Devil, thy tutor, fills each part about thee,
And that I cannot play the exorcist
To dispossess thee – unless I should tear
Thy body limb by limb, and throw it to　　　　　　110
The Furies that expect it – I would now
Pluck out that wicked tongue that hath blasphemed
That great Omnipotency at whose nod
The fabric of the world shakes. Dare you bring
Your juggling Prophet in comparison with　　　　　115
The most inscrutable and infinite Essence
That made this all and comprehends his work?
The place is too profane to mention him
Whose only name is sacred. Oh, Donusa!
How much in my compassion I suffer　　　　　　120
That thou – on whom this most excelling form
And faculties of discourse beyond a woman
Were, by his liberal gift, conferred – shouldst still
Remain in ignorance of him that gave it?
I will not foul my mouth to speak the sorceries　　　125

---

108 **exorcist** Because of its ritualistic character, exorcism was viewed with suspicion by many Protestants.
109 **dispossess** free from demonic possession (*OED v.* 2)
111 **Furies** classical deities responsible for revenge; more generally, tormenting spirits
113–16 **great Omnipotency . . . Essence** circumlocutions designed to avoid the blasphemy of pronouncing God's name onstage
115 **juggling** conjuring, cheating. The libelling of Mahomet with accusations of witchcraft and fraudulent magic was a standard trope of anti-Islamic propaganda; see Parker.
116 **Essence** the 'substance' or absolute being of God (*OED n.* 4)
117 **this all** the totality of creation
comprehends includes in himself

(*OED v.* 8)
119 **only name** name alone
120 **compassion** four syllables here
125–31 **I . . . Alcoran** Vitelli cites recurrent slanders against the Prophet going back to medieval times. Cf. Sandys (sigs F2ᵛ–F3ʳ): '*Mahomet* the Saracen law-giver . . . [was] a man of obscure parentage . . . being disdained by the better sort for the basenesse of his birth; to avoid contempt, he gave it out, that he attained not to that honour by military favour, but by divine appointment. That he was sent by God to give a new law unto mankind; and by force of armes to reduce the world unto his obedience. That he was the last of the prophets; being greater then Christ, as Christ was greater then *Moses* . . . Being much subject to the falling sicknesse,

Of your seducer, his base birth, his whoredoms,
His strange impostures; nor deliver how
He taught a pigeon to feed in his ear,
Then made his credulous followers believe
It was an angel that instructed him   130
In the framing of his Alcoran. Pray you, mark me.

ASAMBEG [*to Mustapha*]

These words are death, were he in nought else guilty.

VITELLI

Your intent to win me
To be of your belief proceeded from
Your fear to die. Can there be strength in that   135
Religion that suffers us to tremble
At that which every day – nay hour – we haste to?

DONUSA

This is unanswerable and there's something
Tells me I err in my opinion.

---

he made them beleeve that it was a propheticall trance; and that he conversed with the Angel *Gabriel.* Having also taught a Pigeon to feed at his eare, he affirmed it to be the holy Ghost, which informed him in divine precepts . . . he had a subtill wit, though viciously employed, being naturally inclined to all villainies. Amongst the rest, so insatiably lecherous, that he countenanced his incontinencie with a law: wherein he declared it, not onely to be no crime to couple with whom soever he liked, but an act of high honour to the partie, and infusing sanctitie.' Biddulph similarly writes that the Prophet's 'parentage was . . . so meane and base that both his birth and infancie remained obscure' and that 'many could not abide the basenesse of his birth, nor the odiousnesse of his former life', denouncing him

as the begetter of 'a monstrous and most divelish Religion', calling him a 'dissembler and deceiver . . . first a theefe, afterwards a seditious souldier, then a runnagate, after that a Captaine of a rebellious hoste' and a man who, by his own confession, was 'destitute altogether of the heavenly gift to worke miracles' (sigs I2ʳ–I4ʳ).

128 **pigeon** three syllables here
131 This hexameter line requires the elision of *of his* ('of's').
138–9 **This . . . opinion** Donusa's intellectual capitulation may be related to an extensive literary tradition of disputation in which the Muslim participants are invariably shown as yielding to the superior reason of Christianity (see Matar, 'Anglo–Muslim', 34).
139 **opinion** Renaissance moral philosophy consistently opposed the promptings of mere *opinion* (the product of passion and will) to those of reason.

132 SD] *this edn*   138–9] *this edn; Q lines* mee / opinion, / it /

VITELLI   Cherish it:
It is a heavenly prompter. Entertain   140
This holy motion, and wear on your forehead
The sacred badge he arms his servants with.
[Marks her forehead with the sign of the cross.]
You shall, like me, with scorn look down upon
All engines tyranny can advance to batter
Your constant resolution. Then you shall   145
Look truly fair, when your mind's pureness answers
Your outward beauties.
DONUSA   I came here to take you,
But I perceive a yielding in myself
To be your prisoner.
VITELLI   'Tis an overthrow
That will outshine all victories. Oh, Donusa!   150
Die in my faith like me and 'tis a marriage
At which celestial angels shall be waiters,
And such as have been sainted welcome us.
Are you confirmed?
DONUSA   I would be – but the means
That may assure me?
VITELLI   Heaven is merciful,   155
And will not suffer you to want a man
To do that sacred office: build upon it.
DONUSA
Then thus I spit at Mahomet.   *[She spits.]*

141 **motion** inward prompting, stirring of the soul (by God) (*OED n.* 9 a, b)
141–2 Cf. *Jew of Malta*, 3.4.125–6: 'True sign of holinesse, / The badge of all his Souldiers that professe him'.
144 **engines** ingenious snares, wiles (*OED n.* 3); siege-engines (*OED n.* 5a)
147–50 **I came . . . victories** Cf. *Virgin Martyr*, 3.1.199–202.
152 **waiters** bridesmaids (*OED n.* 6b)
154 **confirmed** convinced; spiritually strengthened (*OED n.* 9, 4)
would want to
155 **assure me** not simply 'give me confidence' (*OED v.* 9), but part of the play's theological language: 'give me assurance of salvation' (*OED* assurance *n.* 8b)
156 **suffer . . . want** allow you to be without
158 SD Cf. Paulina's behaviour when she repudiates Asambeg's advances at 2.5.124; but Donusa's gesture –

142 SD] *this edn*   158 SD] *this edn*

ASAMBEG   Stop her mouth!
In death to turn apostata! I'll not hear
One syllable from any. Wretched creature,   160
With the next rising sun prepare to die!
Yet Christian, in reward of thy brave courage –
Be thy faith right or wrong – receive this favour:
In person I'll attend thee to thy death;
And boldly challenge all that I can give   165
But what's not in my grant – which is to live.   *Exeunt.*

5.1   *Enter* VITELLI [*and*] FRANCISCO.

FRANCISCO
You are wondrous brave and jocund.
VITELLI   Welcome, father.
Should I spare cost or not wear cheerful looks
Upon my wedding day, it were ominous
And showed I did repent it, which I dare not,
It being a marriage – howsoever sad   5
In the first ceremonies that confirm it –
That will forever arm me against fears,
Repentance, doubts or jealousies, and bring
Perpetual comforts, peace of mind and quiet
To the glad couple.
FRANCISCO   I well understand you;   10
And my full joy to see you so resolved

an unimaginable blasphemy from a Muslim perspective – is obviously designed as the counterpart of Grimaldi's disruption of the Mass, marking Donusa as an example of virtuous renegadism. The princess's expression of contempt echoes Armusia's in *Island Princess* (4.5.131).

159 **apostata** apostate or renegado
165 **challenge . . . give** 'demand any-

thing of me that is within my power to give'

5.1 Location: the prison
1 **jocund** cheerful
5 **marriage** Vitelli has in mind not just his literal marriage to Donusa, but also the familiar trope of death-as-wedding (in turn partly dependent on the idea of orgasm as a 'little death'). Cf. *AC* 4.14.100–2.

6 **first ceremonies** i.e. their executions

160 any. Wretched creature,] *this edn;* any; wretched creature. *Q;* any; wretched creature! *Oxf.*   166 SD] *Exeunt. / The end of the fourth Act Q*   **5.1**] *(Actus Quintus, Scaena Prima.)*

Weak words cannot express. What is the hour
Designed for this solemnity?

VITELLI   The sixth:
Something before the setting of the sun
We take our last leave of his fading light,   15
And with our souls' eyes seek for beams eternal.
Yet there's one scruple with which I am much
Perplexed and troubled, which I know you can
Resolve me of.

FRANCISCO   What is't?

VITELLI   This, sir: my bride –
Whom I first courted and then won, not with   20
Loose lays, poor flatteries, apish compliments,
But sacred and religious zeal – yet wants
The holy badge that should proclaim her fit
For these celestial nuptials. Willing she is,
I know, to wear it as the choicest jewel   25
On her fair forehead; but to you, that well
Could do that work of grace, I know the Viceroy
Will never grant access. Now in a case
Of this necessity, I would gladly learn
Whether in me, a layman without orders,   30
It may not be religious and lawful,

---

13 **solemnity** (religious) ceremony (*OED n.* 1, 2)

14 **Something** somewhat, a little

20–2 **I... zeal** This may appear disingenuous as an account of their 'first' wooing, but Vitelli presumably has in mind the process by which he persuaded her to marry him, rather than his initial seduction by Donusa.

21 **Loose lays** erotically suggestive lyrics

22 **wants** lacks

23–5 **holy badge ... choicest jewel** i.e. the spiritual sign of baptism (cf. 4.3.141)

27 **work of grace** baptism – considered, in sacramental dispensations, a vehicle of divine grace that magically washed away all sins. This idea, while anathema to Calvinists – like the doctrine of salvation by works with which Vitelli's turn of phrase seems to link it – would have commended itself to more moderate Anglicans and Arminians.

28 **access** i.e. to Donusa

28–32 **Now ... office** Because they believed in the salvific power of the sacraments, opponents of Calvinist predestinarianism – including Arminians in the Church of England, as well as Catholics – maintained that baptism by lay persons must be justified in what were called 'cases of necessity', where no priest was available. Dunn (190) cites a parallel case in *Don Quixote*, 1.37.

As we go to our deaths, to do that office?

FRANCISCO

A question in itself with much ease answered:
Midwives upon necessity perform it,
And knights that in the Holy Land fought for   35
The freedom of Jerusalem, when full
Of sweat and enemies' blood, have made their helmets
The font out of which with their holy hands
They drew that heavenly liquor. 'Twas approved then
By the Holy Church, nor must I think it now   40
In you a work less pious.

VITELLI   You confirm me:
I will find a way to do it. In the meantime,
Your holy vows assist me!

FRANCISCO   They shall ever
Be present with you.

VITELLI   You shall see me act
This last scene to the life.

FRANCISCO   And though now fall,   45
Rise a blessed martyr.

VITELLI   That's my end, my all.   *Exeunt.*

5.2   *Enter* GRIMALDI, MASTER, BOATSWAIN [*and*] *Sailors.*

BOATSWAIN

Sir, if you slip this opportunity,
Never expect the like.

---

31 **religious** four syllables
34 i.e. in the case of newborns that would not survive
35–9 **knights . . . liquor** Robinson cites an episode from Tasso's *Gerusalemme Liberata* (12.66–9), in which Tancred, having by an unlucky accident mortally wounded his beloved, the Ethiopian Clorinda, baptizes her with water from his helmet. Thus, Robinson

argues, 'the effort to redeem the Holy Land is mapped onto Vitelli's effort to redeem Donusa' ('Turks', 229, 237 n. 51).
41 **confirm me** both 'strengthen me spiritually' and 'confirm my belief' (*OED v.* 4, 7)
5.2 Location: a street in Tunis
1 **slip** neglect, miss, let slip (*OED v.* 7b, 21b)

5.2] *(Actus Quintus, Scaena Secunda.)*

MASTER   With as much ease now
We may steal the ship out of the harbour, captain,
As ever gallants in a wanton bravery
Have set upon a drunken constable   5
And bore him from a sleepy rug-gowned watch:
Be therefore wise.

GRIMALDI   I must be honest too –
And you shall wear that shape, you shall observe me,
If that you purpose to continue mine.
Think you ingratitude can be the parent   10
To our unfeigned repentance? Do I owe
A peace within here kingdoms could not purchase
To my religious creditor, to leave him
Open to danger, the great benefit
Never remembered? No, though in her bottom   15
We could stow up the tribute of the Turk –
Nay, grant the passage safe too – I will never
Consent to weigh an anchor up till he
That only must, commands it.

BOATSWAIN (*to Master*)   This religion

4–6 Careless or incompetent constables
and watchmen, like Dogberry's troupe
in *Much Ado*, were familiar targets of
satire; cf. *Maid of Honour*, 1.1.73–4.
4   **wanton** lawless (*OED a.* 1c)
     bravery act of bravado (*OED n.* 1a)
6   **rug-gowned** Watchmen typically
     wore 'rug-gowns', garments of rough
     woollen material or 'rug'.
7   **honest** honourable, virtuous, upright
     (*OED a.* 1a, 3)
8   **wear that shape** i.e. be honest like me
     observe imitate
13   **my religious creditor** i.e. Francisco;
     the commercial metaphor is charac-
     teristic of the way the play's language
     brings together the worlds of trade and
     religion. Grimaldi may also be playing
     on a further meaning of *creditor* as 'one
     who believes (in me)' (*OED n.* 4).

to leave only to leave
14–15 **the great . . . remembered** 'as
       though I had completely forgotten
       his great goodness (in helping me to
       salvation)'
14   **benefit** kindness, favour, gift (*OED
     n.* 2). The reciprocal obligations
     established by 'benefits' were a
     favourite topic of Renaissance moral
     philosophy, which took its cue from
     Seneca's *De Beneficiis*; but the context
     (following *creditor*, 13) also activates
     the word's commercial sense ('profit,
     gain').
15   **her bottom** i.e. the hold of the ship in
     which they plan to escape
16   **tribute . . . Turk** i.e. all tribute levied
     by the Sultan (*the Turk*) from his
     dominions
19   **That only** who alone

19, 20, 23 SDD] *this edn*

Will keep us slaves and beggars.

MASTER (*to Boatswain*)   The fiend prompts me   20
  To change my copy. Plague upon't! We are seamen:
  What have we to do with't, but for a snatch or so
  At the end of a long Lent?

BOATSWAIN (*to Master*)   Mum! See who is here?

Enter FRANCISCO.

GRIMALDI
  My father!

FRANCISCO   My good convert. I am full
  Of serious business which denies me leave   25
  To hold long conference with you. Only thus much
  Briefly receive: a day or two, at the most,
  Shall make me fit to take my leave of Tunis,
  Or give me lost for ever.

GRIMALDI   Days nor years –
  Provided that my stay may do you service –   30
  But to me shall be minutes.

FRANCISCO   I much thank you.
  In this small scroll you may in private read
    [*giving him a paper*]
  What my intents are; and, as they grow ripe,
  I will instruct you further. In the meantime,

---

21 **change my copy** alter my behaviour;
assume another character (*OED* copy
n. 11a) – i.e. turn Turk. The same
phrase is used by Gazet at 3.4.32 (see
n.).
22 **with't** i.e. with religion
snatch brief spell (*OED n.* 5); quick
screw (Williams, *Dictionary*, 2.1266–
7)
23 **Lent** the period of penitential abstinence from Ash Wednesday to Easter
Saturday, commemorating Christ's 40
days of fasting in the wilderness
Mum hush

24 **convert** See the verbal sense of this
word at *OED v.* II 3: 'to turn from
a sinful to a religious life'; but the
implication may be that Grimaldi, like
many other renegades, has also been
guilty of apostasy and converted to
Islam before returning to the Christian
fold.
28 **fit** ready (*OED a.* 5a)
29 **give me** render me up as
29–31 **Days . . . minutes** 'Days, or even
years, will seem no longer than minutes to me, if I can be of service to you
by remaining here.'

32 SD] *this edn*

Borrow your late distracted looks and gesture: 35
The more dejected you appear, the less
The Viceroy must suspect you.
GRIMALDI   I am nothing
But what you please to have me be.
FRANCISCO   Farewell, sir.
[*to Master*] Be cheerful, Master, something we will do
That shall reward itself in the performance,   40
And that's true prize indeed.
MASTER   I am obedient.
BOATSWAIN
And I – there's no contending.
FRANCISCO   Peace to you all.
          Exeunt Grimaldi, Master, Boatswain [*and Sailors*].
Prosper, thou great Existence, my endeavours,
As they religiously are undertaken
And distant equally from servile gain   45
Or glorious ostentation!

          Enter PAULINA, CARAZIE *and* MANTO.

                    I am heard
In this blest opportunity, which in vain
I long have waited for. I must show myself.
          [*Paulina sees Francisco.*]
Oh, she has found me! Now, if she prove right,

---

35 another image of theatrical disguise
  late previous, recent
  distracted deranged, crazed (*OED*
  ppl.a. 5)
40 **reward . . . performance** proverbial; cf. Tilley, A26: 'Neither praise
  nor dispraise thyself, thy actions serve
  this turn.' The context animates the
  theatrical connotations of *performance*.
41 **prize** Addressed to a former cor-

sair, the word deliberately recalls the
'prizes' (captured vessels) of piracy
(cf. 5.8.17).
43 **Existence** Massinger's euphemism
  avoids naming God directly in order
  to evade censorship, but plays on the
  biblical formula for the deity, 'I am'
  (Exodus, 3.14).
46–7 **I . . . opportunity** 'this blessed
  opportunity shows that my prayers
  have been heard'

39 SD] *this edn*   42 SD *and Sailors*] *Gifford*   46 SD] *this edn; opp. 45–6 Q*   48 SD] *this edn*

All hope will not forsake us.

PAULINA [*to Carazie and Manto*]   Farther off!   50
And, in that your distance, know your duties too.
You were bestowed on me as slaves to serve me,
And not as spies to pry into my actions
And after to betray me. You shall find,
If any look of mine be unobserved,   55
I am not ignorant of a mistress' power,
And from whom I receive it.

CARAZIE [*aside to Manto*]   Note this, Manto!
The pride and scorn with which she entertains us,
Now we are made hers by the Viceroy's gift!
Our sweet-conditioned princess, fair Donusa –   60
Rest in her death wait on her! – never used us
With such contempt. I would he had sent me
To the galleys – or the gallows – when he gave me
To this proud little devil.

MANTO [*aside to Carazie*]   I expect
All tyrannous usage, but I must be patient;   65
And though ten times a day she tears these locks,
Or makes this face her footstool, 'tis but justice.

PAULINA [*to Francisco*]
'Tis a true story of my fortunes, father –
My chastity preserved by miracle,
Or your devotions for me – and, believe it,   70
What outward pride soe'er I counterfeit,

---

49 **right** upright, virtuous (*OED a.* 5)
56–60 **mistress' power . . . princess**
a classic example of the Fletcherian
tragicomic technique of 'change,
and counterturn' (see p. 7); Paulina
temporarily appears to have assumed
Donusa's role of oriental 'tyranness'
(5.3.174), and Donusa that of the
'sweet saint' Paulina (2.5.164).
60 **sweet-conditioned** sweet-natured

61 **rest . . . her** may she rest in peace
69–70 **miracle . . . devotions**   Here,
as elsewhere, the play links the
Christians' success to the sacramental
power of the priesthood, something
that must surely have been disturbing
to many in the audience, even if its
effect was diluted by the purely material trick that ensures the captives'
escape from Tunis.

50 SD] *Vitkus*   57 SD] *this edn*   64, 68 SDD] *this edn*

Or state to these appointed to attend me,
I am not in my disposition altered,
But still your humble daughter, and share with you
In my poor brother's sufferings all hell's torments.   75
Revenge it on accursed Grimaldi's soul,
That in his rape of me gave a beginning
To all the miseries that since have followed.

FRANCISCO

Be charitable and forgive him, gentle daughter;
He's a changed man, and may redeem his fault   80
In his fair life hereafter. You must bear, too,
Your forced captivity – for 'tis no better,
Though you wear golden fetters – and of him,
Whom death affrights not, learn to hold out nobly.

PAULINA

You are still the same good counsellor.

FRANCISCO   And who knows –   85
Since what above is purposed is inscrutable –
But that the Viceroy's extreme dotage on you
May be the parent of a happier birth
Than yet our hopes dare fashion? Longer conference
May prove unsafe for you and me, however –   90
Perhaps for trial – he allows you freedom.
    (*Delivers a paper.*)

71–2 'whatever outward show of pride or
solemn pomp (*state*) I may put on for
the benefit of my servants'. Paulina's
pretence continues the motif of virtuous counterfeiting.
75 **In** through
77 **rape** abduction
81 **fair** unblemished, virtuous (*OED a.* 9)
83 **golden fetters** Cf. *Knight of Malta*,
5.1.82–5: 'Who yeeldeth unto pleasures, and to lust / Is a poore captive,

that in Golden Fetters / (And
pretious (as he thinkes) but holding gyves) / Frets out his life'; and
Believe, 5.1.40–5: 'how many borne
unto / ample possessions . . . carried
headlonge with ambition contend /
to weare the golden fetters of imployment'.
of from
87 **dotage** doting passion
90 **however** even though

79 FRANCISCO Be] *MS ADD (*franci: Be*);* be *Q*   90–1 however . . . he] *this edn, Q* (howeuer /
Perhaps for triall he)*; however. / Perhaps for trial he *Vitkus*   91 SD] *opp. 93*

From this learn therefore what you must attempt,
Though with the hazard of yourself. Heaven guard you,
And give Vitelli patience! Then I doubt not
But he will have a glorious day, since (some   95
Hold truly) such as suffer overcome.   *Exeunt.*

5.3   *Enter* ASAMBEG, MUSTAPHA, AGA [*and*] KAPIAGA.

ASAMBEG

What we commanded, see performed; and fail not
In all things to be punctual!

AGA   We shall, sir.
                                        Exeunt Aga [*and*] *Kapiaga.*

MUSTAPHA

'Tis strange that you should use such circumstance
To a delinquent of so mean condition.

ASAMBEG

Had he appeared in a more sordid shape   5
Than disguised greatness ever deigned to mask in,
The gallant bearing of his present fortune
Aloud proclaims him noble.

MUSTAPHA   If you doubt him
To be a man built up for great employments,
And as a cunning spy sent to explore   10
The city's strength or weakness, you by torture
May force him to discover it.

ASAMBEG   That were base;
Nor dare I do such injury to virtue
And bold assured courage; neither can I

---

93 **Though . . . yourself** even if it means risking your own life

95 **glorious day** i.e. a day that will confer brilliant renown on him (*OED* glorious *a*. 5b)

96 **such . . . overcome** proverbial (Tilley, E136) – a Christian Stoic truism

5.3 Location: Asambeg's audience-chamber

3 **circumstance** ceremony and ado (*OED n*. 7a)

8 **doubt** suspect (*OED v*. 6c)

14 **assured** assurèd

14–26 ***neither . . . with** Misled by Q's

5.3] *(Actus Quintus, Scaena Tertia.)*

Be won to think – but if I should attempt it,   15
I shoot against the moon – he that hath stood
The roughest battery that captivity
Could ever bring to shake a constant temper,
Despised the fawnings of a future greatness
By beauty in her full perfection tendered,   20
That hears of death as of a quiet slumber,
And from the surplusage of his own firmness
Can spare enough of fortitude to assure
A feeble woman, will now, Mustapha,
Be altered in his soul for any torments   25
We can afflict his body with.

MUSTAPHA   Do your pleasure!
I only offered you a friend's advice,
But without gall or envy to the man
That is to suffer. But what do you determine
Of poor Grimaldi? The disgrace called on him,   30
I hear, has ran him mad.

ASAMBEG   There weigh the difference
In the true temper of their minds. The one –

full stop after 'Moone' (16), editors
have attempted to make sense of
this passage by turning 16–26 into
a negative statement, substituting an
exclamation mark for Q's question
mark after *with* (26); but in fact the
whole passage, marked as it is by
Massinger's characteristically sinuous
syntax, constitutes a single elaborate
sentence, in which the framing statement is 'neither can I / Be won to
think . . . [that] he . . . will now . . . Be
altered in his soul for any torments /
We can afflict his body with', while
'that hath . . . woman' (16–24) gives
the evidence for Vitelli's firmness.
16 **shoot . . . moon** proverbial for
attempting the impossible; see Tilley,

M1114: 'He casts beyond the moon',
and cf. M1123: 'To bark at the moon'.
stood withstood
17 **battery** assault, beating – but beyond
this literal sense another metaphor from
siege warfare may also be intended.
19 **fawnings** i.e. flattering prospect
22 **surplusage** surplus, excess; cf. *Curate*,
5.3.53–4 ('And (as a surplusage) offer'd
her selfe / To be at my devotion'), and
London, 35.
23 **assure** give confidence to (*OED v.* 8)
28 **gall** bitterness
30 **called on** proclaimed (*OED v.* 3); or
perhaps 'called down on'
31 **ran** obsolete past participle of 'run'
There in that
32 **temper** disposition; tempering

16 moon – he] *this edn;* moon. He *Q*   24 now, Mustapha,] *Q (*now, *Mustapha);* now, *Mustapha,* never
Coxeter; not, *Mustapha* | *Gifford*   26 with.] with? *Q;* with! *Oxf*

A pirate sold to mischiefs, rapes and all
That make a slave relentless and obdurate,
Yet of himself wanting the inward strengths   35
That should defend him – sinks beneath compassion
Or pity of a man; whereas this merchant –
Acquainted only with a civil life,
Armed in himself, entrenched and fortified
With his own virtue, valuing life and death   40
At the same price – poorly does not invite
A favour, but commands us do him right,
Which unto him, and her we both once honoured,
As a just debt I gladly pay 'em. They enter:
Now sit we equal hearers.

> *A dreadful music. [Enter] at one door, the* AGA,
> Janizaries, VITELLI, FRANCISCO *[and]* GAZET*; at the*
> *other,* DONUSA, PAULINA, CARAZIE *[and]* MANTO.

MUSTAPHA   I shall hear   45
And see, sir, without passion; my wrongs arm me.
VITELLI

A joyful preparation! To whose bounty
Owe we our thanks for gracing thus our Hymen?
The notes, though dreadful to the ear, sound here
As our epithalamium were sung   50
By a celestial choir, and a full chorus

33–4 **all / That make** *all* is treated as a plural.
34 **obdurate** obdùrate
41 **poorly . . . invite** does not abjectly beg
43 **her . . . honoured** i.e. Donusa
45 **equal** impartial
45.1 *dreadful* inspiring dread, grim
46 **my . . . me** 'my suffering has made me stronger (and therefore better able to confront what is about to happen without giving way to emotion)'
47 **preparation** observances preliminary to the celebration of a rite or festival (*OED n.* 7); referring to the ceremonial entry above
48 **Hymen** wedding (from Hymen, Roman god of marriage)
49 **though . . . ear** although the sound of them fills one with dread
50 **As** as if
epithalamium marriage song

41 price – poorly does] *Q;* price – poorly – does *Vitkus* 44 pay 'em] *Coxeter;* pay'm *Q;* pay 'em *Rawl.;* pay *Gifford* 45.1 *Enter*] *this edn*

Assured us future happiness. These that lead me
Gaze not with wanton eyes upon my bride,
Nor for their service are repaid by me
With jealousies or fears; nor do they envy   55
My passage to those pleasures from which death
Cannot deter me. [*to Francisco*] Great sir, pardon me:
Imagination of the joys I haste to
Made me forget my duty; but, the form
And ceremony past, I will attend you,   60
And with our constant resolution feast you –
Not with coarse cates, forgot as soon as tasted,
But such as shall, while you have memory,
Be pleasing to the palate.
FRANCISCO [*to Vitelli*]   Be not lost
In what you purpose.   *Exit.*
GAZET   Call you this a marriage?   65
It differs little from hanging: I cry at it.
VITELLI

See where my bride appears! In what full lustre –
As if the virgins that bear up her train
Had long contended to receive an honour
Above their births in doing her this service!   70
Nor comes she fearful to meet those delights
Which, once passed o'er, immortal pleasures follow.
I need not therefore comfort or encourage

---

62 **cates** dishes
65–6 **Call . . . hanging** 'English and
foreign visitors at Tyburn were
struck by the fact that the condemned malefactors treated the day
of their hanging as a wedding. "He
that is to be hang'd or otherwise
executed," wrote a Swiss visitor,
"first takes care to get himself
shav'd, and handsomely drest either

in Mourning or in the dress of a
Bridegroom"' (Linebaugh, 112;
Linebaugh's evidence comes from
the late 17th and 18th centuries, but
the practice is presumably older).
71 **delights** i.e. their marriage-in-death
(playing on the familiar idea of orgasm
as erotic death); cf. 5.1.5, and see n.
72 **passed o'er** passed through, consum-
mated (*OED v.* 67 a, b)

57 SD] *this edn*   64 SD] *this edn*   65 SD] *Exit Francisco*

Her forward steps, and I should offer wrong
To her mind's fortitude, should I but ask   75
How she can brook the rough high-going sea,
Over whose foamy back our ship, well rigged
With hope and strong assurance, must transport us.
Nor will I tell her when we reach the haven –
Which tempests shall not hinder – what loud welcomes   80
Shall entertain us, nor commend the place,
To tell whose least perfection would strike dumb
The eloquence of all boasted in story,
Though joined together.

DONUSA   'Tis enough, my dearest:
I dare not doubt you. As your humble shadow,   85
Led where you please, I follow.

VITELLI [*to Asambeg*]   One suit, sir,
And willingly I cease to be a beggar;
And, that you may with more security hear it,
Know 'tis not life I'll ask, nor to defer
Our deaths but a few minutes.

ASAMBEG   Speak, 'tis granted.   90

VITELLI
We being now to take our latest leave

---

74 **forward** onward (*OED a.* 3a); ready, zealous (*OED a.* 6c)

76–8 Ironically, Vitelli, unaware of Francisco's plans for escape by sea, speaks in metaphor here. The commonplace figure of the soul as a ship looks forward, with a benign irony, to the literal circumstances of the lovers' escape from Tunis.

76 **brook** endure

78 **assurance** faith, conviction of salvation

79 **when . . . haven** qualifies *entertain* rather than *tell*
haven punning on 'heaven'

81 **nor** nor will I

83–4 **all . . . together** i.e. every comparable event of which legend boasts, even if all rolled into one

85–6 ***As . . . follow*** The princess's new-found humility echoes Ruth, 1.16–17: 'Intreat me not . . . to return from following after thee: for whither thou goest, I will go . . . Where thou diest, I will die.' Q's 'lead' is ambiguous, since 'lead' appears elsewhere (4.1.123) as a spelling for 'led'. Thus this passage can mean (as Vitkus and those who prefer 'lead' suppose) 'Wherever you choose to lead me, I will follow, like your humble shadow', or (as this edition assumes) 'I follow like your humble shadow, led wherever you please to take me'.

86 **One suit** grant me one favour

90 **but** but for

91 **latest** final

86 Led] *this edn;* Lead *Q*   SD] *this edn*

And grown of one belief, I do desire
I may have your allowance to perform it
But in the fashion which we Christians use
Upon the like occasions.

ASAMBEG   'Tis allowed of.   95

VITELLI

My service – haste, Gazet, to the next spring,
And bring me of it.

GAZET   Would I could as well
Fetch you a pardon, I would not run but fly,
And be here in a moment.   [*Exit.*]

MUSTAPHA   What's the mystery
Of this? Discover it!

VITELLI   Great sir, I'll tell you.   100
Each country hath its own peculiar rites:
Some, when they are to die, drink store of wine,
Which poured in liberally does oft beget
A bastard valour – with which armed, they bear
The not-to-be-declined charge of death   105
With less fear and astonishment; others take
Drugs to procure a heavy sleep, that so
They may insensibly receive the means
That casts them in an everlasting slumber;
Others –

Enter GAZET *with water.*

Oh, welcome!

---

96 **My service** my service to you; I am
  obliged to you
  next nearest
97 **of it** i.e. some water from it
99 **mystery** Mustapha means only 'secret
  meaning', but Massinger plays on the
  idea of the sacrament of baptism as a
  mystery (*OED n.* 3).

100 **Discover** reveal
101 **peculiar** particular
102 **store** abundance
104 **bastard** false – but punning on *bastard* = a sweet Spanish wine (*OED n.* 4)
105 **declined** declinèd
106 **astonishment** dismay, dread (*OED
  n.* 3)

99 SD] *Vitkus*

ASAMBEG   Now, the use of yours?   110

VITELLI

The clearness of this is a perfect sign
Of innocence; and, as this washes off
Stains and pollutions from the things we wear,
Thrown thus upon the forehead, it hath power
To purge those spots that cleave upon the mind,   115
   (*Throws it on her face.*)
If thankfully received.

ASAMBEG   'Tis a strange custom!

VITELLI

How do you entertain it, my Donusa?
Feel you no alteration? No new motives?
No unexpected aids that may confirm you
In that to which you were inclined before?   120

DONUSA

I am another woman: – till this minute
I never lived, nor durst think how to die.
How long have I been blind! Yet on the sudden,
By this blest means, I feel the films of error
Ta'en from my soul's eyes. O divine physician,   125
That hast bestowed a sight on me which death,

---

110 **the use of yours?** 'What is the purpose of your ritual?'

111–14 **sign . . . power** Vitelli's gloss appears to include both the Protestant understanding of the sacrament as a metaphor (or *sign*) of spiritual truth, and the Catholic/Arminian belief in its magical efficacy. This staged performance of a sacrament was unparalleled in theatre of the period; perhaps the fact that it was performed by a layman rather than a priest sufficiently reduced its controversial character to enable Massinger to take the risk.

115 **spots** marks of sin

117 **entertain** admit to consideration (*OED v.* 15b)

118 **motives** inward promptings (*OED n.* 2b); cf. 'motion' (4.3.141)

123–5 **How . . . eyes** Cf. St Paul's conversion experience in Acts, 9.18: 'And immediately there fell from his eyes as it had been scales; and he received sight forthwith, and arose, and was baptized.' The echo takes on a peculiar ironic resonance in the presence of Paulina, whose name links her with the apostle, but who at this point appears to have undergone a conversion in the opposite direction.

124 **blest means** Cf. 'sanctified means', 4.1.32 and n.

125 **divine physician** presumably Vitelli – but perhaps referring to Christ, for whom he acts

110 SD] *after* welcome   SP] *Qa (Asam.), MS ADD (underlined); Vitelli Qb*   111 SP] *MS ADD (*Vitelli:*); Vit: Rawl.; not in Q*

221

Though ready to embrace me in his arms,
Cannot take from me! Let me kiss the hand
That did this miracle, and seal my thanks
Upon those lips from whence these sweet words
    vanished   130
That freed me from the cruellest of prisons –
Blind ignorance and misbelief. False Prophet,
Impostor Mahomet!

ASAMBEG   I'll hear no more –
You do abuse my favours. [*to Janizaries*] Sever 'em! –
Wretch, if thou hadst another life to lose,   135
This blasphemy deserved it: instantly
Carry them to their deaths!

VITELLI   We part now, blest one,
To meet hereafter in a kingdom where
Hell's malice shall not reach us.

PAULINA   Ha, ha, ha!

ASAMBEG
What means my mistress?

PAULINA   Who can hold her spleen,   140
When such ridiculous follies are presented –
The scene, too, made religion? O my lord,
How from one cause two contrary effects
Spring up upon the sudden!

ASAMBEG   This is strange.

PAULINA
That which hath fooled her in her death wins me   145
That hitherto have barred myself from pleasure
To live in all delight.

---

140 **hold her spleen** suppress her laughter (*OED* spleen *n.* 6); contain her indignation (*OED n.* 1c); the spleen was the supposed seat of both mirth and rage.
142 **scene** stage performance; the place where a piece of theatrical action is imagined to take place; the stage or theatre itself (*OED n.* 2, 4). Paulina's language (*follies . . . presented . . . scene*) echoes Calvinist indictments of ritual as empty theatre.

134 SD] *this edn* 145–6] *Rawl, Coxeter; Qa lines* death, / mee, / pleasure, / ; *Qb lines* death, / pleasure, /

222

ASAMBEG   There's music in this.

PAULINA

I now will run as fiercely to your arms
As e'er longing woman did, borne high
On the swift wings of appetite.

VITELLI   O devil!   150

PAULINA

Nay, more – for there shall be no odds betwixt us –
I will turn Turk.

GAZET (*aside*)   Most of your tribe do so
When they begin in whore.

ASAMBEG   You are serious, lady?

PAULINA

Serious? But satisfy me in a suit
That to the world may witness that I have   155
Some power upon you, and tomorrow challenge
Whatever's in my gift – for I will be
At your dispose.

GAZET (*aside*)   That's ever the subscription
To a damned whore's false epistle.

ASAMBEG   Ask this hand –
Or, if thou wilt, the heads of these. I am rapt   160
Beyond myself with joy! Speak, speak – what is it?

PAULINA

But twelve short hours' reprieve for this base couple.

---

151 **odds** difference, dispute
152 **your tribe** i.e. women
  do so Gazet plays on one of the colloquial meanings of *turn Turk* (= become a whore; see Williams, *Dictionary*, 3.1439–40).
153 **in** to
  serious A sly metatheatrical joke is probably involved, since (as Burton points out) while 'no representation of a Christian['s] . . . genuine conversion to Islam exists in the canon . . . we repeat-

edly find Christians *acting* the part of the apostate' (*Traffic*, 30); cf. 5.5.6.
156–7 **challenge . . . gift** demand anything that is in my power to give
158 **subscription** the concluding phrases and signature at the end of a letter
159 **Ask this hand** ambiguous: either 'ask for this hand in marriage' or 'ask me to cut off this hand and give it to you'
160 **heads . . . these** i.e. the severed heads of Vitelli and Donusa

152 SD] *after* whore *153*   154 Serious?] *Qb*; Serious: *Qa*   158 SD] *after* epistle *159*

223

ASAMBEG

The reason – since you hate them?

PAULINA   That I may

Have time to triumph o'er this wretched woman:

I'll be myself her guardian; I will feast   165

Adorned in her choice and richest jewels.

Commit him to what guards you please. Grant this,

I am no more mine own, but yours.

ASAMBEG   Enjoy it –

Repine at it who dares. Bear him safe off

To the Black Tower; but give him all things useful –   170

                    [*Exeunt Janizaries with Vitelli.*]

The contrary was not in your request.

PAULINA

I do contemn him.

DONUSA   Peace in death denied me?

PAULINA

Thou shalt not go in liberty to thy grave:

For one night a sultana is my slave.

MUSTAPHA

A terrible little tyranness.

ASAMBEG   No more!   175

Her will shall be a law. [*aside*] Till now, ne'er happy! *Exeunt.*

5.4   *Enter* FRANCISCO, GRIMALDI, MASTER,
                    BOATSWAIN *and* Sailors.

GRIMALDI

Sir, all things are in readiness: the Turks

165–6 **I will . . . jewels** an implied stage
    direction for the costuming and stag-
    ing of 5.5
170 **Black Tower** According to Sandys
    (sig. E3ʳ), the name of the castle
    guarding the Bosphorus north of

Constantinople (see 5.7n., and
    Fig. 16), but here relocated to Tunis.
174 **sultana** woman belonging to the
    Sultan's family
175 **tyranness** female tyrant
5.4 Location: a street

164 woman:] *Qb;* wo *Qa*   167 Grant this,] *Qb;* Gra *Qa*   170 SD] *this edn*   176 SD1] *this edn*
5.4] *(Actus Quintus, Scaena quarta.)*

That seized upon my ship stowed under hatches,
My men resolved and cheerful. Use but means
To get out of the ports, we will be ready
To bring you aboard, and then – heaven be but pleased –   5
This for the Viceroy's fleet!   [*Gestures contemptuously.*]
FRANCISCO   Discharge your parts;
In mine I'll not be wanting. Fear not, Master,
Something will come along to fraught your bark
That you will have just cause to say you never
Made such a voyage.
MASTER   We will stand the hazard.   10
FRANCISCO
What's the best hour?
BOATSWAIN   After the second watch.
FRANCISCO
Enough – each to his charge!
GRIMALDI   We will be careful.   *Exeunt.*

5.5   *Enter* PAULINA [*, adorned in Donusa's jewels*],
         DONUSA, CARAZIE [*and*] MANTO. [*A table with
                  a rich banquet laid out.*]

6   **This** Though no SD appears in Q,
    This clearly calls for some contemptu-
    ous gesture – perhaps the obscene
    'spanish fig', made by thrusting the
    thumb between the index and mid-
    dle fingers. The ironic juxtaposition
    of this gesture with Grimaldi's pious
    deference to heaven's will (5) suggests
    that something of his old sinful and
    violent self has survived his transfor-
    mation.
    Discharge perform (*OED n.* 11)
8   **fraught your bark** load your ship
10 **such** i.e so profitable
11 **second watch** Naval practice divided
    the day into four-hour 'watches', the
    second (or middle) *watch* running from

    midnight until 4 a.m.
5.5 Location: Paulina's chamber in the
    palace
0.1–3 ***adorned . . . jewels . . . A
    table . . . out*** Paulina's request that
    Donusa *Sit* while she waits upon her
    (1) and her enquiry as to whether the
    princess *cannot eat* (37), suggests that
    this scene is meant to stage the feast
    that Paulina promised at 5.3.165; that
    being the case she will presumably be
    'Adorned in [Donusa's] choice and
    richest jewels' (5.3.166) – the same
    finery worn by the princess in the
    seduction scene (2.4). The *bake-meat*
    sent to Vitelli (29) will be among the
    dishes on the table.

6 SD] *this edn* **5.5**] *(Actus Quintus, Scaena quinta.)* 0.1 *adorned . . . jewels*] *this edn* 0.2–3 *A
table . . . out*] *this edn*

PAULINA

    Sit, madam, it is fit that I attend you;
      [Donusa sits at the table.]
    And pardon, I beseech you, my rude language –
    To which the sooner you will be invited
    When you shall understand no way was left me
    To free you from a present execution   5
    But by my personating that which never
    My nature was acquainted with.

DONUSA   I believe you.

PAULINA

    You will, when you shall understand I may
    Receive the honour to be known unto you
    By a nearer name; and, not to rack you further,   10
    The man you please to favour is my brother –
    No merchant, madam, but a gentleman
    Of the best rank in Venice.

DONUSA   I rejoice in't.

    But what's this to his freedom? For myself,
    Were he well off, I were secure.

PAULINA   I have   15

    A present means – not plotted by myself,
    But a religious man, my confessor –
    That may preserve all, if we had a servant
    Whose faith we might rely on.

DONUSA   She that's now

    Your slave was once mine: had I twenty lives   20
    I durst commit them to her trust.

MANTO   O madam,

---

1 **attend** serve, wait upon – reversing the roles that Paulina established at the end of 5.3, when she claimed Donusa as her 'slave'

3 **which** i.e. pardoning her
    invited induced (*OED v.* 1d)

6 **personating** Cf. 5.3.153n., on *serious*.

10 **rack** stretch upon the rack (the most common form of torture used in early modern England)

15 **off** away (from Tunis)

1 SD] *this edn*   10 rack] *(*wrack*)*

I have been false: forgive me! I'll redeem it
By anything, however desperate,
You please to impose upon me.

PAULINA   Troth, these tears
I think cannot be counterfeit: I believe her   25
And, if you please, will try her.

DONUSA   At your peril.
There is no further danger can look towards me.

PAULINA
This only, then – canst thou use means to carry
This bake-meat to Vitelli?

MANTO   With much ease –
I am familiar with the guard; beside,   30
It being known it was I that betrayed him,
My entrance hardly will of them be questioned.

PAULINA
About it, then: say that it was sent to him
From his Donusa; bid him search the midst of 't;
He there shall find a cordial.

MANTO   What I do   35
Shall speak my care and faith.   *Exit.*

DONUSA   Good fortune with thee!

PAULINA
You cannot eat?

DONUSA   The time we thus abuse
We might employ much better.

---

26 **try** test (*OED v.* 7a)
29 **bake-meat** pie, pastry
31 *To judge by the corrections in Q, this was a line that gave Massinger some trouble; neither the corrected nor the uncorrected version is metrically satisfactory. The version printed here, as in most other editions, combines the two readings. By eliding Q's 'it was' to

"twas' and stressing the first syllable of *betrayed* it is possible to deliver the line as a more-or-less acceptable pentameter.
32 **hardly . . . questioned** is unlikely to be questioned by them
35 **cordial** 'medicine, food, or beverage which invigorates the heart' (*OED n.* B)

31 It being] *Qb;* Being *Qa, Rawl.*   betrayed him] *Qa, Rawl;* betrayde *Qb*   36 SD] *(Exit Manto)*

PAULINA   I am glad
   To hear this from you. As for you, Carazie,
   If your intents do prosper, make choice whether   40
   You'll steal away with your two mistresses
   Or take your fortune.
CARAZIE   I'll be gelded twice first –
   Hang him that stays behind!
PAULINA   I wait you, madam.
   Were but my brother off by the command
   Of the doting Viceroy, there's no guard dare stay me.   45
   And I will safely bring you to the place
   Where we must expect him.
DONUSA   Heaven be gracious to us!

                                                   Exeunt.

5.6   *Enter* VITELLI, AGA *and* GUARDS.

VITELLI [*aside*]
   Paulina to fall off thus! 'Tis to me
   More terrible than death, and like an earthquake
   Totters this walking building – such I am –
   And in my sudden ruin would prevent,
   By choking up at once my vital spirits,   5

42 **take your fortune** take your chances
   (by remaining here)
   twice a second time
44 **off** free
47 **be gracious** grant us grace
5.6 Location: the Black Tower
1 **fall off** become estranged, change
   allegiance (*OED* fall *v.* 92e)
4 **prevent** forestall
5 **choking up** clogging, blocking the
   flow of
   vital spirits subtle fluids supposed
   to permeate the blood and to be
   responsible for maintaining life: see
   Thomas Walkington, *The Optick*

Glasse of Humors (1631): 'A spirit is
a most subtile, aery and lightsome
substance, generated of the purest
part of bloud, whereby the soule
can easily performe her functions
in the naturall body . . . they be of
three sorts, vital, natural and animall: vitall in the heart, naturall in
the liver, animall in the braine. Vital,
because they give power of motion
& pulsion unto the arteries: which
motion any living creature hath, so
long as it hath a being, and that
being extinct, the life is also extinct'
(sig. G5ʳ).

40 your] *Q;* our *Mason*   whether] *Qb;* whither *Qa*   **5.6**] *(Actus Quintus, Scaena Sexta.)*   0 SD
GUARDS] *Vitkus; a Garde Q*   1 SD] *this edn*

This pompous preparation for my death.
But I am lost. – That good man, good Francisco,
Delivered me a paper, which till now
I wanted leisure to peruse.   (*Reads the paper.*)

AGA   This Christian

Fears not, it seems, the near approaching sun   10
Whose second rise he never must salute.

Enter MANTO *with the bake-meat.*

1 GUARD

Who's that?

2 GUARD   Stand!

AGA   Manto!

MANTO   Here's the Viceroy's ring

Gives warrant to my entrance, yet you may
Partake of anything I shall deliver;
'Tis but a present to a dying man   15
Sent from the princess that must suffer with him.

AGA

Use your own freedom.

MANTO   I would not disturb

This his last contemplation.

VITELLI [*aside*]   Oh, 'tis well!

He has restored all, and I at peace again
With my Paulina.

MANTO   Sir, the sad Donusa,   20

Grieved for your sufferings more than for her own,
Knowing the long and tedious pilgrimage
You are to take, presents you with this cordial,

---

6 **pompous** stately, ceremonious (*OED*
  a. 1)
7 **lost** desperate, hopeless (*OED ppl.a.* 1c)

21 **Grieved** distressed, full of grief
23 **cordial** referring to the pie; see
   5.5.35n.

11 SD *bake-meat*] *this edn; Bak't-meat Q*   18 SD] *this edn*

Which privately she wishes you should taste of –
[*aside to Vitelli*] And search the middle part, where
   you shall find   25
Something that hath the operation to
Make death look lovely.

VITELLI   I will not dispute
What she commands, but serve it.   *Exit.*

AGA   Prithee, Manto,
How hath the unfortunate princess spent this night
Under her proud new mistress?

MANTO   With such patience   30
As it o'ercomes the other's insolence,
Nay, triumphs o'er her pride. My much haste now
Commands me hence; but, the sad tragedy passed,
I'll give you satisfaction to the full
Of all hath passed, and a true character   35
Of the proud Christian's nature.   *Exit.*

AGA   Break the watch up. –
What should we fear in the midst of our own
   strengths?
'Tis but the Pasha's jealousy. Farewell, soldiers.   *Exeunt.*

5.7   *Enter* VITELLI *with the bake-meat, above.*

24 'which she wishes you to eat in private'
26 **operation** efficacy (*OED n.* 3a)
35 **character** description (*OED n.* 9)
5.7 Location: Vitelli's cell in the Black
Tower. The action of this scene
appears to be modelled on an episode from Sandys (see Fig. 16): 'on
the *Europe* side [of the Bosphorus]
there standeth a Castle called formerly
Damalis, and now the *Blacke Tower*:
strongly fortified, and commanding
that entrie . . . This is also a prison
for captives of principall quality. At
such time as the deservedly beloved

Maister *Barton* lay here, Embassador
for our Nation, there was a certain
Hollander, called *Hadrian Cant*, who
being taken by a *Renegado*, then
Captaine of two gallies, was by the
Grand Signiors commandment shut
up in this place . . . Where after he
had remained three yeeres; arising one
morning before day, and finding the
doores open, he descended without
the privitie of his keepers into the
Court of the Castle. When advising
himselfe of his escape, and casting his
eyes about him, he found a rope that

25 SD] *this edn* 28 SD] *(Exit Vitelli)* 36 SD] *(Exit Manto)* 5.7] *(Actus quintus. Scaena Septima.)* 0 SD *bake-meat*] *this edn;* bak't-meates *Q*

VITELLI

There's something more in this than means to cloy
A hungry appetite, which I must discover.
She willed me search the midst. Thus, thus I pierce it.
    [*Cuts open the bake-meat.*]
Ha! What is this? A scroll bound up in pack-thread?
What may the mystery be?   5
([*Reads*] *the scroll.*) *Son, let down this pack-thread at the*
west window of the castle. By it you shall draw up a ladder
of ropes, by which you may descend. Your dearest Donusa
with the rest of your friends below attend you. Heaven
prosper you!   10
                                          Francisco

    [*Lets down the thread.*]
O best of men! He that gives up himself
To a true religious friend leans not upon
A false deceiving reed, but boldly builds
Upon a rock, which now with joy I find   15
In reverend Francisco, whose good vows,
Labours and watchings in my hoped-for freedom
Appear a pious miracle. [*Pulls up the rope.*] I come,

was tied to a tree, not farre from the wall, which he ascending, by the benefit thereof without danger descended on the other side; and from thence conveyed himselfe into the house of our Embassador; then (as now) a Sanctuary for escaped captives: where for three dayes they hid him under a wood-stacke, and not long after shipt him for *Holland.* In the morning the Captaine of the Castle . . . vainely sought for his prisoner' (sig. E3ʳ).

1   **something** both figuratively and literally
    means the means
4   **pack-thread** stout thread for tying up bundles. In both 'The Captive's Tale' and *Los Baños*, the Moorish heroine engineers her lover's escape by using a thread to let down a cane to the window of her beloved's cell; it contains gold with which to engineer his escape. In *Barnavelt* (1619), a prisoner receives a message from his wife in a hollowed-out pear.

13–15 **leans . . . rock** a paraphrase, as Oxf points out, of Isaiah, 36.6 ('Lo, thou trustest in the staff of this broken reed, on Egypt; whereon if a man lean, it will go into his hand, and pierce it: so *is* Pharaoh king of Egypt to all that trust in him') and Matthew, 7.25 ('And the rain descended, and the floods came, and the winds blew, and beat upon that house; and it fell not: for it was founded upon a rock')

3 SD] *this edn*   6 SD *Reads*] *Vitkus*   11 SD] *this edn*   18 SD] *this edn*

I come, good man, with confidence: though the descent
Were steep as hell, I know I cannot slide,   20
Being called down by such a faithful guide.

> [*Descends by the rope.*] *Exit.*

5.8   [*Enter*] ASAMBEG, MUSTAPHA [*and*] Janizaries.

ASAMBEG

Excuse me, Mustapha, though this night to me
Appear as tedious as that treble one
Was to the world when Jove on fair Alcmena
Begot Alcides, were you to encounter
Those ravishing pleasures which the slow-paced hours –   5
To me they are such – bar me from, you would
With your continued wishes strive to imp
New feathers to the broken wings of Time,
And chide the amorous Sun for too long dalliance
In Thetis' watery bosom.

MUSTAPHA   You are too violent   10
In your desires, of which you are yet uncertain,

---

21 **faithful** loyal; full of faith
21 SD ***Descends . . . rope** Massinger's
implied stage direction ('I come, / I
come', 18–19) requires Vitelli to descend
by the rope-ladder from the gallery.
5.8 Location: Asambeg's audience-
chamber
2 **Appear** obsolete form of the verb
used in the conditional mood
3–4 **when . . . Alcides** When Jove/
Jupiter (Zeus) seduced Alcmena in
the guise of her husband Amphitryon,
he delayed the sunrise for three days
so that he could extend his pleasure
with her; the offspring of this union
was Hercules (Alcides). Massinger
probably knew Plautus' version of the
story in his mythological burlesque,
Amphitryon; cf. *Roman Actor*, 4.2.110–

12. Asambeg identifies himself with
the disguised god, but ironically it is he
who has been deceived by the guise of
pretended conversion adopted by his
expected conquest, Paulina.
7 **imp** engraft; cf. *Great Duke*, 1.1.244;
Roman Actor, 5.2.22; *Emperor*, 4.1.20.
The Renaissance iconography of
Father Time, which borrowed from
medieval representations of Death,
as well as from the iconography of
Saturn/Cronos (punningly associated
with Chronos) showed him as a winged
figure, an old (and often crippled)
man, equipped with an hourglass and
a scythe (see Panofsky, 82–3).
10 **Thetis' watery bosom** the ocean;
Thetis was a sea-nymph, one of the
nereids.

21 SD *Descends . . . rope*] *this edn*   5.8] *(Actus Quintus, Scaena Vltima.)*   0 SD *Enter*] *this edn*

Having no more assurance to enjoy 'em
Than a weak woman's promise, on which wise men
Faintly rely.

ASAMBEG   Tush! She is made of truth,
And what she says she will do holds as firm   15
As laws in brass that know no change.

    (*The chamber shot off.*)

            What's this?

Some new prize brought in, sure.

      Enter AGA.

          Why are thy looks

So ghastly? Villain, speak!

AGA   Great sir, hear me,
Then after, kill me: we are all betrayed!
The false Grimaldi, sunk in your disgrace,   20
With his confederates have seized his ship,
And those that guarded it stowed under hatches;
With him the condemned princess and the merchant,
That with a ladder made of ropes descended
From the Black Tower in which he was enclosed,   25
And your fair mistress –

ASAMBEG   Ha!

AGA   With all their train
And choicest jewels are gone safe aboard.
Their sails spread forth, and with a foreright gale

---

16 **in brass** engraved in brass (proverbially impervious to decay and therefore
 everlasting)
16 SD *chamber* small cannon used for
 salutes, and for artillery effects in theatres
23 **condemned** còndemned
27 **choicest jewels** In *The Captive's Tale*
 Zoraida similarly makes her escape 'in
 festive attire' and 'wearing all [her]

jewels' (113).
28 ***foreright gale** wind favourable for
 steering a direct course; *foreright gale*
 seems to have been a standard term
 in navigation (*OED* foreright *adv.*; *a.*
 1b); cf. also *Parliament*, 3.3.94–5: 'You
 did but poynt mee out a fore right
 waie / To leade to certaine happines.'
 Massinger's MS correction of Q 'fore-

---

16 SD] *after 15* What's this] *Qb;* what' this *Qa* 17 SD] *Vitkus; opp.* speake *18 Q* 28 foreright gale]
*MS ADD (*foreright-gale*);* fore-gale *Q*

Leaving our coast, in scorn of all pursuit,
As a farewell they showed a broadside to us.   30

ASAMBEG

No more!

MUSTAPHA   Now note your confidence.

ASAMBEG   No more!

O my credulity! I am too full
Of grief and rage to speak. Dull, heavy fool,
Worthy of all the tortures that the frown
Of thy incensed master can throw on thee   35
Without one man's compassion! I will hide
This head among the deserts or some cave
Filled with my shame and me, where I alone
May die without a partner in my moan.   *Exeunt.*

FINIS

gale' is necessary for the metre as well
as for the sense.

30 **showed a broadside** 'swung round to
show the full side of the ship and fired
a broadside at us'; *broadside* = simulta-
neous discharge of all the cannon on
one side of a ship

32–3 **I . . . rage** Asambeg is consumed
by the passion proverbially associated
with Turks. As Linda McJannet has
shown, the origins of the stereotype
celebrated in the title of a well-known

academic play (Goffe's *Raging Turk*,
c. 1618) can be traced back through the
impotent fury of the captive Bajazeth
in Marlowe's *Tamburlaine* to the rant-
ing Herod of medieval mystery plays
(McJannet, 16–25, 64–89). Theatrical
rage was typically expressed by stamp-
ing and staring.

33 **heavy** slow-witted (*OED a.* 18); sor-
rowful (*OED a.* 25a)

35 **incensed** incensèd
master the Sultan

LONGER NOTE

TITLE A *renegado* was a renegade, or apostate; however, the Spanish form seems to have been used with a more specific reference to Christians who gave their allegiance to Islam and turned Turk. In 1599 the term was still sufficiently novel for Hakluyt to feel the need for a gloss: 'He was a Renegado, which is one that was first a Christian, and afterwards becommeth a Turke' (2.1.186). Christian renegades formed a significant part of the population in the cities of the North African Barbary Coast: in Algiers, for example, they made up more than half of the population by 1581, and from 1568 all the beylerbeys of the city were chosen from this caste (Garcés, 36). According to de Nicolay, 'The most part of the Turkes of Alger, whether they be of the kings houshold or the Gallies, are Christians renied, or Mahumetised, of al Nations, but most of them Spaniards, Italians, and of Provence . . . given to all whoredome, sodometrie, theft and all other most detestable vices, lyving onely of rovings, spoyles, & pilling at the Seas' (sig. B45ʳ). Renegades, whom Sandys describes as 'the most terrible adversaries [to the Christians]' (sig. F1ʳ), were indeed disproportionately represented amongst the corsairs.

In Herbert's licence for performance (17 April 1624) the play is entitled *The Renegado, or the Gentleman of Venice*; and this, presumably, was the version he found in the company's official manuscript (the 'allowed copy'), though, for whatever reason, it did not survive in Q. The subtitle must have invited comparison with Shakespeare's *Merchant of Venice*, and perhaps also with *Othello, the Moor of Venice* (see pp. 8–9). Shirley, whose commendatory verses are printed on pp. 76–7, wrote a tragicomedy entitled *The Gentleman of Venice* in 1639; although it appears to have no direct relation to Massinger's play, it too has connections with Shakespeare's *Merchant of Venice*, especially through its thematization of mercy.

English writers, such as Lewkenor, though often suspicious of Venice's Catholicism and its reputation as a notorious centre of prostitution, often liked to stress the Republic's resemblances to England, as a small but expansionist maritime power, whose mixed constitution – with its regard for the rule of law and the liberties of subjects – seemed analogous to their own, with the Doge and his Council standing in for King and Parliament.

APPENDIX

THE UNVEILING SCENE
FROM CERVANTES,
LOS BAÑOS DE ARGEL,
SECOND DAY

Translated by Gwyn Fox[1]

This scene[2] provides the basis for *The Renegado*, 1.3.98–179, the episode at Vitelli's market stall where Donusa overwhelms the hero by removing her veil and exposing him to the power of her extraordinary beauty.

Enter DON LOPE *and* VIVANCO.

DON LOPE   We find ourselves here and free as a result of the most extraordinary event captivity ever saw.

VIVANCO   You don't think that this was just a matter of random chance? It's a true divine mystery! God, who is determined that this Moorish woman should go to a   5
land where his name is adored, inspired her to become the instrument of a good deed that will benefit all three of us.

DON LOPE   She said in her last note that perhaps one Friday she would go out into the countryside by the Al   10
Wad Gate, and she promised to find a way to reveal her identity to us. At the end of the note she also suggested that we might know her father Agi Morato's garden,

1   The full translation is available on the internet at http://www.ardenshakespeare.com.
2   *Los Baños*, Second Day, 631–790.

where our play and our dealings are to have their happy
ending. 15

VIVANCO   Over these several occasions she's given us a
total of three thousand escudos.

DON LOPE   Our freedom has cost us two thousand.

VIVANCO   We've gained more than we've lost – and we'll
gain more still if, through our good works, we can 20
manage to bring this soul to Christianity, even though it
lives in a Moorish body. But is that her coming?

DON LOPE   If it is, then by heaven she's proud!

> *Enter* ZAHARA *and* HALIMA, *their faces covered with
> white* al-milhafas *and with them, dressed as Moors,*
> COSTANZA *and the* Lady CATALINA *(who does not
> have to speak more than two or three times).*

I don't know which of the two she is, but the others
with them are captives. 25

HALIMA   Anyway, I know that if you were to speak with
him . . .

COSTANZA   Don't give up hope, for I'm going to speak
with him, to tempt or force him into adoring you; but
you have to give me the space in which to deal with 30
him.

HALIMA   You can have as much as you wish, friend; so
there's no need for you to stay here just to relieve my
fatigue.

ZAHARA   Walk, Halima, if you are able. 35

COSTANZA   I am much obliged to your goodness.

ZAHARA   Costanza, look and see whether you recognize
either of those two.

COSTANZA   I don't know either of them.

VIVANCO   If she's the one, it is indeed a stroke of good 40
fortune, because in her elegance she's exceedingly
lovely.

23.2 **al-milhafas** a type of over-garment worn by Moorish women in the street

ZAHARA   They're spirited young dogs. Oh, to be able to
          speak to them!

HALIMA   If my one were there I would go and speak to   45
          them.

ZAHARA   Costanza, look at them again and tell me if their
          bearing is noble.

CATALINA Why?

ZAHARA   So I can buy them.   50

COSTANZA The one on the left looks like a gentleman;
          and even the other one's no rustic.

ZAHARA   I want to look at them more closely.

HALIMA   If only my Christian were here!

ZAHARA   I like the look of both of them.   55

VIVANCO   They really do make it hard to leave! Let's go
          over to them.

DON LOPE No, they're coming to us.

VIVANCO   They're so delightfully pretty and vivacious.

ZAHARA   By Allah! Something has stung me. Look here,   60
          Costanza, see if it's a wasp. It stings as badly as if I'd
          been speared in the throat. Shake out my veil – I'm
          going mad trying to see what it is. Oh misery! Have you
          killed it? Can't you see it? Shake it more, look and feel
          for it. There it is!   65

COSTANZA I can't see anything.

ZAHARA   The invisible sting has gone straight to my heart.

COSTANZA A wasp sting is extremely painful; but I fear it
          may have been a spider.

ZAHARA   If it were a spider it must have come from Spain, 70
          because the Algerian ones are harmless.

DON LOPE Have you ever seen such artifice? Such a clever
          trick?

HALIMA   Zahara, you mustn't uncover yourself: put your
          veil back over your face.   75

ZAHARA   There's a bad smell in the air.

HALIMA   It's only a slight one, but it's spoiled our party.

VIVANCO   What do you think?

DON LOPE   Fate seems to be offering me everything I
could desire.   80

VIVANCO   The sun's eclipsed; all her brightness has
vanished.

ZAHARA   Do you know whether that prisoner is Spanish,
Costanza?

COSTANZA   I am glad to say that he is.   85

DON LOPE   Come out again, sun: your light will restore my
being, my understanding, my courage, and the promise
of all the happiness I would attain in possessing you!

ZAHARA   Ask him, Costanza.

HALIMA   How do you feel now?   90

ZAHARA   I feel better.

COSTANZA   Sir, are you from Spain?

DON LOPE   Yes, lady; from a land without poisonous
spiders, where fraud, deceit and trouble are unheard
of, where everyone is honest and straightforward, and   95
where promise and fulfilment are one and the same.

ZAHARA   Ask him if he is married and if his wife is
beautiful.

COSTANZA   Are you married?

DON LOPE   No, lady; but I shall be, very soon – to a   100
Moorish Christian.

COSTANZA   How can that be?

DON LOPE   How? Anyone who doesn't know that doesn't
know much. Moorish in her unbelief, and Christian in
her goodness is what my mistress must be.   105

COSTANZA   I'm at a loss to understand what on earth
you're talking about!

ZAHARA   Pray Allah you speak true!

HALIMA   Ask him if he is a slave or free.

DON LOPE   I know what you're getting at, and I'm happy   110
to be a prisoner.

ZAHARA   I understand everything he says, and I'm dying
   to know more.

DON LOPE   With what pleasure and glory I'll soon step
   ashore in Spain, and then I'll show you how I keep my   115
   word.

ZAHARA   Thanks be to Allah – and to a certain cane.

HALIMA   Stay here, Christians, for we're going into the
   city.   *Exeunt women.*

VIVANCO   We shall obey you.   120

DON LOPE   We are left in darkness. Beautiful sun, how
   can you leave me like this? You ransomed my body
   from captivity with your generosity: but your beauty
   has put my soul in chains. From everything I've seen in
   you – all that repressed passion – I can't help adoring   125
   you – not for being beloved of Mahomet but for being
   beloved of Christ. I'll take you wherever you want to
   go and bring you everything you desire, even if it costs
   me a thousand lives.

VIVANCO   Let's go – this is painful for you. Not that way,   130
   let's take a more roundabout route.   *Exeunt.*

117   **a certain cane** Zahara is referring to the piece of cane in which she first conveyed
   a message to Don Lope and which she subsequently used to send him the money for
   his ransom.

ABBREVIATIONS AND REFERENCES

Quotations and references relating to *The Renegado* are keyed to this edition. Other plays by Massinger are cited from Philip Edwards and Colin Gibson (eds), *The Plays and Poems of Philip Massinger* (Oxford, 1976), and works by Shakespeare are cited from the most recent Arden editions. *OED* references are to *OED²*, accessed before 2009. Unless otherwise indicated, biblical quotations are cited from the King James Authorized Version of the Bible. Place of publication is London unless otherwise noted.

ABBREVIATIONS

ABBREVIATIONS USED IN NOTES

*	precedes commentary notes involving readings altered from the base text
conj.	conjectured
LN	Longer note
LR	List of roles
MS	manuscript
n.	commentary note
SD	stage direction
SP	speech prefix
subst.	substantially
this edn	a reading adopted or proposed for the first time in this edition
t.n.	textual note

SHORT TITLES FOR WORKS BY MASSINGER

Bashful Lover	*The Bashful Lover*
Believe	*Believe as You List*
Bondman	*The Bondman*
City Madam	*The City Madam*
Combat	*The Unnatural Combat*
Dowry	*The Fatal Dowry*
Duke of Milan	*The Duke of Milan*

Emperor	*The Emperor of the East*
Great Duke	*The Great Duke of Florence*
Guardian	*The Guardian*
London	*London's Lamentable Estate*
Maid of Honour	*The Maid of Honour*
New Way	*A New Way to Pay Old Debts*
Parliament	*The Parliament of Love*
Picture	*The Picture*
Roman Actor	*The Roman Actor*
Very Woman	*A Very Woman*

WORKS BY AND PARTLY BY SHAKESPEARE

AC	*Antony and Cleopatra*
AYL	*As You Like It*
1H4	*King Henry IV, Part 1*
2H4	*King Henry IV, Part 2*
H5	*King Henry V*
3H6	*King Henry VI, Part 3*
JC	*Julius Caesar*
KL	*King Lear*
MND	*A Midsummer Night's Dream*
Oth	*Othello*
Per	*Pericles*
R2	*King Richard II*
Tem	*The Tempest*
TN	*Twelfth Night*
TS	*The Taming of the Shrew*

SHORT TITLES FOR OTHER PLAYS

Alchemist	*The Alchemist*
Arden	*Arden of Faversham*
Barnavelt	*The Tragedy of John van Olden Barnavelt*
Changeling	*The Changeling*
Curate	*The Spanish Curate*
Custom	*The Custom of the Country*
Double Marriage	*The Double Marriage*
1 Edward IV	*King Edward IV, Part 1*
1 Fair Maid	*The Fair Maid of the West, Part 1*
Fair Quarrel	*A Fair Quarrel*
False	*The False One*
Faustus	*Doctor Faustus*
Goose Chase	*The Wild Goose Chase*
2 Honest Whore	*The Honest Whore, Part 2*
Island Princess	*The Island Princess*

Jew of Malta	*The Jew of Malta*
Knight of Malta	*The Knight of Malta*
Law	*The Old Law*
Lawyer	*The Little French Lawyer*
Maid's Tragedy	*The Maid's Tragedy*
Malfi	*The Duchess of Malfi*
Revenger's	*The Revenger's Tragedy*
Sea-Voyage	*The Sea-Voyage*
Spanish Tragedy	*The Spanish Tragedy*
1 Tamburlaine	*Tamburlaine the Great, Part 1*
Triumph of Beautie	*The Triumph of Beautie*
Turned Turk	*A Christian Turned Turk*
Virgin-Martyr	*The Virgin-Martyr*
White Devil	*The White Devil*

REFERENCES

EDITIONS OF *THE RENEGADO* COLLATED

Coleridge	Hartley Coleridge (ed.), *The Dramatic Works of Massinger and Ford* (1840)
Coxeter	Thomas Coxeter (ed.), *The Dramatic Works of Philip Massinger*, 4 vols (1761)
Cunningham	Francis Cunningham (ed.), *The Plays of Philip Massinger* (1867)
Folger Harbord	See MS ADD
Gifford	William Gifford (ed.), *The Plays of Philip Massinger* (1805)
Gifford²	William Gifford (ed.), *The Plays of Philip Massinger* (1813)
Mason	J. Monck Mason, revision of Thomas Coxeter (ed.), *The Dramatic Works of Philip Massinger*, with an introduction by Thomas Davies, 4 vols (1779)
MS ADD	Massinger's manuscript alterations and corrections in the Folger Harbord copy of Q, Folger Shakespeare Library, STC 17641, copy 1
Oxf	Philip Edwards and Colin Gibson (eds.), *The Plays and Poems of Philip Massinger*, 5 vols (Oxford, 1976)
Q	*The Renegado, A Tragæcomedie* (1630)
Rawl.	MS. Rawl. poet. 20 (?late seventeenth-century manuscript revision held in Bodleian library)
Senob	A. Senob (ed.), *The Renegado* (Chicago, 1939)
Vitkus	Daniel Vitkus (ed.), *Three Turk Plays from Early Modern England* (New York, 2000)

OTHER WORKS CITED

Adler	Doris Adler, *Philip Massinger* (Boston, 1987)
Alchemist	Ben Jonson, *The Alchemist*, STC 14755, ed. C. H. Herford and Percy and Evelyn Simpson, in Jonson
Arden	*The Tragedy of Master Arden of Faversham*, STC 733, ed. Martin White (1982), 2nd edn (2007)
Barnavelt	John Fletcher [and Philip Massinger], *The Tragedy of Sir John van Olden Barnavelt*, BL Add. MS 18653, ed. Fredson Bowers, in Beaumont and Fletcher
Beaumont and Fletcher	*The Dramatic Works in the Beaumont and Fletcher Canon*, ed. Fredson Bowers, 10 vols (Cambridge, 1966–96)
Bentley	G. E. Bentley, *The Jacobean and Caroline Stage*, 7 vols (Oxford, 1941–68)
Biddulph	William Biddulph, *The Travels of certaine Englishmen into Africa, Asia, Troy, Bithynia, Thracia, and to the Blacke Sea* (1609), STC 3051
Bisaha	Nancy Bisaha, *Creating East and West: Renaissance Humanists and the Ottoman Turks* (Philadelphia, 2006)
Browne	Sir Thomas Browne, *Pseudodoxia Epidemica* (1646), Wing B5159
Burton, *Anatomy*	Robert Burton, *The Anatomy of Melancholy*, STC 4159, ed. Holbrook Jackson, 3 vols (1948)
Burton, *Traffic*	Jonathan Burton, *Traffic and Turning: Islam and English Drama, 1579–1624* (Newark, 2005)
Cervantes, *Los Baños*	Miguel de Cervantes Saavedra, *Los Baños de Argel*, trans. Gwyn Fox, http://www.ardenshakespeare.com
Cervantes, *Captive's Tale*	Miguel de Cervantes Saavedra, *The Captive's Tale*, trans. Donald P. McCrory (Oxford, 1994)
Cervantes, *El Trato*	Miguel de Cervantes Saavedra, *El Trato de Argel*, in Cervantes, *Works*
Cervantes, 'Liberall Lover'	*Exemparie nouells in sixe books. The two damosels. The Ladie Cornelia. The liberall lover. The force of bloud. The Spanish ladie. The jealous husband . . . Turned into English by Don Diego Puede-Ser* (1640), STC 4914
Cervantes, *Novels*	Miguel de Cervantes Saavedra, *The Exemplary Novels*, trans. Walter K. Kelly (1882)
Cervantes, *Works*	Miguel de Cervantes Saavedra, *Obras Completas*, ed. Florencio Sevilla Arroyo (Madrid, 1999)
Changeling	Thomas Middleton and William Rowley, *The Changeling*, Wing M1980, ed. Douglas Bruster, in Middleton
Chaucer	*The Works of Geoffrey Chaucer*, ed. F. N. Robinson, 2nd edn (1957)

Chelli	Maurice Chelli, *Le Drame de Massinger* (Lyon, 1923)
Christian Turned Turk	Robert Daborne, *A Christian Turned Turk*, STC 6184, ed. Daniel J. Vitkus, in Vitkus, *Turk Plays*
Cogswell	Thomas Cogswell, *The Blessed Revolution: English Politics and the Coming of War, 1621–1624* (Cambridge, 1989)
Collinson	Patrick Collinson, *The Elizabethan Puritan Movement* (Oxford, 1990)
Coryat	Thomas Coryat, *Coryats Crudities* (1611), STC 5808
Cressy	David Cressy, *Birth, Marriage, and Death: Ritual, Religion, and the Life-Cycle in Tudor and Stuart England* (Oxford, 1997)
Curate	John Fletcher [and Philip Massinger], *The Spanish Curate*, Wing B1581, ed. Fredson Bowers, in Beaumont and Fletcher
Custom	John Fletcher [and Philip Massinger], *The Custom of the Country*, Wing B1581, ed. Fredson Bowers, in Beaumont and Fletcher
Daborne	Robert Daborne, *A Christian Turned Turk*, STC 6184, ed. Daniel J. Vitkus, in Vitkus, *Turk Plays*
D'Amico	Jack D'Amico, *The Moor in English Renaissance Drama* (Tampa, 1991)
Degenhardt	Jane Degenhardt, 'Catholic prophylactics and Islam's sexual threat: preventing and undoing sexual defilement in *The Renegado*', *JEMCS*, 9 (2009), 62–92
Dekker	*The Works of Thomas Dekker*, ed. Fredson Bowers, 4 vols (Cambridge, 1953–64)
de Nicolay, *Navigations*	Nicolas de Nicolay [Daulphinois], *The Navigations, Peregrinations and Voyages made into Turkie*, trans. T. Washington the younger (1585), STC 18574
Dent	R. W. Dent, *Shakespeare's Proverbial Language: An Index* (Berkeley, 1981)
Dimmock	Matthew Dimmock, *New Turkes: Dramatizing Islam and the Ottomans in Early Modern England* (Aldershot, 2005)
Donne	*The Poems of John Donne*, ed. Herbert J. C. Grierson (1951)
Double Marriage	John Fletcher [and Philip Massinger], *The Double Marriage*, Wing B1581, ed. Fredson Bowers, in Beaumont and Fletcher
Dunn	T. A. Dunn, *Philip Massinger* (1957)
ELR	*English Literary Renaissance*
Faerie Queene	Edmund Spenser, *The Faerie Queene*, in *The Poetical Works*, ed. J. C. Smith and E. De Selincourt (1912)

Fair Quarrel	Thomas Middleton, *A Fair Quarrel*, STC 17911, ed. Suzanne Gossett, in Middleton
Falk	Bernard Falk, *The Berkeleys of Berkeley Square* (1944)
False	John Fletcher [and Philip Massinger], *The False One*, Wing B1581, ed. Fredson Bowers, in Beaumont and Fletcher
Faustus	Christopher Marlowe, *Doctor Faustus*, STC 17429, 17432, ed. Roma Gill, in Marlowe
Fletcher	See Beaumont and Fletcher
Fuchs	Barbara Fuchs, 'Faithless empires: pirates, renegadoes, and the English nation', *ELR*, 67 (2000), 45–69
Garcés	Maria Antonia Garcés, *Cervantes in Algiers: A Captive's Tale* (Nashville, 2002)
Gibson, 'Behind the arras'	C. A. Gibson, '"Behind the arras" in Massinger's *The Renegado*', *N&Q*, 24 (1969), 296–7
Goose Chase	John Fletcher, *The Wild Goose Chase*, Wing B1616, ed. Fredson Bowers, in Beaumont and Fletcher
Greg	W. W. Greg, 'More Massinger corrections', *The Library*, 4th series, 5 (1924), 59–95
Hakluyt	Richard Hakluyt, *The Principal Navigations, Voyages, Traffiques & Discoveries of the English Nation* (1589), STC 12625, 12 vols (Glasgow, 1903–5)
Harington	Sir John Harington, *A New Discourse of a Stale Subject, Called the Metamorphosis of Ajax*, STC 321, ed. E. S. Donno (1962)
Harris	Jonathan Gil Harris, *Sick Economies: Drama, Mercantilism, and Disease in Shakespeare's England* (Philadelphia, 2004)
Heywood, *1 Edward IV*	Thomas Heywood, *The First and Second Parts of King Edward IV*, STC 13341, ed. Richard Rowland (Manchester, 2005)
Heywood, *1 Fair Maid*	Thomas Heywood, *The Fair Maid of the West, Parts 1 and 2*, STC 13320, ed. Robert K. Turner (1968)
2 Honest Whore	Thomas Dekker, *The Second Part of The Honest Whore*, STC 6506, ed. Fredson Bowers, in Dekker
Hope	Jonathan Hope, *Shakespeare's Grammar* (2003)
Howard, D.	Douglas Howard (ed.), *Philip Massinger: A Critical Reassessment* (Cambridge, 1985)
Island Princess	John Fletcher [and Philip Massinger], *The Island Princess*, Wing B1581, ed. Fredson Bowers, in Beaumont and Fletcher
JEMCS	*Journal for Early Modern Cultural Studies*
Jew of Malta	Christopher Marlowe, *The Jew of Malta*, STC 17412, ed. Roma Gill, in Marlowe

Jonson	*Ben Jonson*, ed. C. H. Herford, Percy and Evelyn Simpson, 11 vols (Oxford, 1925–52)
Jowitt, 'Another woman'	Claire Jowitt, '"I am another woman": the Spanish and French matches in Massinger's *The Renegado* (1624) and *The Unnatural Combat* (1624–5)', in Alexander Samson (ed.), *The Spanish Match: Prince Charles's Journey to Madrid, 1623* (Aldershot, 2006), 151–71
Jowitt, *Voyage*	Claire Jowitt, *Voyage Drama and Gender Politics 1589–1642* (Manchester, 2003)
Juvenal	*Juvenal and Persius*, ed. and trans. Susanna Morton Braund (Cambridge, Mass., 2004)
Kamps and Singh	Ivo Kamps and Jyotsna G. Singh (eds), *Travel Knowledge: European 'Discoveries' in the Early Modern Period* (New York, 2001)
Kerrigan	John Kerrigan (ed.), *Motives of Woe: Shakespeare and 'Female Complaint': A Critical Anthology* (Oxford, 1991)
Knapp	Jeffrey Knapp, *An Empire Nowhere: England, America, and Literature from 'Utopia' to 'The Tempest'* (Berkeley, 1992)
Knight of Malta	John Fletcher [, Nathan Field and Philip Massinger], *The Knight of Malta*, Wing B1581, ed. Fredson Bowers, in Beaumont and Fletcher
Knolles	Richard Knolles, *The Generall Historie of the Turkes* (1603, repr. 1621), STC 15053
Korda	Natasha Korda, 'Household Kates: domesticating commodities in *The Taming of the Shrew*', SQ, 47 (1996), 109–31
Kyd, *Spanish Tragedy*	Thomas Kyd, *The Spanish Tragedy*, STC 766, ed. Philip Edwards (1959)
Law	[William Rowley,] Thomas Middleton [, and Thomas Heywood], *The Old Law*, Wing 1048, ed. Jeffrey Masten, in Middleton
Lawyer	John Fletcher [and Philip Massinger], *The Little French Lawyer*, Wing B1581, ed. Fredson Bowers, in Beaumont and Fletcher
Lewkenor	Gasparo Contarini, *The Commonwealth and Government of Venice*, trans. Lewis Lewkenor (1599), STC 5642
Linebaugh	Peter Linebaugh, 'The Tyburn riot against the Surgeons', in Douglas Hay *et al.*, *Albion's Fatal Tree* (1975), 65–117
Linthicum	M. Channing Linthicum, *Costume in the Drama of Shakespeare and his Contemporaries* (New York, 1972)
Lithgow	William Lithgow, *Discourse of a Peregrination in Europe, Asia, and Affricke* (1614), STC 15710
McIlwraith	A. K. McIlwraith, *The Life and Works of Philip Massinger*, unpublished doctoral thesis, Oxford University (1931)

McJannet Linda McJannet, *The Sultan Speaks: Dialogue in English Plays and Histories about the Ottoman Turks* (New York, 2006)

Maid's Tragedy Francis Beaumont and John Fletcher, *The Maid's Tragedy* (1611), Wing 1595, ed. Fredson Bowers, in Beaumont and Fletcher

Malfi John Webster, *The Duchess of Malfi*, STC 25176, ed. Gunby *et al.*, in Webster

Malieckal Bindu Malieckal, '"Wanton irreligious madness": conversion and castration in Massinger's *The Renegado*', *Essays in Arts and Sciences*, 31 (2002), 25–6

Marlowe *The Plays of Christopher Marlowe*, ed. Roma Gill (1971)

Mason, *The Turk* John Mason, *The Turk*, ed. Fernand Lagarde (Salzburg, 1979)

Matar, 'Anglo-Muslim' Nabil Matar, 'The Anglo-Muslim disputation in the early modern period', in Matthew Birchwood and Matthew Dimmock (eds), *Cultural Encounters Between East and West* (Newcastle-upon-Tyne, 2005), 29–43

Matar, *Turks* Nabil Matar, *Turks, Moors, and Englishmen in the Age of Discovery* (New York, 1999)

Middleton *Thomas Middleton: The Collected Works*, ed. Gary Taylor and John Lavagnino (Oxford, 2007)

Milton Anthony Milton, *Catholic and Reformed: The Roman and Protestant Churches in English Protestant Thought, 1600–1640* (Cambridge, 1995)

Montagu [Richard Montagu,] *A New Gagg for an Old Goose* (1624), STC 18038

Moryson Fynes Moryson, *An Itinerary* (1617), STC 18205

Neill, 'Materiall flames' Michael Neill, '"Materiall flames": romance, empire and mercantile fantasy in John Fletcher's *The Island Princess*', in Michael Neill, *Putting History to the Question: Power, Politics, and Society in English Renaissance Drama* (New York, 2000), 311–39

Neil, 'Turn' Michael Neil, 'Turn and counterturn: merchanting, apostasy and tragicocomic form in Massinger's *The Renegado*', in Subha Mukherji and Raphael Lyne (eds), *Early Modern Tragicomedy* (Woodbridge, Suffolk, 2007), 154–74

'N.H.' 'N.H.', *The Complete Tradesman* (1684), Wing H97

OED *Oxford English Dictionary*, ed. J. A. Simpson and E. S. C. Weiner, 2nd edn, 20 vols (Oxford, 1989)

Ovid *Shakespeare's Ovid*, trans. Arthur Golding, ed. W. H. D. Rouse (1961)

Panofsky	Erwin Panofsky, *Studies in Iconology: Humanistic Themes in the Art of the Renaissance* (New York, 1939)
Parker	Patricia Parker, 'Preposterous conversions: turning Turk, and its "Pauline" rewriting', *JEMCS*, 2 (2002), 1–34
Paster	Gail Kern Paster, *Humoring the Body: Emotions and the Shakespearean Stage* (Chicago, 2004)
Patterson	W. B. Patterson, *King James VI and I and the Reunion of Christendom* (Cambridge, 1997)
Peck	Linda Levy Peck, *Consuming Splendor: Society and Culture in Seventeenth Century England* (Cambridge, 2005)
Percy	William Percy, *Mahomet and his Heaven*, ed. Matthew Dimmock (Aldershot, 2006)
Policy	*The Policy of the Turkish Empire* (1597), STC 24335
Puttenham	George Puttenham, *The Arte of English Poesie* (1589), STC 20519.5
Revenger's	[Thomas Middleton,] *The Revenger's Tragedy*, STC 24149, ed. Macdonald P. Jackson, in Middleton
Rice	Warner G. Rice, 'The sources of Massinger's *The Renegado*', *Philological Quarterly*, 11 (1932), 65–75
Robinson, 'Commodities'	Benedict Robinson, 'Strange commodities', in *Islam and Early Modern English Literature: The Politics of Romance from Spenser to Milton* (New York, 2007), 117–43
Robinson, 'Turks'	Benedict Robinson, 'The "Turks", Caroline politics, and Massinger's *The Renegado*', in Adam Zucker and Alan B. Farmer (eds), *Localizing Caroline Drama: Politics and Economics of the Early Modern Stage, 1625–1642* (New York, 2006), 213–37
Sandys	George Sandys, *A Relation of a Journey begun Anno Domini 1610* (1621), STC 21727, copy 2
Sea-Voyage	John Fletcher and Philip Massinger, *The Sea-Voyage*, Wing B1581, ed. Fredson Bowers, in Beaumont and Fletcher
Shell	Alison Shell, *Catholicism, Controversy and the English Literary Imagination, 1558–1660* (Cambridge, 1999)
Shirley, *Poems &c*	James Shirley, *Poems &c* (1646), Wing S3481
Shirley, *Triumph of Beautie*	James Shirley, *The Triumph of Beautie* (1646), Wing S3488
Smyth	John Smyth, *The Berkeley Manuscripts: The lives of the Berkeleys* (Gloucester, 1883–5)
Spanish Tragedy	Thomas Kyd, *The Spanish Tragedy*, STC 15086, 15089, ed. Philip Edwards (Manchester, 1981)
SQ	*Shakespeare Quarterly*

STC	Short-Title Catalogue. *A Short-Title Catalogue of Books Printed in England, Scotland, & Ireland and of English Books Printed Abroad 1475–1640*, compiled by A. W. Pollard and G. R. Redgrave (1969)
1 Tamburlaine	Christopher Marlowe, *The First Part of Tamburlaine the Great*, STC 17425, ed. Roma Gill, in Marlowe
Tilley	M. P. Tilley, *A Dictionary of the Proverbs in England in the Sixteenth and Seventeenth Centuries* (Ann Arbor, 1950)
Tyacke	Nicholas Tyacke, *Anti-Calvinists* (Oxford, 1987)
Virgin-Martyr	Thomas Dekker and Philip Massinger, *The Virgin-Martyr*, STC 17644, ed. Fredson Bowers, in Dekker
Vitkus, 'Conversion'	Daniel J. Vitkus, 'Turning Turk: the conversion and damnation of the moor', *SQ*, 28 (1997), 145–77
Vitkus, *Piracy*	Daniel J. Vitkus, *Piracy, Slavery, and Redemption: Barbary Captivity Narratives from Early Modern England* (New York, 2001)
Vitkus, *Turk Plays*	See Vitkus, under Editions of *The Renegado* collated
Vitkus, *Turning Turk*	Daniel J. Vitkus, *Turning Turk: English Theater and the Multicultural Mediterranean, 1570–1630* (New York, 2003)
Volpone	Ben Jonson, *Volpone, or the Foxe*, STC 14783, ed. C. H. Herford, Percy and Evelyn Simpson, in Jonson
Warner	G. Rice Warner, 'The sources of Massinger's *The Renegado*', *Philological Quarterly*, 11 (1932), 65–75
Webster	*The Works of John Webster*, ed. David Gunby, David Carnegie, Antony Hammond and MacDonald P. Jackson, 3 vols (Cambridge, 1995–2007)
White Devil	John Webster, *The White Devil*, STC 25178, ed. Gunby *et al.*, in Webster
Williams, *Dictionary*	Gordon Williams, *A Dictionary of Sexual Language and Imagery in Shakespearean and Stuart Literature*, 3 vols (1994)
Williams, *Glossary*	Gordon Williams, *A Glossary of Shakespeare's Sexual Language* (1997)
Wing	Donald Wing (ed.), *A Short-Title Catalogue of Books Printed in England, Scotland, Ireland, Wales and British America and of English Books Printed in Other Countries 1641-1700*, 3 vols (New York, 1945–51)
Wotton	Sir Henry Wotton, *The state of Christendom* (1657), Wing 3654

INDEX

if they, all of them,
really didn't want me,
then it's gonna take a
little time but I'll push
through it. I'm ~~a~~ attached
to all of them, and I want
~~many them~~ as many people
to love me as possible.

wanting stranger
to be mine

I am loving. Losing life

Lightning Source UK Ltd.
Milton Keynes UK
UKHW020625150822
407311UK00006B/386

9 781904 271611